THE ACCOUNT

of

CABEZA DE VACA

THE ACCOUNT

of

CABEZA DE VACA

A Literal Translation

With Analysis and Commentary

Original text by
Alvar Núñez Cabeza de Vaca

Translated and Edited by
David Carson

For information about this title, contact the publisher:
Living Water Specialties
P.O. Box 720
Friendswood, Texas 77549
lws@lwspecialties.com

Paperback edition
ISBN 978-1-7326874-1-7
Library of Congress Control Number: 2018912461

Cover art licensed from artmajeur.com

Table of Contents

Preface i

Introduction..ix

Table of Figures xv

Prologue to the Narváez Expedition xvii

Chapter 1 - Organizing the Expedition 3

Chapter 2 - From Cuba to Florida 13

Chapter 3 - The Arrival at Florida 17

Chapter 4 - The Initial Exploration of Florida..................19

Chapter 5 - The Journey to Apalache 27

Chapter 6 - At Apalache..35

Chapter 7 - From Apalache to Aute 37

Chapter 8 - Building Boats 45

Chapter 9 - Leaving the Bay of Horses 51

Chapter 10 - Trouble on the Sea 59

Chapter 11 - On an Island 67

Chapter 12 - Losing the Boat 69

Chapter 13 - More Survivors on the Island....................75

Chapter 14 - The Natives of the Island of Misfortune 79

Chapter 15 - Becoming Healers 85

Chapter 16 - A Group Leaves the Island 89

Chapter 17 - A Happy Reunion 99

Chapter 18 - The Mariames and Iguaces 109

Chapter 19 - The Plan to Escape 117

Chapter 20 - Accepted by the Avavares 121

Chapter 21 - Cabeza de Vaca Gets Lost........................ 123

Chapter 22 - Life with the Avavares and Their Neighbors 127

Chapter 23 - A Village with Fifty Houses 137

Chapter 24 - The Indians' Customs Regarding Disputes 141

Chapter 25 - How the Indians Fight 145

Chapter 26 - The Indians' Drinking Ceremony 147

Chapter 27 - The Mesquite Eaters at the Large River 153

Chapter 28 - The Custom of Robbery 159

Chapter 29 - In a Land of Plenty 165

Chapter 30 - The People of the Cows 173

Chapter 31 - Gifts of Turquoise 183

Chapter 32 - News of Other Christians 187

Chapter 33 - Contact with Other Spaniards 195

Chapter 34 - Saying Goodbye to the Indians 199

Chapter 35 - Melchior Díaz, the Alcalde of Culiacan 203

Chapter 36 - On to Mexico City 209

Chapter 37 - The Voyage to Europe 215

Chapter 38 - Of Narváez's Ships 221

Epilogue to the Narváez Expedition 227

Chronology 243

Glossary 253

Bibliography 257

Index 259

About the Author 267

Preface

When I began doing an in-depth study of Cabeza de Vaca's *La Relación* for a project for my web site, TexasCounties.net, I found that there was no shortage of English translations to read and analyze. I also found, however, that any time I compared a passage in two or more translations, there were almost always discrepancies, not just in style and phrasing, but in content. In one translation, men are sailing on the ocean in "boats," and in another, their vessels are "barges." In one translation, a group of soldiers is three days ahead of Cabeza de Vaca, and in another translation, the same group is three days behind him. I consider differences like these to be important. Surely, at least one of these translations is incorrect.

In such cases, I would, logically, turn to Cabeza de Vaca's text in Spanish, which I am quite good at reading (even though I am not fluent in speaking it), and there I found even more surprises: the translators were frequently making additions and changes to the text, apparently just to add color to the story: a "wave" would become a "great wave," a man who died "later" ended up dying "soon," and translators would arbitrarily (it would seem) decide that the Spanish word for "gourd" meant "pumpkin" in one passage, "squash" in another, and plain-old "gourd" in another. These translations took too many liberties for my purposes. I did not want to read an interpretation or paraphrase of the work; I wanted one that simply told me what the author *wrote*. Unable to find a pure translation of *La Relación* that is faithful to the author's words and voice, I decided to create one myself.

It is easy to see why others who have worked with *La Relación* have so often crossed the line from translator to editor and interpreter. The original text can be confusing and even incoherent in some places. The fact that it is 500 years old certainly has a lot to do with its unwieldiness. Writers in the 16th century used extremely long, unorganized sentences of hundreds of words that often changed subjects more than once from start to finish. Cabeza de Vaca himself must also bear some of the blame. He was a soldier and government official, not an author, and *La Relación* is an expedition report, not a historical novel. He tends to employ plain, all-purpose words, and he can be repetitive. His story contains very little dialogue; it is almost all narration. His writing has a dry, unemotional tone that often does not do his subject justice. Translators can hardly be blamed for reorganizing and streamlining his sentences and adding a few colorful flourishes here and there.

Perhaps it is because there are so many paraphrase-translations and interpretive translations of *La Relación* that I feel the English-speaking world needs a more literal one. As difficult and wordy as Cabeza de Vaca can be to read, I believe there are many readers who would appreciate knowing, as exactly as possible, what he wrote, rather than a cleaned-up, punched-up, interpretation of what he wrote. Anyone doing an analysis of his route, or who is using *La Relación* for any other kind of serious project, should require such a translation. This translation is for those readers.

This is not to say that the translation in your hands or on your screen is entirely literal, word-for-word. A Spanish work translated into English needs to read as if it were written in English. Translators must be allowed to take great liberties with syntax. Still, it should be possible, most of the time, to keep the "meat" words of the sentence – the nouns, verbs, adjectives, and adverbs – the same, without dropping any or adding any new ones. It should be possible, most of the time, to keep the tenses of the verbs the same. The key to making a literal translation, as I see it, is to concentrate on rearranging the connective tissue of the text - the syntax, punctuation, conjunctions, prepositions, etc. - to make natural-sounding sentences without making any more changes than are necessary.

I will give an example that compares Cabeza de Vaca's original words with several existing translations. Consider this phrase from Chapter 10, in which the author describes his arrival on land in a boat:

cerca de tierra nos tomó una ola, que echó la barca fuera del agua un juego de herradura

The word-for-word translation is:

close to/near land us took a wave, that threw the boat out of the water a game of horseshoe

Translating this phrase should be a straightforward matter of rearranging "us took a wave" to "a wave took us," removing the comma, and figuring out what to do with "a game of horseshoe." Let us see, then, how three existing translations read. Since the purpose of this exercise is to demonstrate a difference in method rather than to critique other translations for criticism's sake, I am withholding the translator's names:

A. close to shore a wave took us and hurled the barge a horse's length out of water
B. near the shore a wave took us, that knocked the boat out of water the distance of the throw of a crowbar
C. near land a great wave took us and cast the boat out of the water as far as a horseshoe can be tossed

Even before getting to "a game of horseshoe," all three translations make significant modifications to the author's words. A and B translate *tierra* as "shore" instead of "land." Yes, it is obvious that the scene being described occurs offshore, but that is not the point: if Cabeza de Vaca had wanted to write "shore," he would have written *costa*, a word he uses quite often elsewhere. The translators wrote "shore" because that was the picture formed in their heads when they read the passage, but the author wrote "land," so that is how it should be translated. All three translations correctly state "a wave took us," but C makes it a "great" wave, adding an adjective where one was not written. None of the translations stick to the simple meaning of *echó* of "threw"; A and C go with more colorful synonyms - "hurled" (*tiró*) and "cast" (*lanzó*), while B uses "knocked" (*golpeó*), which is not even a synonym. A's identification of the boats (*barcas*) as "barges" (*barcazas*) is a serious and recurring flaw of her translation. Thus, all three translations are guilty of taking liberties with the author's words seemingly just to make them more colorful or interesting.

The real fun begins with *un juego de herradura*, "a game of horseshoe." The first thing to know is that the translation of *herradura* is locked to "horseshoe"; there are no synonyms. Just as in English, it can refer to either the iron object that is nailed to a horse's hoof, to another object or curve that has the same shape as a horseshoe, or to the game involving the tossing of horseshoes. It cannot mean "horse," as in A, or "crowbar," as in B. Furthermore, we do not have to wonder whether the author is referring to the object, the shape, or the game: he explicitly tells us, *un juego de herradura* – "a game of horseshoe." Even so, all three translations drop the noun "game." At least C alludes to it, but A and B do not. In place of "game," all three translations add words meaning "distance" or "length." A's rendition, "a horse's length," is ridiculous. Why would a man who always measures short distances in palms, spans, cubits, or fathoms come up with something like "a horse's length," especially when out on the water in a boat? (I have never heard of anyone using "horse" as a unit of length, except in a horserace.) As for B, if the translator thinks the author is describing the distance an iron object is thrown, why not stick with "horseshoe"? Where did "crowbar" come from? B and C each require a verb – "throw" and "tossed," respectively – to translate "a game of horseshoe."

Cabeza de Vaca's wording is admittedly vague and open to interpretation. What does he mean, it threw the boat "a game of horseshoe"? The problem all three translators have is that they formed an interpretation of what he meant first, then they changed *his* words to match *their* interpretation. You are no longer reading what Cabeza de Vaca wrote; you are reading their interpretation of what he wrote – an interpretation, by the way, I believe to be incorrect.

So how does one translate "threw the boat out of the water a game of horseshoe" literally, while still making sense of it? All we have to do is realize that author is using a metaphor or simile – comparing two dissimilar things to make a description more emphatic or vivid. We may not know exactly how he arrived at this comparison, or what he intended it to mean, but the fact that it is a comparison should be obvious. Let us try phrasing Cabeza de Vaca's comparison first as a metaphor, then as a simile:

near land, a wave took us and the boat thrown out of the water was a game of horseshoe
near land, a wave took us and threw the boat out of the water like a game of horseshoe

There is no question that the second form is better. It only needs a couple of adjustments. First, the word "threw" should be changed to "tossed" because, in English, in the context of a game, horseshoes are "tossed," not "thrown." Second, we need to make the horseshoe, not the game, the object that is being tossed. We end up with:

near land, a wave took us and tossed the boat out of the water like a horseshoe in a game.

Every noun and verb the author wrote, including "game," is preserved. No new nouns, verbs, adjectives, or adverbs are added, nor are the concepts of distance or length introduced. All I did was add a couple of prepositions and articles to make a natural-sounding English sentence out of the author's original words.

Hopefully, readers can see, from the above example, the pitfalls of forming an interpretation of the text, then presenting that interpretation as if it were a translation. All three of the other translators decided Cabeza de Vaca was describing the *distance* that the boat was thrown from the water, and they translated the phrase so that is the only way it can be read. I, however, do not think that is what he was describing. First of all, I doubt that the boat was thrown more than a few inches out of the water – it was lifted by a wave, not a hurricane. More importantly, the phrase that follows this one describes the bone-rattling jolt that everyone on the boat felt when it crashed back down. I think he was describing the *motion* of the boat - the feeling of being in it as the water tossed it up high, and then it hit the water again, like a horseshoe being tossed up high in a pronounced arc and hitting the dirt with a heavy thud. This is what I think the author meant, but my translation does not force that interpretation on anyone – it leaves the meaning a little ambiguous, just like the author himself did.

I hope that this example will suffice to convince readers of the need for a more literal translation of *La Relación*. It is not a translator's job to make a work more exciting – that is an editor's job. It is not a translator's job to take a text that a Spanish speaker would find ambiguous or unclear and make its meaning apparent to an English speaker – that is a job for a commentator. This being said, there are still numerous instances of where the original Spanish would be clear to a Spanish speaker, but a literal translation to English would sound wrong. Take, for example, the author's statement about an argument he was having:

viendo que conmigo no aprovechaba

Word-for word this is: "seeing that with me he did not take advantage of/make use of." This does not make sense in English, but to a Spanish-speaking person, the meaning is clear, and it is:

seeing that he had gotten nowhere with me

The other translations read:

A. Seeing that he could not change my determination
B. Seeing that what he said to me availed nothing
C. Seeing that he was getting nowhere with me

All of these translations say the same thing – the third almost identically to mine, so there is no loss of meaning in any of them. Still, mine is the most literal, because it is the only one that both preserves *conmigo* as "with me" and replicates the imperfect past tense of the verb, *aprovechaba*. Even when some of the author's wording has to be changed to make sense, we should still attempt to preserve as much of it as we can, replicating his own voice as much as possible. The goal is to translate, not to paraphrase.

Where the above passage appears in my translation, I added a footnote in the text that gave the author's original wording in Spanish, plus the literal translation, to alert the reader to the fact that the passage was translated idiomatically. I tried to always do that. Additionally, there were places where I went ahead and stuck with a literal translation, but used the footnotes to provide a more idiomatic rendition. An example of the latter would be where I translated *un tiro de ballesta*, an expression that means "a long distance," literally as "a crossbow shot." The reader should be told that this is only an expression, so that he does not waste time researching the length of a crossbow shot, but I think the expression should be translated as-is. In every instance where the literal and idiomatic translations do not match, I try to give both of them to the reader. I do this because I want to gain the reader's trust that at all times, reading the translation of *La Relación* presented here is the closest thing there is to reading it in Spanish.

Introduction

La Relación was published fewer than 50 years after Christopher Columbus's discovery of the New World and almost 80 years before the Mayflower Compact. This makes it one of the earliest documents of the history of the present-day United States. *La Relación* tells the story of Spain's third attempt to colonize Florida: the Narváez Expedition. Pánfilo de Narváez failed in his attempt, just like his predecessors, Juan Ponce de León and Lucas Vázquez de Ayllón, did in theirs. The Narváez Expedition was not a total loss, however, for some eight years after Narváez's ships dropped him and his army of 300 men off near Tampa Bay, four of those men emerged from the wilderness of northwestern Mexico with an amazing story to tell.

The tale of the Narváez Expedition was told twice. Three of the four survivors - but primarily Cabeza de Vaca, who was Narváez's second-in-command, and Andrés Dorantes, one of the army captains – collaborated while in Mexico City to produce a 30-page summary of their journey. This document has been called the "Joint Report." Cabeza de Vaca carried a copy of it with him back to Cuba and from there, it was sent to Spanish historian Gonzalo Fernández de Oviedo in Santo Domingo, Hispaniola. Oviedo included rewritten and paraphrased material from the Joint Report in his immense work, *General and Natural History of the Indies*, which was completed sometime between 1552 and Oviedo's death in 1557. Regrettably, the original, unedited Joint Report no longer survives, but the material Oviedo preserved is nevertheless quite valuable.

After Cabeza de Vaca returned to Spain, he wrote his own account, which is translated to English and presented in this book. *La Relación*, or "The Account," was completed in 1540 and published in 1542, after the author had departed for a government position in South America. Back in Spain again in 1555, Cabeza de Vaca re-published *La Relación*, with some slight changes. The differences between these two editions are few and unimportant; they are essentially the same work. The majority of *La Relación* takes place in Texas, making it the earliest surviving written record of Texas history.

A Spanish historian, Andrés González de Barcia, wrote a volume entitled *Historiadores Primitivos de las Indias Occidentales*, or "Early Historians of the West Indies," which included *La Relación*. Cabeza de Vaca's story was retitled as *Naufragios*, which can mean both "shipwrecks" and "the shipwrecked ones" (or "those who were shipwrecked.") This volume was published in 1749, after Barcia's death. A photocopy of *Naufragios* from this publication served as my master source text for this translation. As a secondary source, I used an online copy of the second edition of *La Relación* published by the Cervantes Virtual Library (www .cervantesvirtual.com). The only differences I found between the 1749 printing and the online version were the latter version's more modern spelling and punctuation.

Another secondary source text was Buckingham Smith's translation of *La Relación*, which was published posthumously in 1871. Smith had access to the rare 1542 first edition, and made footnotes where there were differences between it and the more widely-available second edition, allowing us to compare them.

I did make some minor formatting changes. The source text is divided into chapters, with headings. I kept the chapter divisions as they were, but because the headings appeared to me to have been based on the first few lines of the chapter, rather than the chapter as a whole, I supplied chapter headings of my own. I preserved the source text's headings as subheadings. In the source text, most chapters consist of a single paragraph. Some chapters have two paragraphs; none have more than two. To improve readability, I divided each chapter into multiple paragraphs. In many cases, my paragraphs represent individual sentences in the original. I indicated the few paragraph divisions in the source text by inserting a blank line. To aid in this translation's usefulness as a reference to writers and students, I also added paragraph numbers.

I added some words in brackets where I felt they were required for comprehension. Most of the time, this had to do with the Spanish practice of omitting nouns and pronouns in places where English expects them to be written. I also had to make sure, when breaking up excessively long sentences, that each new sentence had a subject; this sometimes required the addition of a noun or pronoun. On rare occasions, I reluctantly added words purely for clarity's sake, such as where the author wrote, "we lost the other boat," when what he meant was "we lost [sight of] the other boat." Strictly speaking, insertions like this work against my goal of not making the English translation any more or less comprehensible than the original Spanish, but more than just making the text read more smoothly, they keep the reader from making mistakes in important places. These insertions are also infrequent and are always indicated with brackets.

The footnotes serve a variety of important purposes and are essential for getting the most out of this translation. They provide chronological and geographical information to help the reader keep up with when and where the story is taking place. They provide biographical information about the people in the story, as well as technical and historical information on a variety of topics, such as ships, flora and fauna, and the culture of 16th-century Spanish expeditions. Sometimes the footnotes are used to explain parts of the source text that are tricky to translate or confusing to read. Occasionally, I make footnotes simply to comment on parts of the text that I find especially interesting.

Barcia's text uses some archaic spellings, such as *vno* for *uno, iá* for *ya,* and *paſar* for *pasar.* When I bring the source text into the footnotes, I preserve it exactly the way it is written – spelling, capitalization, accenting, and all. Note that the source text seldom puts accent marks over lower-case i's, which means *aquí* is printed as *aqui*, *día* as *dia*, etc.

Where personal names appear in the English translation, written accents are placed according to modern rules, regardless of how the names are accented in the source text. I used the digital copy provided by the Cervantes Virtual Library to determine the correct accentuation of names. Accent marks are only written with personal names, not toponyms. For example, the names *Narváez* and *Andrés* are written with accent marks, but the towns named *Pánuco* and *Culiacán* in Spanish are written here as "Panuco" and "Culiacan."

All of the information in the footnotes was independently researched, but there are some references that were especially valuable. No study of *La Relación* would be thorough without comparing it with the other contemporary account of the Narváez Expedition, which is Oviedo's paraphrase of the Joint Report. I believe that Cabeza de Vaca may have had a copy of the Joint Report at hand when writing *La Relación*, owing to the heavy amount of overlap between them. While the two accounts never vary that far from each other, they do have some discrepancies. A footnote in my translation that reads, "According to Oviedo ..." does not necessarily mean I consider Oviedo to be superior; it just means that he and Cabeza de Vaca differ.

I also make occasional references in the footnotes to Buckingham Smith and Fanny Bandelier's translations. These were the first two English translations of Cabeza de Vaca. They influenced most of the work done on *La Relación* in the 20th and 21st centuries, and many subsequent translations rely heavily upon them. They are also both in the public domain, meaning they are easy to find on the internet and are often the first translations a student reads. Unfortunately, neither is very literal, and Bandelier's is, in my humble opinion, downright unsound. I refer to them in the footnotes sometimes not to heap criticism upon them, but because I feel that certain widely-held misconceptions about *La Relación* and Cabeza de Vaca's journey need to be addressed at the source. This is not to say that I find them worthless; on the contrary, both of them were a big help to me, and I also noted a few places in the footnotes where they were particularly insightful.

Readers who wish to learn more about Cabeza de Vaca and the other Narváez Expedition survivors' route through Florida, the Gulf coast, Texas, and Mexico are invited to read my book, *Children of the Sun: Following in the Footsteps of Narváez and Cabeza de Vaca*. I also have some articles focusing on the Texas portion of their route on my web site, TexasCounties.net. Both resources provide a treatment that is more comprehensive and organized than what I was able to provide in these footnotes.

The footnotes, as ample as they are, are not the only resource accompanying the translation. The back matter includes a chronology and a glossary. The chronology includes events that occur in *La Relación* as well as those that are part of its context. The glossary consists of words that appear repeatedly in *La Relación* and for which some explanation is warranted, but it would be too repetitive to provide that explanation through footnotes. The first instance in each chapter of a word that is contained in the glossary is indicated with an asterisk (*).

Table of Figures

Figure 1 - First Page of Barcia's Publication of *La Relación*.......... 2

Figure 2 - Map of the Narváez Expedition in Cuba and Florida...16

Figure 3 - Pineda's 1519 Map of the Gulf of Mexico 34

Figure 4 - Map of the Narváez Expedition on the Gulf................ 58

Figure 5 - Map of the Narváez Expedition on the Texas Coast ... 98

Figure 6 - Map of the Native Tribes of Coastal Texas.................158

Figure 7 - Map of the Journey of the Four Ragged Castaways .. 198

Prologue to the Narváez Expedition

For the first few decades after Christopher Columbus discovered the New World, Spain's focus was on colonizing the main islands in the Caribbean Sea – Hispaniola, Puerto Rico, Cuba, and Jamaica – and nearby parts of the North American mainland, including Panama and Mexico. Juan Ponce de León and others made some sporadic, unsuccessful attempts to explore and colonize Florida. Spain claimed the entire continent surrounding the Gulf of Mexico from Florida to the Yucatan Peninsula for an undetermined distance inland, but knew nothing about most of it except for what a few ships saw as they sailed along the coast.

Pánfilo de Narváez was born in Spain around 1478 and came to the New World as a young man. He aided Diego Velázquez de Cuellar in the conquest of Cuba from 1511 to 1514 and became one of his favorite captains. When Velázquez received reports of a kingdom of advanced natives and a fortune in gold in present-day Mexico, he probably would have sent Narváez to command a mission of conquest had Narváez not been in Spain at the time. As it happened, he sent Hernán Cortés.

Once Cortés established a foothold on the continent, he proclaimed the creation of the province of "New Spain," independent of Cuba and Velázquez and subject only to the Spanish crown, and installed himself as governor. Enraged, Velázquez sent Narváez, who had come back to Cuba, with a fleet and an army in 1520 to either kill Cortés or arrest him.

Alarmed at the prospect of one Spanish army going to war against another, the royal court at Santo Domingo sent one of its judges, Lucas Vázquez de Ayllón, to mediate between Narváez and Cortés. Narváez, finding Ayllón to be an impediment to his mission, had him arrested. This was a huge mistake in judgment on Narváez's part, and he paid a dear price for it, both politically and militarily. He arrived in New Spain with about a 4-to-1 advantage over Cortés in manpower, but he was still outmatched, for Cortés's skill as a general exceeded Narváez's by more than that. By hurling charges of treason in Narváez's direction over his arrest of Ayllón, Cortés persuaded most of Narváez's men to switch sides. Narváez was captured after a short battle in which he lost an eye. He remained in New Spain as Cortés's prisoner for about 3½ years, after which time another official negotiated his release.

Narváez went to Spain to seek redress from the Council of the Indies, a powerful body of ministers who set policies and advised King Charles in matters pertaining to Spain's overseas colonies. The Council's president was partial to Governor Velázquez and hated Cortés, but even he could not excuse Narváez's arrest of Ayllón. When Narváez went to make his case against Cortés before Charles personally, the king laughed out loud at his testimony. He awarded Narváez no relief and decided most of the other lawsuits in Cortés's favor.

Narváez had only to wait a few years to get another chance at glory. As Cortés's fortunes grew, so did the list of people who were against him. While some were merely jealous of his success, others made persuasive arguments that he was a threat to the king's sovereignty. Eventually, Charles decided it would be prudent to place limits on Cortés's power. He took the district of Panuco, which was in the present-day state of Veracruz, near Tampico, away from New Spain and gave it to Nuño de Guzmán, and he authorized the conquest of the neighboring province, which extended along the Gulf coast from Panuco to Florida. The man given the opportunity to become the next great Spanish *conquistador* of North America was Cortés's foe, Pánfilo de Narváez. His commission was issued on December 11, 1526.

The conquistadors were men who Spain invested with the authority to expand the reach and wealth of the Spanish empire into new territories. Like all other Spanish conquistadors, Narváez had to pay for the expedition out of his own funds. He was expected to set up ports and towns in places that would best serve Spain, and they were to be organized with councils and officials according to Spanish customs. Because a main part of every conquistador's duty was to spread Roman Catholicism, churches must be built. Conquistadors were charged with trying to teach the natives about God and Catholicism and invite them to become willing vassals of the Spanish crown. Natives living in territories claimed by Spain were not required to be baptized as Christians, but whether they did or not, they had to forsake certain offensive practices, including idolatry, human sacrifice, and cannibalism. If the natives attacked the Spaniards or refused to submit to their authority, Narváez was permitted to wage war upon them and to make slaves of them.

A conquistador's powers to command the army and govern his province were broad, but his actions, especially in financial matters, were carefully monitored. His contract stipulated the size of the territory and number of slaves he was allowed to have for his personal estate, as well as the number of years he was exempt from paying taxes. The most important stipulation was that one-fifth of all gold, silver, and other wealth his province produced had to be sent to the king. To make sure this was done properly, the crown always sent officials to every new province to handle the money. The authority of the king's treasury officials was so high that it was common for them, on occasions when the governor was absent, to function as lieutenant governors in his place.

The most important of these officials had the title of treasurer. The treasurer kept physical custody of the province's valuables in a chest that was fastened by three locks, and he carried one of the keys. His duties also included collecting rents and fines, paying salaries, and transporting the king's fifth – or *quinto real* - to Spain. The treasurer of the Narváez Expedition, and Narváez's second-in-command, was Álvar Núñez Cabeza de Vaca, the author of the following document.

Little is known of Cabeza de Vaca's life before the expedition. He was born circa 1490 into a respected family; his paternal grandfather was a major figure in the conquest of the Canary Islands. His surname is Cabeza de Vaca, which translates as "cow's head"; referring to him in shorthand as "Cabeza" or "de Vaca" is incorrect. He had some previous military service in Italy, among other places. His commission to serve as Narváez's treasurer was issued by King Charles on February 15, 1527. There are no records of him holding any government office prior to this. He was about 37 years old when he embarked on the voyage that would ensure his place in history.

THE SHIPWRECKED ONES

BY ALVAR NUÑEZ

CABEZA DE VACA

AND

THE ACCOUNT OF THE JOURNEY

THAT HE MADE TO FLORIDA WITH THE GOVERNOR

PANFILO DE NARVAEZ

NAVFRAGIOS
DE ALVAR NUÑEZ
CABEZA DE VACA,
Y
RELACION DE LA JORNADA,
QUE HIZO A LA FLORIDA CON EL ADELANTADO

PANFILO DE NARVAEZ.

CAPITVLO I. En que cuenta quando partiò el Armada, i los
Oficiales, i Gente, que iba en ella.

Diez i siete días del Mes de Junio de mil quinientos i veinte i siete, partiò del Puerto de Sant Lucar de Barrameda, el Governador Panfilo de Narvaez, con Poder, i mandado de V. Mag. para conquistar, i governar las Provincias, que estan desde el Rio de las Palmas, hasta el Cabo de la Florida, las quales son en Tierra-firme; i la Armada, que llevaba eran cinco Navios, en los quales, poco mas, ò menos, irian seiscientos Hombres. Los Oficiales que llevaba (porque de ellos se ha de hacer mencion) eran estos, que aqui se nombran: Cabeça de Vaca, por Tesorero, i por Algoacil Maior; Alonso Enriquez, Contador; Alonso de Solis, por Factor de V. Mag. i por Veedor; iba vn Fraile de la Orden de Sant Francisco por Comisario, que se llamaba Fr. Juan Suarez, con otros

quatro Frailes de la misma Orden : llegamos à la Isla de Santo Domingo, donde estuvimos casi quarenta i cinco dias, proveiendonos de algunas cosas necesarias, señaladamente de Caballos. Aqui nos faltaron de nuestra Armada mas de ciento i quarenta Hombres, que se quisieron quedar alli, por los partidos, i promesas, que los de la Tierra les hicieron. De alli partimos, i llegamos à Santiago (que es Puerto en la Isla de Cuba) donde en algunos dias, que estuvimos, el Governador se rehiço de Gente, de Armas, i de Caballos. Sucedio alli, que vn Gentil-hombre, que se llamaba Vasco Porcalle, Vecino de la Trinidad (que es en la misma Isla) ofreciò de dàr al Governador ciertos Bastimentos, que tenia en la Trinidad, que es cien Leguas del dicho Puerto de Santiago. El Governador, con toda la Armada, partio para allà : mas llegados à vn Puerto, que se dice Cabo de Santa Cruz, que es mitad del camino : parecióle, que era bien esperar alli, i embiar vn Navio, que truxese aquellos Bastimentos; i para esto

A maq

Figure 1 - First Page of Barcia's Publication of *La Relación*

Chapter 1
Organizing the Expedition
Which tells when the fleet left, and the officers and men
that went in it

On the seventeenth day of June of one thousand five hundred and twenty-seven,[1] Governor Pánfilo de Narváez[2] left the port of San Lucar de Barrameda[3] on the authority and orders from Your Majesty[4] to conquer and govern the provinces that extend from the River of Palms to the cape of Florida, which are on

---

[1] All dates herein are according to the Gregorian calendar. For more information, see the chronology at the back of this book.

[2] Narváez possessed the titles of governor, captain-general, and *adelantado,* which granted him executive, military, and judicial powers, respectively. He was 49 or in his early 50's at the beginning of the expedition. See the prologue for more information about Narváez.

[3] By law, all ships sailing from Spain to the Americas had to depart from and return to the city of Seville, which is about 50 miles up the Guadalquivir River. San Lucar de Barrameda, at the mouth of the Guadalquivir on Spain's south coast, is where the ships entered the Atlantic Ocean.

[4] Born in 1500, King Charles I of Spain was the grandson of Ferdinand and Isabella, the Spanish monarchs who sponsored Columbus's discovery of the New World. He inherited the throne of Spain in 1516. (Technically, he ruled the separate kingdoms of Aragon and Castile as regent on behalf of his mother, Queen Juana, who was confined to a monastery and exercised no power.) In 1519, he was named Holy Roman Emperor Charles V. The original publications of *La Relación* include a short proem, or preface, in which Cabeza de Vaca assures the king how diligently he worked to compose the narrative, how he hopes it will be useful to the king's service, etc. Barcia omitted this proem from his printing, which serves as my master text. The proem adds no value to the work, so I consider its omission to be entirely justifiable.

the mainland.[1] The fleet he took had five ships, in which went six hundred men, a few more or less. The officers he took (since they must be mentioned) were those named here: Cabeza de Vaca, treasurer and master-at-arms;[2] Alonso Enríquez, accountant;[3]

---

[1] The River of Palms was the name then given to the Soto La Marina River in the Mexican state of Tamaulipas. South of it was the territory of Panuco, which was the northernmost Spanish settlement on the Gulf of Mexico. The cape of Florida was the boundary between Narváez's territory and a separate province on the Atlantic coast that had most recently been awarded to Lucas Vázquez de Ayllón. Narváez's grant was essentially the same as the one previously awarded to Francisco de Garay in 1521, minus the hotly-contested district of Panuco. It took in the coasts of half of Tamaulipas, all of Texas, Louisiana, Mississippi, and Alabama, and two-thirds of Florida. Narváez's contract did not specify how far inland his territory extended because Spain had no idea what existed beyond the coast.

[2] See the prologue for more information about Cabeza de Vaca and his appointment as treasurer. His second title was *alguacil mayor*, which was a law-enforcement post somewhat analogous to a sheriff on land and a master-at-arms at sea. In this position, he had the power to make arrests. Narváez's petition to become governor of Florida included a request that he be made *alguacil mayor*, and the king's grant conferred it to him "for the present." Cabeza de Vaca's commission as treasurer says nothing about him being appointed *alguacil mayor*, so the author's statement here in *La Relación* that he held this office is something we must take at his word. What it all boils down to, and what the reader will see in due time, is that Cabeza de Vaca was Narváez's second-in-command.

[3] Lit. *contador*, from the verb *contar*, "to count." The accountant's job was to keep records of the payments received and made by the treasurer. He held one of the three keys needed to unlock the king's treasure chest and was the third highest-ranking member of the expedition, behind the governor and the treasurer. His job title is frequently translated to English as "comptroller" to better convey his level of authority. Nothing is

Alonso de Solís, Your Majesty's agent and inspector.[1] A friar of the Order of Saint Francis named Juan Suárez went as the commissary,[2] along with four other friars from the same order.[3]

2 We arrived at the island of Santo Domingo,[4] where we stayed about forty-five days,[1] gathering the things we needed,

---

known of this Alonso Enríquez other than what is told in *La Relación* and Oviedo.

[1] Lit. *factor* and *veedor*. The *factor* was the king's commercial agent, meaning he had the authority to represent the king in business matters. He was also the third keyholder. The *veedor* (from the verb *ver*, "to see") inspected gold mines and other wealth-producing assets and their output. These were normally two different positions; perhaps a separate *veedor* was not sent with Narváez because there was as yet no knowledge of whether his province contained gold mines. I wonder why Cabeza de Vaca always referred to Solís hereafter as "the inspector," when *factor* was the higher of his two titles. Nothing is known of this Alonso de Solís other than what is told in La Relación and Oviedo. He is not to be confused with Diego Alonso de Solís, who was named the treasurer of Molucca in 1525.

[2] The Franciscans were one of the leading Spanish missionary orders in the Americas. Their mission was to convert the American natives to Christianity. Once Hernán Cortés completed his conquest of the Aztecs and began setting up a civil society and government, he requested that more missionaries come to New Spain. Juan Suárez (also Juárez or Xuárez) was one of the "Twelve Apostles of New Spain" who arrived at Mexico City on June 17 or 18, 1524. He was named the bishop of the River of Palms and Florida and thus was the head, or "commissary," of the Franciscan delegation that went with Narváez.

[3] Also see 5:1.

[4] That is, the island of Hispaniola. Santo Domingo, the capital, was the first city Spain founded in the New World, dating to 1496. By 1527, its status as the principal city of Spanish America was starting to be

especially horses. Here, more than a hundred and forty men, who wanted to remain there because of the promises and proposals the people of that country made to them, left our fleet.[2]

3 We left from there and came to Santiago (which is a port on the island of Cuba),[3] where, in the few days we were there, the governor acquired men, arms, and horses. It happened there that a gentleman named Vasco Porcalle,[4] a resident of the town of

---

eclipsed by Mexico, but it was still an important hub in the Caribbean Sea.

[1] Travel times between Spain and the Caribbean varied from about six weeks to several months. Westbound ships typically sailed south to the Canary Islands, off the coast of Morocco, before crossing the Atlantic Ocean. It might have been around mid-October when the fleet left Santo Domingo.

[2] This is the first of many places where Cabeza de Vaca foreshadows the ill fortune that will come to Narváez's expedition. It is also the first of many places where he refers to something that sounds important without telling us what actually happened.

[3] Narváez made his name in Cuba and represented himself in letters and documents sent to the court as a resident of that island. His mentor, Governor Diego Velázquez de Cuellar, died three years before Narváez sailed from Spain, but he still had many other friends there, not to mention a wife and an estate, so it is natural that he would go to Cuba before heading to Florida. Santiago, on the island's east end, was the province's capital and largest city at that time. It was also where Velázquez had lived.

[4] Vasco Porcallo de Figueroa was a prominent, wealthy landowner in Cuba. Like Narváez, he had been a protégé of Velázquez. He was supposedly considered to lead the expedition to New Spain that Cortés was later chosen to lead, but he preferred to keep his comfortable life in Cuba. He apparently went to New Spain with Narváez in 1520, for his name is among more than 500 signatures on a document accompanying a letter Cortés wrote to the emperor on October 30, 1520. Soon after this let-

Trinidad (which is on the same island), offered to give the governor certain supplies that he had in Trinidad, which was a hundred leagues* from the said port of Santiago.[1] The governor left for there with the whole fleet, but when we arrived at a port called Cape Santa Cruz, which was halfway on the route, it seemed to him that it was better to wait there and send one ship to bring the supplies. For this, he ordered one Captain Pantoja[2] to go with his ship, and for I, for better security, go with him [in another ship], and he remained with four ships, for on the island of Santo Domingo he had bought another ship.

4 We arrived on these two ships at the port of Trinidad.[3] Captain Pantoja went with Vasco Porcalle to the town, which is one league from there, to receive the supplies. I remained at sea with the pilots, who told us that we should leave as quickly as

---

ter was written, Cortés allowed some of Narváez's supporters to return to Cuba.

[1] Trinidad, at the middle of Cuba's south coast, was Cuba's third-largest city at the time. The given distance from Santiago to Trinidad of 100 leagues is undoubtedly an approximation, but nevertheless it supports my conclusion that Cabeza de Vaca's league was the 3.46-mile *legua común*, or common league, not some of the shorter estimates that are frequently assumed. The distance by sea between the two ports, going by way of Santa Cruz, is about 380 miles (608 km).

[2] A book called *The Encomenderos of New Spain, 1521-1555* has a listing for a Juan Pantoja, who came to New Spain with Narváez in 1520. Some researchers have taken this Pantoja to be the same one who appears as a recurring character in *La Relación*. They cannot be the same, however, because the *encomendero* stayed in New Spain and participated in the conquest of New Galicia, a province that did not exist until 1531.

[3] They arrived on a Friday – presumably November 1, and certainly no later than that. See 1:10.

possible, because it was a very bad port, and many ships had been lost in it.

5 Because what happened to us there was very notable, it seemed to me that it would not be outside of the purpose and end with which I wanted to write this narrative to tell it here. The next morning, there were signs of bad weather.[1] It started to rain, and the sea was intensifying so much that, although I gave the men permission to go ashore, when they saw what was happening with the weather, and that the town was a league away, many returned to the ship rather than be wet and cold. At this time, a canoe came from the town, bringing me a letter from a resident of the town, greatly urging me to go there so that they could give me the supplies which they had, and were necessary. I excused myself of that, saying that I could not leave the ships.

6 At midday, the canoe returned with another letter asking the same thing, with great insistence, and it brought a horse for me to go on.[2] I gave the same response I had given the first time, saying that I would not leave the ships, but pilots and the men begged me greatly to go, to hurry and bring the supplies as quickly as possible, so we could leave from there, where they were in great fear that the ships would be lost if they stayed there much longer. For this reason, I decided to go to the town, although before I went, I left instructions and ordered the pilots that if the south wind, which had often destroyed ships there, should blow and they saw themselves in great danger, to bring the ships across

---

[1] Lit. *el tiempo a dar no buena señal*, "the weather to give no good sign."

[2] Cabeza de Vaca was surely given a reason why his presence was needed, but he chose not to disclose it. Since he never passes up an opportunity to cast Pantoja in a bad light, that leaves me to suspect that Sr. Porcallo was the problem. Perhaps he was demanding payment or a promissory note for supplies that Narváez thought were being given freely.

the beam[1] in a place where the men and the horses could be saved. With that, I left, although I wished to take some people with me, to go together, but they did not want to leave, saying it was wet and cold, and the town was very far, and that the next day, which was Sunday, they would come, God willing, to hear Mass.

7 An hour after I left, the sea started to become very ferocious, and the north wind became so severe that neither did the boats dare to land, nor was there any way to bring the ships across the beam, because of the wind from the bow. With very great difficulty,* with two contrary winds and much rain, they stayed that day and Sunday, until the night. At that time, the rain and the tempest began increasing, making no less trouble in the village than on the sea. All of the houses and churches fell, and to be able to protect from the wind carrying us, it was necessary for seven or eight men to go arm-in-arm. We were no less afraid of walking among the trees than in the houses, of being killed beneath them when they fell. We went about all night in danger in this tempest, without finding any place or anywhere that we could be safe for half an hour.[2]

8 Following this, we heard all night, especially after midnight, a lot of racket - a roar of voices, and a great sound of bells, flutes, tambourines, and other instruments - which lasted until

---

[1] Lit. *al través*. In nautical terms, this means to turn a ship at a right angle to the wind or, to put it simply, sideways. Most translations render this as an order to run the ships aground. The author's order to bring the ships sideways "in a place where the men and horses could be saved" suggests to me that he wanted to shorten the distance between the ships' decks and the shore in order to expedite the process of getting the men and horses safely off of them.

[2] This is not the earliest record of a tropical storm or hurricane in the Gulf of Mexico, but it is the oldest eyewitness account of one.

morning, when the terror ceased.[1] Nothing so fearful has ever been seen in these parts. I sent a testimony proving it to Your Majesty.[2]

9 On Monday morning, we went down to the port, and did not find the ships. When we saw their buoys in the water, we knew they were lost. We went along the coast to see if we could find anything of them. Not finding anything, we went into the woods. A fourth of a league from the water, we found a boat from one of the ships atop some trees. Ten leagues from there, by the coast, we found two men from my ship and some box covers. The bodies were so disfigured from the blows of the rocks that they could not be identified. We also found a cape and a quilt rent to pieces; nothing else was apparent. Sixty people and twenty horses on the ships were lost.[3] Those who went ashore the day the ships

---

[1] It is odd that the author does not offer his opinion of who or what was responsible for this terrifying concert. I can think of no logical explanation other than that it was a response to the storm by natives who lived outside the town. Some commentators suggest that the reason Cabeza de Vaca was so afraid of the noise is because he thought the natives were mounting an uprising.

[2] This is the point in Cabeza de Vaca's narrative where Oviedo's account begins. Presumably, the survivors began their Joint Report here because Cabeza de Vaca had already reported on the preceding events, so there was no need to create a duplicate record. Oviedo, who, unfortunately, was quite error-prone as an editor, states that Cabeza de Vaca's letter was dated February 15, 1527. The best we can do is assume Oviedo got the month and day correct and meant to write February 15, 1528. Cabeza de Vaca's letter to King Charles has never been found.

[3] The loss of two ships, sixty men, and twenty horses was quite significant, and it happened while Cabeza de Vaca was in charge. The reader will notice how he has taken great pains to point out that these losses were everyone's fault but his – Pantoja's for not being able to do his job, the men for refusing to go ashore, the townspeople for insisting that he

arrived, which would be up to thirty, were what remained from both ships.

10 We were there several days, with much hardship,* and in need, for the provisions and supplies the village had, and some livestock, were lost. The country was left such that it was a great pity to see it: trees were fallen, forests were burned,[1] all leafless and barren. And so we waited until the fifth day of the month of November,[2] when the governor arrived with his four ships, also having been through a great storm and also having escaped by getting to a safe place in time. The people he had in them, and those he found, were so frightened by what had happened that they were very afraid to go back out to sea in the winter, and begged the governor to wait there. He, seeing their will and that of the residents, wintered there. He put me in charge of the ships, and of the people, to go with them to spend the winter at the port of Xagua, which is twelve leagues from there,[3] and where I stayed until the twentieth day of the month of February.

---

leave his post, and the pilots for not following his instructions. I have no doubt that this avoidance of blame was the main theme and purpose of his letter to King Charles.

[1] Lit. *quemados*, "burned." The author was probably saying that the trees looked the same as if they had been burned, not that they had literally burned.

[2] November 5, 1527 was a Tuesday. Presumably, this means Cabeza de Vaca inspected the aftermath of the storm on Monday, November 4 and the storm occurred on Saturday, November 2, which is November 12 on our calendar. Hurricane season officially runs through November 30. While tropical storms in November are uncommon, they do occur. The most deadly hurricane in Cuban history occurred on November 9, 1932.

[3] Xagua is the present-day city of Cienfuegos. It is 40 miles (64 km) by sea from Trinidad. At 3.46 miles (5.54 km) per league, this converts to

11.6 leagues. This is further confirmation that my conversion factor of 3.46 is correct.

Chapter 2
From Cuba to Florida

How the governor came to the port of Xagua and brought a pilot with him

At this time, the governor arrived there with a brigantine[1] that he bought in Trinidad, and he brought with him a pilot named Miruelo. He had taken him on because he said he knew the River of Palms and had been there, and was a very good pilot on all of the North coast.[2] He also left, on the coast of Havana,[3] another ship he bought, in which he left Álvaro de la Cerda as captain, with forty men and twelve horsemen.[4]

---

[1] A brigantine was a small, two-masted sailing ship designed for maneuverability.

[2] A typed copy of an official handwritten record of Francisco de Garay's 1523 expedition to Panuco and the River of Palms records Garay's pilot's name as Diego Murillo, and his signature is rendered as Diego Fernández de Mirnedo. These spelling variations are most likely the typist's best efforts to render handwriting that is difficult to read. There are several other references to Diego Miruelo from this period which always find him in the waters near Florida. Barcia, the Spanish historian, states that there were two Diego Miruelos – an uncle and a nephew – that the uncle died in 1526 on Ayllón's expedition, and that Narváez's pilot was the nephew. Barcia gets nearly everything wrong about Ayllón's expedition, however, so he could well have been mistaken about there being two Cuban pilots named Diego Miruelo.

[3] Lit. *la Habana*, the second-largest city in Cuba at that time.

[4] Lit. *con cuarenta Hombres, i doce de Caballo*, "with forty men, and twelve of horse." This could easily be read as saying that there were 52 men in all, but I believe it means "forty men, twelve of whom had horses." Also see my comments on the next paragraph.

2 Two days after the governor arrived, he embarked.[1] The people he was carrying were four hundred men and eighty horses,[2] on four ships and one brigantine.[3] The pilot we had newly taken put the ships into the shallows called Canarreo, so that the next day, we were on dry land. We stayed there fifteen days - the keels of the ships touching dry land many times. At the end of [the fifteen days], a storm from the south put so much water on the shallows that we were able to leave, although not without much danger.

3 Having left here and arrived at Guaniguanico, another storm took us, and we were at the moment of being lost. At Cape Corrientes we had another; we were there three days. After this, we rounded Cape San Antonio,[4] and we went with contrary winds

---

[1] February 22, 1528.

[2] This kind of statement - the enumeration of ships, men, horses, and so on – is a standard feature of 16th-century Spanish expedition reports, and they are notoriously difficult to follow. Is the author saying that there were 400 footmen and 80 horsemen, or 400 men altogether, 80 of whom had horses? Some of these censuses count the soldiers only, while others include sailors, priests, slaves, women, etc. Considering that after Narváez took 300 men with him (5:1), there were "almost a hundred people left" (38:2), the above figure of 400 must be pretty inclusive.

[3] The author does not say what kind of ships the four were, but since he considered it worth noting that Narváez brought in a brigantine, it stands to reason that they were of a larger, three or four-masted class, designed more for their carrying capacity than their maneuverability. A galleon would be an example of such a ship.

[4] The places mentioned – Canarreo, Guaniguanico, Cape San Corrientes, and Cape San Antonio – are all geographic features on the south coast of western Cuba. The Canarreos Archipelago is the chain of islands that includes the large Isla de Juventud. Guaniguanico refers to a mountainous area on the west end of the main island of Cuba. Cape Corrientes and Cape San Antonio are the two small peninsulas at the island's western

until we were twelve leagues* from Havana. On the next day, when we tried to enter, a wind from the south kept us away from the land, so we went across to the coast of Florida. We arrived at the land on Tuesday, the twelfth day of April[1] and we sailed along the coast of Florida. On Holy Thursday, we anchored on the same coast, in the mouth of a bay,[2] at the end of which we saw some houses and habitations of Indians.

---

tip. (Also see Figure 2, "The Narváez Expedition in Cuba and Florida," on page 16.)

[1] April 12, 1528 was Easter Sunday. Oviedo makes the same error; this is one of many reasons why I believe Cabeza de Vaca wrote *La Relación* with a copy of the Joint Report on his desk. If we assume that the author correctly remembered that their arrival was on the Tuesday before Easter, then the actual date was April 7.

[2] It took 44 days for Narváez to sail from Cienfuegos to Tampa Bay. A canoe could have gotten there faster! Narváez and his men were, under-standably, eager to get to Florida, but his decision not to stop at Havana deprived him of some much-needed men, horses, and supplies and probably cost the lives of some of the horses he did have.

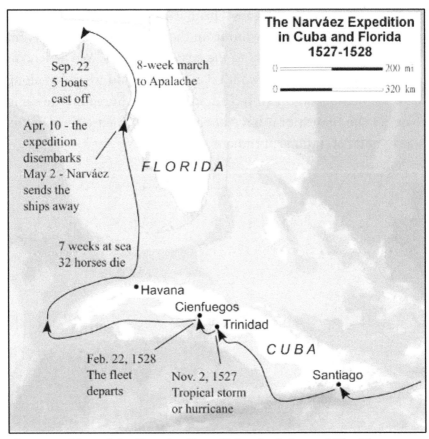

Figure 2 - Map of the Narváez Expedition in Cuba and Florida

Chapter 3
The Arrival at Florida

How we arrived at Florida

On this same day,[1] the accountant, Alonso Enríquez, went to an island that was in the same bay and called to the Indians, who came and were with him for a good bit of time. By way of exchange, they gave him fish and some pieces of venison. The following day, which was Holy Friday,[2] the governor disembarked with as many men as the little boats he brought could hold. We came to the Indian huts or houses we had seen, and found them deserted and empty, because the people had gone that night in their canoes. One of those huts was very large; it could fit more than three hundred people. The others were smaller. We found a gold rattle among the nets.

2 The next day, the governor raised banners on behalf of Your Majesty, took possession of the land in your Royal Name, presented his credentials, and was acknowledged as governor, as Your Majesty commanded him. At this time, we presented those [credentials] of ours before him, and he acknowledged them according to their contents.[3] Afterward, he commanded that all of the rest of the men disembark, with the horses we had left, which were no more than forty-two, because the rest of them died due to the great storms and the long time he had been at sea, and these few we had left were so thin and exhausted, that they could be of little use to us at the present.

---

[1] April 9, 1528. It is now sixteen months since Narváez received his commission to explore and colonize Florida. Thirteen months after Cortés received his commission to explore New Spain, he was ruling the Aztecs.

[2] Good Friday.

[3] Lit. *como en ellos fe contenia,* "as in them was contained."

3 The next day,¹ the Indians of that village came to us. Although they spoke to us, we did not understand them, since we did not have an interpreter.* They did make many signs and threats, and it seemed to us that they were telling us to leave the country. With that, they left, without making any problems for us, and they went away.

---

¹ This should be Easter Sunday. According to Oviedo, it was.

Chapter 4
The Initial Exploration of Florida

How we entered the country

O n the following day,[1] the governor decided to go forth into the country, to explore it and see what was in it. We went with him - the commissary, the inspector, and I - with forty men. Six among them had horses,[2] which were able to be of little benefit to us. We went to the north[3] until at the hour of vespers* we came to a very large bay, which appeared to go far inland.[4] We stayed there that night.

2 The next day, we returned to where the ships and men were. The governor ordered that the brigantine go sail along the way of the coast of Florida and look for the port that the pilot, Miruelo, had said he knew (yet he had erred, and did not know where we were, nor where the port was). He ordered that if the brigantine did not find it, it should cross over to Havana, look for Álvaro de la Cerda's ship, take on some supplies, and return to look for us.

---

[1] April 13, 1528, if the author has not omitted any days.

[2] Oviedo writes that there were 40 footmen plus 6 on horseback, with Narváez being one of the latter.

[3] Northeast, according to Oviedo.

[4] The ships landed north of Tampa Bay. The proof of this will be made as the story progresses, and any remaining doubts will be put to rest in Chapter 38. The fact that the men discovered a large bay by walking north (or northeast) of their landing site indicates that they landed in Pinellas County, on the west side of Tampa Bay. The bay they discovered here is called Old Tampa Bay. Their specific landing site cannot be known, but I believe they anchored their ships at Johns Pass in Boca Ciega Bay, 4 miles (6.4 km) south of Seminole. Also see 38:4-5.

3 After the brigantine left,[1] we returned to explore the country - the same ones as before, plus some more men. We followed the coast of the bay[2] we had found for four leagues,* then encountered four Indians. We showed them corn* to see if they knew what it was, because up to that point, we had not seen any sign of it. They told us that they would take us to where it was, and they took us to their village, which is at the end of the bay, close to there, and in it they showed us a little corn that was not ready for picking. There we saw many boxes of Castilian[3] merchandise, and in each one of them was a dead person's body. The bodies were covered with some painted deerskins. To the commissary, this appeared to be some form of idolatry, and he burned the box with the bodies. [4] We also found pieces of linen and cloth and helmet crests[5] that appeared to be from New Spain.[6] We also

---

[1] Cabeza de Vaca does not make this clear, but Miruelo piloted the departed brigantine.

[2] Cabeza de Vaca uses the verb *costear*, a nautical term that means "to follow the coast," and he uses the same word elsewhere when sailing is obvious, as in 4:2. I am sure, however, that they did not board the galleons for this. It sounds more like they returned on foot and horseback to the place where they found the bay, then walked along the shore of that bay.

3 The kingdom of Spain was a union of the kingdoms of the crowns of Castile and Aragon. Castile was more than twice as large as Aragon, was where the seats of government were, and was where Narváez and most of his men were from, so "Castilian" usually fits as a synonym for "Spanish."

4 Oviedo writes, "It appeared to them, the *fray comisario* and the friars, that those objects were idolatrous, and the Governor had them burned."

5 Lit. *Penachos*, the plumage often attached to the helmets of the period, which resembled the tuft of feathers on the heads of some birds, such as parrots.

6 The province of New Spain was the nucleus of present-day Mexico.

found samples of gold. Using signs, we asked the Indians where they had found those things.[1] They signed to us that very far from there was a province called Apalache,[2] where there was much gold. They made signs that there was a great quantity of everything we valued in it.[3] They said that in Apalache, there was plenty.[4]

4 Taking some of these Indians as guides,[5] we left there. Having walked ten or twelve leagues, we found another village with fifteen houses, where there was a good patch of sewn corn that was ready to pick. We also found some that was already harvested.[6]

5 After two days there, we returned to where the accountant, the men, and the ships were. We told the accountant and the pilots what we had seen and the news that the Indians had given us.

---

[1] Oviedo writes that the Spaniards found pieces of shoes, canvas, and cloth, and some iron. They asked the Indians, by signs, where they found the items, and they said they found them in a shipwreck in the bay. The governor then showed them some gold and asked them if they knew where any more was.

[2] The territory of the Apalachee Indians, at present-day Apalachee Bay, west of the Florida peninsula and south of Tallahassee.

[3] Narváez and his men did not realize that these natives were now just trying to get rid of these foreigners, who were causing a commotion in their village and even starting fires in it. Other Spanish explorers, both before and after Narváez, observed that whenever they showed something foreign to American natives, the natives informed them that there was plenty of that item far away or in the land of their enemies.

[4] Lit. *mucho*, "much."

[5] Most likely, against their will, which would have been the norm in those situations. In Oviedo, they are "captive Indians."

[6] Lit. *eftaba iá feco*, "was already dry."

6 The next day, which was the first of May,[1] the governor called aside the commissary, the accountant, the inspector, myself, a sailor named Bartolomé Fernández,[2] and a scribe named Gerónimo de Alaniz.[3] Once gathered, he told us that he had the desire to explore inland, while the ships go along the coast until they reach the port that the pilots said and believed was the way to the Palms,[4] which was very close to there. He asked us to give him our opinions of this.

7 I responded that it seemed to me that we should not leave the ships for any reason until they were in a safe and settled port,[5] and that it looked like the pilots were unsure and did not agree on one thing, nor did they know where we were. Beyond this, the horses were such that we could not take advantage of them for any need that may arise. Above all, we were going around mute, without an interpreter,* where we understood the

---

[1] Two weeks passed that the author did not account for in his narration.

[2] Nothing is known of this man, but he evidently became the chief pilot after Miruelo's departure. It would stand to reason that he was also Narváez's chief pilot prior to Miruelo's joining the expedition, unless that man was one of those who stayed behind in Santo Domingo or who died in Trinidad.

[3] Cabeza de Vaca calls him *Eſcrivano*, a word that is often translated as "notary." Every Spanish expedition had a notary whose duties included reading orders, letters, and other official documents, writing them, and being a witness or signatory to them. Of all the Narváez Expedition members, Alaniz's name is the easiest to find in official documents. He was a royal scribe in Santiago, Cuba, starting apparently in 1525, and he was working in his official capacity there at least as late as May 27, 1527. Narváez undoubtedly picked him up during his stopover in Santiago that autumn.

[4] I.e., the River of Palms – see 1:1 and 2:1.

[5] In 38:2, Cabeza de Vaca writes that one of the ships had already been lost on the dangerous coast.

Indians poorly, nor [did they] know what we wanted from the land. We were entering a land that we had no records of, and did not know of what sort it was, neither what was in it, nor what kind of people lived there, nor what part of it we were in. Above all this, we did not have supplies to explore the unknown, in view of the fact that the ships did not have more than a pound of biscuit and a pound of bacon to give each man as rations for entering the country. My opinion was that we should embark and go look for a port and country that was better for settlement, since that which we had seen was the most deserted and poorest ever found in those parts.

8 To the commissary, everything seemed to the contrary. He said that we should not embark, but we should go in search of the port, always staying along the coast, for the pilots said it was not but ten or fifteen leagues from there, on the way to Panuco.[1] He said it was impossible, by always going along the coast, not to come to it, since he said the land came inward twelve leagues.[2] The first ones to find it should wait there for the others. He said that for us to embark was to tempt God, because after we left Castile so many hardships had taken place – we had so many storms,

---

[1] Panuco was a town near present-day Tampico, Mexico that was about 100 miles south of the River of Palms. "On the way to Panuco" means following the Gulf coast in a counter-clockwise direction, i.e. keeping the sea to their left and the land to their right. To the members of the expedition, Panuco was a safety net – if they got hopelessly lost, they could always sail ahead until they reached Panuco. The great tragedy of this moment is that the entrance to the port they were looking for was only a few miles in the opposite direction.

[2] It is unclear what this means, but Tampa Bay's south shore is about 30 miles (48 km) long. This is nine leagues, not twelve, but no other bay on Florida's west coast is larger.

so many losses of ships and men prior to arriving there.[1] For these reasons, he would have us go by the length of the coast until arriving at the port, and the other ships, with the other men, would go the same way until they arrived at the same port.

9 It seemed good to everyone who was there, except for the scribe, that was what should be done. He said that before we abandon the ships, they should be left in a known and safe port, in a place that could be settled. Once that is done, we could explore the interior of the land and do as we wished.

10 The governor held to his opinion, and to that which the others advised. Seeing his determination, I required him, on Your Majesty's behalf, not to leave the ships until they were left in a port and secured. I asked for a testament from the scribe of what transpired there with us.[2] [Narváez] responded that he was satisfied with the opinions of the majority of the other officers and commissary, that I had no part in making those requirements, and he asked the scribe for a testament how, since that country had no sustenance to be able to populate it, nor a port for the ships, he took up the people that had settled there, and they went with him in search of a port and a country that would be better. He then gave an order to notify the men who were going with him

---

[1] Here we see the ultimate effect of the decisions and mistakes made earlier in the expedition – the 45 days spent at Santo Domingo, the 2½-month layover in Cuba, and the bad piloting and excruciatingly long trip from Cuba to Florida. Everyone at that meeting, except Alaniz, had been on the expedition for 11 months, and they had spent way too much of that time at sea. I imagine that their problem with Cabeza de Vaca's proposal was not so much that finding a place to build a town and then building it would take time, but that they would have to board the ships again to do it. I can envision heads nodding in agreement when Suárez said, "to embark was to tempt God."

[2] Lit. *lo pedí por Teftimonio al Efcrivano, que alli teníamos*, "I asked the scribe for testimony, what there we had."

to prepare themselves with whatever they were going to need for the journey. After that decree, he said to me, in the presence of everyone there, because I was so opposed, and afraid of exploring the country, that I would stay and take charge of the ships and the men remaining on them, and settle [the port] if I arrived before him. I excused myself of this.

11 That same evening, after leaving there, saying that it did not seem to him that there was anyone he could trust with that, [Narváez] sent word to me to ask me to take charge of it. In view of how it bothered me so much, I still excused myself. He asked me what the reason was that I avoided accepting it, to which I responded that I avoided charging myself with that because I felt certain, and knew, that he would never again see the ships, nor the ships him, and that I understood this, seeing how he was so poorly equipped for exploring the interior country. I would much rather risk the danger that he and the others were risking, and endure what he and they would endure. [I told him] not to put me in charge of the ships and give occasion for saying that I had opposed the expedition and remained out of fear, placing my honor in dispute, and that I would much rather risk my life than put my honor in that position. Seeing that he had gotten nowhere[1] with me, he asked many others to speak to me about it and plead with me. I responded the same to them as to him. So, he arranged for his lieutenant to stay on the ships - an alcalde* he brought whose name was Caravallo.

---

[1] Lit. *conmigo no aprovechaba*, "with me not did take advantage of/make use of."

Chapter 5
The Journey to Apalache

How the governor left the ships

On Saturday, the first of May, the same day that this happened,[1] [Narváez] ordered that each man going with him be given two pounds of biscuit and a half pound of bacon. We then left to explore the country. The sum of all the men that we took was three hundred.[2] Among them were the commissary, Friar Juan Suárez, another friar named Juan de Palos,[3] three clerics,[4] and the officers. The horsemen who went with us, we were forty horsemen. And so, we proceeded with the provisions that we brought for fifteen days, without finding anything else to eat, ex-

---

[1] The officers' meeting described in the previous chapter occurred on Friday, May 1, but Narváez and Cabeza de Vaca were still arguing about it later that evening. Narváez then consented to let Cabeza de Vaca go on the overland journey and leave the ships in charge of someone else. That final decision may be the "this" referred to here. Presumably, the march to Apalache actually commenced on Saturday, May 2.

[2] Cabeza de Vaca will report the deaths of three individuals in separate incidents (5:6, 7:5, and 7:10) ten in one incident (8:5), "more than forty" of sickness and hunger (8:7), and have 251 depart on boats (8:7), making a sum of more than 304.

[3] Juan de Palos, like Juan Suárez, was one of the "Twelve Apostles to New Spain." Also see the footnotes to 1:1.

[4] Lit. *Clerigos*. In 1:1, Cabeza de Vaca writes that "four other friars" (*Frailes*) were with Suárez, while this passage refers to two friars and three clerics. It is unclear whether these clerics were counted with the friars in 1:1, or whether three of the friars stayed with the ships, and the clerics are being mentioned here for the first time. If I had to guess, I would say it was the former. One of the clerics is mentioned a few times in the middle of the narrative; the other two are not mentioned again.

cept for palmettos,[1] like those of Andalusia. In all this time, we found not one Indian, nor saw one house or village.

2 At the end [of these fifteen days],[2] we came to a river that we crossed with very great effort,*[3] swimming and on rafts. It took us a day to cross it because of its very strong current. On the other side, some two hundred Indians, more or less, came out to us. The governor went over to them, and after having spoken to them with signs, they signed to us in such a manner that we were obliged to turn against them. We seized five or six of them, and they took us to their houses, which were almost half a league* from there. In them was a great quantity of corn,* which was ready to pick. We gave infinite thanks to our Lord for having helped us in such great need, because we were certainly new to such hardships, beyond exhausted, and we arrived very weakened from hunger.

3 On our third day there,[4] the accountant, the inspector, the commissary, and I came together and requested of the governor that we venture out to the sea to see if we could find a port, because the Indians said that the sea was not very far from there.

---

[1] Saw palmettos, found throughout Florida, bear clusters of edible blue-black berries in autumn. In May, the men would have eaten the hearts, which can be eaten raw and have a color and texture not unlike a potato.

[2] May 16.

[3] This is the first of two significant rivers that the expedition crossed from their landing site to Apalache, and it serves as evidence that they landed on the coast no further south than Pinellas County. This river would be the Withlacoochee. Their route probably had something in common with U.S. Highway 19, which runs from St. Petersburg to Tallahassee. It is about 90 miles (144 km) along that route to the Withlacoochee. In covering only 6 miles (9.6 km) a day, they were moving quite slowly.

[4] May 18.

He responded to us that we would not make ourselves better off[1] by speaking of that, because it was very far from there. Since I was being the most insistent, he told me to go and discover it and look for a port, and to go on foot with forty men. So, the next day I left with Captain Alonso del Castillo[2] and some forty men of his company. We walked thusly until noon, when we arrived at some sandbars that seemed to go far inland. We walked along them for a league and a half, with the water halfway up our legs, stepping on top of oysters, from which we received many puncture wounds on our feet. They were the cause of much trouble for us until we arrived at the river we had crossed earlier, which emptied into the same inlet. Since we could not cross it, on account of having the wrong equipment, we returned to the camp and reported what we had found to the governor - that it was necessary to cross the river again in the same place we had crossed it earlier in order to explore that inlet well and see if there was a port.

4 The next day,[3] [Narvácz] ordered a captain named Valenzuela[4] to cross the river with sixty men and six horsemen, follow it down to the sea, and find out if there was a port. After being out for two days, [Valenzuela] returned and said that he

---

[1] Lit. *no curaſemos*, from *curar*, "to cure." A literal translation of this phrase would be "we would not make ourselves well."

[2] Captain Castillo, who becomes a recurring character in the narrative, is first mentioned here. Very little is known of his background. The signature of one Alonso del Castillo is on the same letter from Segura la Frontera, New Spain signed by Vasco Porcallo in 1520 (see the footnotes to 1:3), but seeing as Alonso was an extremely common given name and Castillo was also a common family name, we must not make any assumptions about that. Castillo presumably came over with the fleet from Spain. His full name was Alonso del Castillo Maldonado.

[3] May 20.

[4] Captain Valenzuela is not mentioned before or after this. Also see the footnotes to 8:7.

had explored the inlet, and the whole bay was knee-deep, and there was no port.[1] Also, he had seen five or six Indian canoes crossing one way or the other, and that the Indians were wearing many feathered headdresses.[2] Knowing this, we left from there the next day, always going in quest of that province that the Indians had called Apalache, bringing as guides those of them who we had taken.

5 And so we continued until the seventeenth day of June,[3] without finding Indians that would dare to wait for us. And then a lord,[4] who an Indian carried on his back, came out to us, covered in a painted deerskin. He brought many people with him. Ahead of him, they came playing flutes made of cane. He came to where the governor was and stayed with him for an hour. By signs, we made him understand that we were going to Apalache. By signs that he made, we took him to be an enemy of those of Apalache, and that he would go to help us against them.[5] We gave him beads, bells, and other items of barter, and he gave the governor

---

[1] Readers are invited to look at a terrain or topographic map of Florida to notice how the Florida coast on the north side of the Withlacoochee River is a vast expanse of wetlands and creeks, with sea depths of four feet or less for dozens of miles offshore.

[2] Lit. *Penachos*, a feathered crest worn on the head or naturally occurring on some birds. See also "helmet crests" in 4:3.

[3] Here the author has skipped ahead about four weeks. His date of June 17 creates some improbable travel speeds for the preceding segment and the next segment, though; a date closer to June 2 would be more internally consistent.

[4] Cabeza de Vaca refers to some native leaders as *señor* ("lord"), and others as *cacique* ("chief"). To Cabeza de Vaca, the lords were more regal-looking and had more authority than the chiefs.

[5] Lit. *contra él*, "against him."

the hide that he was wearing. Then he turned back, and we went following on the path that he went.

6 That night, we came to a river that was very deep and very wide, and the current very strong.[1] Since we could not cross over on rafts, we made a canoe for it. We took a day to cross it. If the Indians had wanted to offend us, they could well have hindered our passing. Even with them helping us, we had great difficulty. One horseman, who was called Juan Velázquez, a native of Cuellar, not wanting to wait, entered the river. The current, which was strong, swept him from the horse. He kept hold of the reins, and so he and the horse drowned. The Indians of that lord, whose name was Dulchanchelín,[2] found the horse. They told us where down the river we would find him, and so they went for him. His death gave us much pain, because until then, we had not lost anyone. The horse made dinner for many that night.[3]

7 Moving on from there, the next day we arrived at that lord's village, and he gave us corn there. That night, where they went to get water, a Christian was shot with an arrow; God willed that they did not hurt him.

———————————————

[1] This is probably the Suwannee River, the largest river on the west coast of Florida north of Tampa Bay, and about 40 miles (64 km) north of the Withlacoochee. According to the Gentleman of Elvas, eleven years later, the De Soto Expedition encountered natives playing flutes after crossing a large river in which one of their horses drowned on their way to Apalache.

[2] This is the only native American Cabeza de Vaca met whose name was recorded.

[3] Many Spaniards, as the author will attest later, had an ethical objection to eating horsemeat, but there may have been some who had no qualms, and in any case, necessity frequently trumps all else. The natives may have also partaken.

8 The next day,[1] we left there without any of the native Indians appearing, for all had fled, but going on our trail, Indians who came to battle appeared. Although we called to them, they did not come back, neither did they wait, but they withdrew, following us by the same trail that carried us. The governor left an ambush of some horsemen on the trail. When they passed it, [the horsemen] came up on them and took three or four Indians, and these we took along as guides from there on. They took us through a country that was very difficult to traverse and marvelous to see, because in it there are many great forests, and the trees are marvelously tall. So many of them were fallen on the ground that they obstructed the trail in such a way that we could not pass them without going a long way around and with a very great effort. Of those that were not fallen, many were split open from top to bottom from lightning, which strikes in that country, as there are always many great storms and tempests.

9 With this difficulty, we traveled until the day after Saint John's,[2] when we came within sight of Apalache, without the Indians of the country sensing us. We gave many thanks to God for seeing we were so close to it, believing that what those of the other country had told us was true: that there the great hardships we had endured would be finished, for our road had been long and bad, and we had endured great hunger. Although we had found corn at times, most of the time we had walked seven or eight leagues without coming across it. There were many among us who, beyond the great fatigue and hunger, were dealing with wounds made on their backs from carrying their weapons, besides

---

[1] June 19.

[2] St. John's Day is June 24, so this is June 25. The author has skipped ahead five days.

other things that occurred.[1] But on seeing ourselves arrived where we wished to be, and where we were told so much sustenance and gold would be, it was as if a great part of our labor and fatigue had been taken away.

---

[1] Lit. *fin otras cofas que fe ofrefcian*, "without other things that to him offered/occurred."

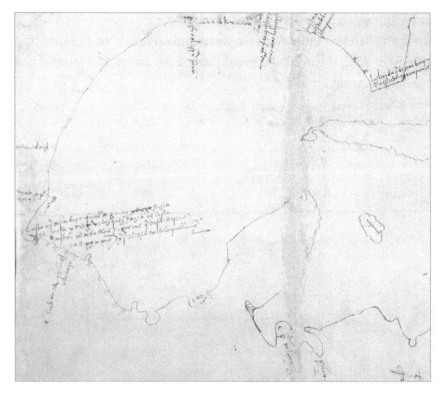

Figure 3 - Pineda's 1519 Map of the Gulf of Mexico

Chapter 6
At Apalache

How we arrived at Apalache

Having arrived within sight of Apalache, the governor ordered that I take nine horsemen and fifty footmen and enter the village. The inspector and I undertook this. We entered, finding nothing except women and children, for the men were not in the village at that time. A little later, as we were walking through it, they came and began to fight. They shot arrows at us, killing the inspector's horse, but finally they fled and left us.

2 There was a great quantity of ripe corn* there, and much dry [corn] that they had stored. We found many deerskins, and among them some small thread blankets, which the women used to cover themselves somewhat; they were no good. They had many vessels for grinding corn. The village had forty small houses and buildings, low and in sheltered locations, for fear of the great tempests that continuously occur in that country. The construction is straw. They are surrounded by a very thick forest, large groves, and many bodies of water, where there are so many and such large fallen trees that they are hindered. They are the reason that it is impossible to walk around without a lot of effort* and danger.

Chapter 7
From Apalache to Aute

On the manner of the country

The land between where we disembarked and this village and country of Apalache is, for the most part, level. The soil is sand and earth. Throughout it there are very large trees and open forests, where there are walnuts, laurels, others that are called sweetgums, cedars, junipers, live oaks, pines, oaks, and low palmettos, of the kind of those of Castile. Throughout it there are many large and small lagoons, some of which are very troublesome* to cross, partly because of the great depth, and partly because there are so many fallen trees in them. Their bottoms are sandy, and we found those in the Apalache region to be much bigger than those on the way there.

2 There are many cornfields in this province. The houses are quite scattered around the countryside, in the manner of those that are in Los Gelves.[1] The animals that we saw there were: three kinds of deer, rabbits, hares, bears, lions, and other wild beasts. Among those we saw an animal that carries its young in a pouch that it has in its belly. The whole time they are small, it carries them there, until they know how to look for food. If it so happens that they are looking for food and people come, the mother does not flee until they have gathered in her pouch. [2] Through

---

[1] Los Gelves is the Spanish name for the island of Djerba, off the coast of Tunisia. Spanish forces captured it in 1520 and remained there until 1524. For Cabeza de Vaca to make this somewhat casual reference to such an obscure place suggests to me that he served in the military there.

[2] This is the first recorded description of the opossum.

there, the country is very cold.¹ It has very good pastures for cattle. There are many kinds of birds: large numbers of geese, common ducks, wild ducks, mallards, flycatchers, egrets, herons, and
partridges; we saw many falcons, female falcons, sparrow hawks,
pigeon hawks, and many other birds.²

3 Two hours after we arrived at Apalache, the Indians that
had fled from there came back to us in peace, asking us for their
women and children. We gave them to them, except that the governor detained one of their chiefs³ with us. For this reason, they
left offended, and the next day, they returned on the warpath and
attacked us with such courage and speed, that they set fire to the
houses we were in.⁴ When we came out, they had fled, taking ref-
uge in the lagoons that were very close by.⁵ Because of this, and
because of the large cornfields that were there, we could not do
them harm, except for one that we killed. The following day, other
Indians from another village that was on the other side came to us
and attacked us with the same skill as the first ones, and fled in
the same manner. One of them also died.

---

¹ Many geologists and historians believe that many parts of the earth, including North America, experienced a "Little Ice Age" from the 1500s to
early 1800s. During this time, winters were longer and colder than they
are today. Even so, Cabeza de Vaca was in Florida from April to September and was writing about the Tallahassee area in June and July. His recollection of it as "very cold" is hard to believe.

² The lack of any mention of the alligator in *La Relación* is most curious.
Then again, alligators dislike very cold climates.

3 Lit. *caciques*. Here, the author uses the standard word for "chief," unlike in Chapter 5, when he referred to Dulchanchelín as a *señor*, or
"lord."

4 Oviedo writes, "There were up to two hundred natives."

5 Oviedo writes, "by the mountain and in the hills." Apalache was in the
vicinity of Tallahassee. There are not any mountains in that area, but
there are many hills of around 150 feet in height.

4 We were in this village twenty-five days,[1] during which we made three trips into the country and found it very thinly populated[2] and very bad for travel, because of the bad crossings, forests, and lagoons it had. We asked the chief that we had detained, and the other Indians that we brought with us, who were neighbors and enemies of theirs, about the manner and population of the country, the quality of its people, and about supplies and everything else about it. They responded to us, each one for himself, that Apalache was the largest village in all that country, and that further on there were fewer people who were much poorer than them, and that the land was not well-populated, and its inhabitants were very scattered. Even further in, there were large lagoons, dense thickets, and vast, unpopulated deserts. We then asked them about the country that was to the south - about the villages and resources it had. They said that nine days' travel[3] in that direction, toward the sea, there was a village called Aute. The Indians there had much corn,* and that they had beans and gourds,* and that by being so close to the sea, they caught fish, and they were friends of theirs.

5 We, in view of the poverty of the country and the bad reports about its population and everything else they gave us, and how the Indians had made constant war on us, wounding the men and horses in the places where we went to collect water - and this from the lagoons, so safe that we could not harm them, because they shot arrows at us while nestled in the them, and they killed a lord of Tescuco named Don Pedro, who came with the commis-

---

[1] This would be from June 25 to July 19, 1528, based on the author's last date check. Oviedo states that they stayed there for 26 days.

[2] Lit. *mui pobre de Gente*, "very poor of people."

[3] Or eight days, according to Oviedo.

sary[1] - decided to leave there and go and look for the sea and that village of Aute that they had told us about. We therefore left at the end of twenty-five days after our arrival.

6 The first day,[2] we passed those lagoons and crossings without seeing an Indian. But on the second day, we came to a lagoon that was very hard to cross, because the water came to our chests, and it had many fallen trees in it. We were in the middle of it when many Indians, who were hidden within the trees so that we could not see them, attacked us. Others were on top of the fallen [trees]. They commenced to shoot arrows in such a manner that they wounded many of our men and horses. They also took from us the guide we had brought. Before we could get out of the lagoon, and after they got out of it, they turned around and continued [the attack], wanting to hinder the crossing in such a way that we could not get an advantage by getting out of it or make ourselves stronger and want to fight them, who would stay hidden in the lake, and from there wound our men and horses. In view of this, the governor ordered that the horsemen dismount and attack them on foot. The accountant dismounted with them. They then attacked. All of [the Indians] fled into a lagoon, and so we won the crossing.

7 Some of our men were wounded in this revolt; the good armor they took did not protect them.[3] There were men this day who swore that they had seen two live oaks, each one of them as

---

[1] I.e., Texcoco, an Aztec city east of present-day Mexico City that Cortés conquered in 1520. The Spaniards gave "Christian" first names to the natives who they baptized.

[2] July 20.

[3] Lit. *que no les valieron buenas Armas, que llevaban.* The verb *valer* can be rendered either as "to protect" or "to have value," so the author could be saying either "the good armor did not protect them" or "the good armor was worthless to them."

thick as a man's lower leg, shot completely through with the Indians' arrows. This is not so amazing if one considers the force and skill with which they shoot; I myself saw an arrow in the base of a poplar, which penetrated it by a span.[1] All of the many Indians we saw throughout Florida are archers. Because their bodies are so large[2] and they go around naked, from afar they appear to be giants. These people are amazingly fit - very slender, and with great strength and agility. The bows they use are as thick as a man's arm - eleven or twelve palms long - and they shoot arrows at two hundred paces with such great care that in no case do they miss.[3]

8 After we made this crossing, we came to one of the same kind one league* from there, except that because it was so long - it went on for half a league - it was much worse. We crossed this one freely and without hindrance from the Indians, because they had spent their whole supply of arrows at the first one; they had none left with which to dare to attack us.

9 The next day, while passing through a similar crossing, I found evidence of people that crossed ahead of us. I notified the governor, who was at the rearguard, of this so that we could be prepared if the Indians should attack us, and they would not be able to harm us. When we came out onto the plain, they were still following us. We turned on them in two groups and killed two In-

---

[1] Lit. *geme*. A Spanish span, or *jeme*, is the distance from the tip of a man's thumb to the tip of his index finger when the angle between them is the widest. This equals about 7½ inches (19 cm).

[2] Lit. *son tan crescidos de cuerpo*, "[they] are so grown of body."

[3] There were 4,000 paces to the league. One pace is approximately 4.6 feet (1.4 m). 200 paces is 913 feet (278 m). There are few people on Earth who can accurately shoot arrows this far, so take Cabeza de Vaca's statement with a grain of salt, especially about how they never missed. He writes that the natives made "constant war" on the Spaniards and wounded many of their men and horses, but he only reports one man killed at this point.

dians. They wounded me and two or three other Christians.¹ They then returned to the forest, and we could not do them any more harm or damage.

10 We traveled eight days in this manner. After the crossing I described previously, no more Indians came out to us until the place to which I said we were going was one league ahead. There, as we were going along our trail, Indians came out without being noticed and struck our rearguard. A boy who was back there, who belonged to a nobleman named Avellaneda, let out some screams. Avellaneda turned around and went back to help, and the Indians hit their mark with an arrow at the edge of his armor. It gave him such an injury that the arrow passed almost all the way through his neck. He then died there, and we carried him to Aute. We arrived there from Apalache in nine days of travel.² When we arrived, we found all of its people gone and the houses burned. There was much corn, gourds,* and beans, all of which were ready to begin to pick.

11 We rested there for two days. After these passed, the governor ordered me to go explore the sea, which the Indians had said was quite close by. On the trip we had just made, we had discovered a very large river that we had given the name, River of the Magdalene.³ Accordingly, I left the following day¹ to explore it,

---

¹ The author uses the word "Christians" to mean anyone on the expedition. The company included at least one Portuguese, one Greek, one Moor, and possibly many other non-Spaniards. It was a requirement for everyone going on an expedition from Europe to the New World, even slaves, to convert to Catholicism.

² The date ought to be July 29.

³ We can be sure this name means the Spaniards discovered the river on the feast day of Mary Magdalene, which is July 22. This means they found it on their third day of travel from Apalache to Aute. In all likelihood, it was the St. Mark's River.

joined by the commissary, Captain Castillo, Andrés Dorantes,[2] seven other horsemen, and fifty footmen. We traveled until the hour of vespers,* when we reached an inlet, or entrance of the sea, where we found many oysters, which the men enjoyed. We gave many thanks to God for having brought us there.

12 The next morning, I sent twenty men to inspect the coast and take a look at its layout. They returned the following night. They said that its inlets and bays were very large and reached far inland, which greatly hindered their discovery of what they wanted, and that the coast was very far from there. With this new knowledge, and seeing how poorly organized and prepared we were for exploring the coast, I returned to the governor.

13 When we arrived, we found the governor ill, along with many others.[3] The previous night, the Indians had struck and put them under the greatest stress, which is why this sickness came upon them so unexpectedly. Also, one horse had died. I reported

---

[1] August 1.

[2] Here, another major figure in Cabeza de Vaca's narrative is mentioned for the first time. Andrés Dorantes de Carranza was a member of Captain Alonso del Castillo's company. Later on, Cabeza de Vaca will begin referring to him with the title of captain, the same as Castillo, but that title is missing in his first few references to him. This suggests to me that he was promoted during the expedition. A royal decree excerpted by the Spanish historian Antonio de Herrera in *Historia General* gives the names of eight men who were to compose the councils of the first two towns Narváez established. Dorantes was one of the councilors designated for the first town. This, and the fact that he was one of the few who brought a slave, suggests that he was a man who possessed some wealth and respect. Two of his cousins were also members of the expedition.

[3] Oviedo writes, "they found the Governor, the purser, and the inspector fallen ill, as well as many others." The purser would be the accountant, Enríquez.

that which I had done and about the poor layout of the country. We remained there that day.[1]

---

[1] August 2, based on working backward from author's next date check.

Chapter 8
Building Boats

How we left Aute

We left Aute the following day[1] and traveled all day until we arrived where I had been. We went on the trail with extreme difficulty,* because neither were the horses sufficient to carry the sick, nor did we know how to cure them. They suffered every day; it was a very painful and pitiful thing to see the need and hardship that they were in. The further we went, I saw how unprepared we were for going forward, because we did not know where to go. Neither even if we did could the men move forward, because they were mostly sick - so sick that few of them were able to be of much good. I refrain from reporting about it at greater length, because any one can imagine what might happen in such a strange and bad country, without any aid of any kind, either for staying there or for leaving it.

2 As much as the surest aid was our Lord God, and of this we never doubted, something happened next that aggravated me more than all of this. Among the horsemen, the largest part of them began to go secretly, thinking they would find their own aid, and abandoning the governor and the sick, who were weak and powerless. Still, since many among them were noblemen and men of a good sort, they did not want this to happen without bidding farewell to the governor and Your Majesty's officials. We then chastised them for their proposal, making our case about abandoning their captain, the sick, and the weak, and separating themselves from Your Majesty's service at such a time. They agreed to stay, and that whatever happened to one, happened to all, with no one abandoning another.

---

[1] August 3, 1528.

3 Upon this, the governor called everyone together, and each person for himself, to give his impression of that bad country, so that we could leave it and look for some aid, for none was to be had there. A third of our people were greatly infirmed, and this grew every hour, so that we were totally certain that if we stayed there, the only way out was death, which that place would make even more dire. Considering this and many other problems, and that we had tried many remedies, we agreed on a very difficult one to put into action, which was to make ships in which we would escape. It seemed impossible to everyone, because we did not know how to make them, neither had we any tools, iron, forges, oakum, pitch, or rigging. In the end, out of all of the many things that would be needed, we had none, nor did anyone know anything about their fabrication. Above all, there was nothing to eat while they did it, and those who had to work the labor that we had said.[1] Considering all this, we agreed to think about it more carefully. This ended our discussion that day. Each one went entrusting it to our Lord God, that He would lead him on the path that would most serve Him.

4 The next day, God willed that one of our company came saying that he would make some tubes from sticks, and some bellows could be made from deerskins. Since we were in such a state that anything that had the resemblance of aid seemed good to us, we told him to put himself to the task. We agreed to make nails, saws, axes, and other tools which we needed so badly from the stirrups, spurs, crossbows, and other iron objects that we had. To give assistance, so to have sustenance for the time that they did this, four incursions were made on Aute, with all of the horses and men that were able to go. On every third day, a horse was

---

[1] This is an instance of where the Spanish text is ungrammatical.

killed[1] and was divided among those who were working on the boat project and those who were sick. The incursions were made with the men and horses that were able; they returned with up to four hundred bushels[2] of corn* - although not without contending and quarreling with the Indians. We gathered many palmettos, making use of their fibers and husks, twisting and preparing them to use in place of oakum for the boats. Work on them was begun by the only carpenter we had in our company.[3] We were so diligent that, starting from the fourth day of August, five boats[4] were

---

[1] Cabeza de Vaca writes that the expedition disembarked with 42 horses (3:2). He subsequently mentions the deaths of three (5:6, 6:1, 7:13), but probably more had died than those. The men were at Aute for 50 days, killed a horse every three days, and had one horse left at the end (8:7). This suggests that they had 17 horses when they came to Aute.

[2] Lit. *hanegas*. The Spanish bushel, or *fanega*, was equivalent to 55.5 liters, which is 1.57 times larger than the 8-gallon bushel used in the U.S. 400 *fanegas* equals about 192 dry barrels. However, the author could have simply been stating that there were 400 containers of corn, rather than giving an estimate of the total volume. This huge amount of corn was the survivors' main sustenance during their upcoming ordeal on the Gulf of Mexico.

[3] Presumably, this was Álvaro Fernández; see 13:4. For the most part, the men who went on Spanish expeditions of conquest, even those who had titles or held rank, were unskilled and did not practice a trade.

[4] The author consistently calls these vessels *barcas*. A *barca* is a small boat, such as a fishing boat, lifeboat, or dinghy. Fanny Bandielier, one of the first translators of *La Relación*, made many poor word choices, one of which was to use the word "barges" for these vessels. Unfortunately, many other translators and interpreters have followed suit. A boat has a keel and a pointed bow, while a barge is flat-bottomed and rectangular. While it is linguistically possible for a barge, or *barcaza*, to be classified as a *barca* if it is small enough, "boat" is a much more typical translation of *barca* than "barge." Furthermore, the stated goal of these men was to "make ships (*Navios*) in which we could escape" (see Paragraph 3), and

completed on the twentieth of September. Each one was twenty-two cubits long.[1] They were caulked with palmetto oakum and tarred with a kind of pitch that a Greek man named Don Teodoro made from some pines. We made ropes and rigging from palmetto fibers and the tales and manes of horses, sails from our shirts, and oars - which we thought were going to be necessary - from the junipers that were there. Such was the land in which our sins had placed us that it was with great effort that we were able to find stones for ballast and anchors for the boats, for we had not seen one in all of it.[2] We also skinned the horses' legs whole and tanned the hides to make pouches in which we could carry water.

5 During this time, some went to the nooks and inlets of the sea to gather seafood. The Indians struck them twice. They killed ten men in view of the camp, without our being able to help them. We found them shot with arrows all the way through. Although some of them were wearing good armor, it was not enough to withstand, because nothing was,[3] because they shot with such skill and force, as I said above.

---

while they may not have known much about how to construct them, surely they knew that barges are used to transport heavy loads along canals and rivers, not to navigate an ocean's bays and coastlines. Cabeza de Vaca mentions, at various places in *La Relación*, the crafts' hulls, waist boards, sails, riggings, oars, and rudder, making them out to be as close to normal boats or small ships as they were capable of making them.

[1] Lit. *codas*, or "elbows." A cubit was reckoned as the distance from a man's elbow to the tip of his third finger. The usual estimate is 18 inches (45.7 cm). 22 cubits is 33 feet (10 m).

[2] The coast of the Gulf of Mexico is not a good place to find large rocks. Also see 18:7, "I surely believe that if there were rocks in that country, they would eat them."

[3] Lit. *para que eſto no ſe hicieſe*, "so that this would not be done."

6 By the statement and oath of our pilots, we had traveled two hundred and eighty leagues,* more or less, from the bay, which we gave the name of the Cross, to here.[1] In this whole country, we did not see a mountain range, nor saw any sign of one in any way.

7 Before we embarked, besides those of us that the Indians killed, more than forty men had died of sickness and hunger.[2] On the twenty-second day of September, they had finished eating the horses,[3] with only one left. On that day, we embarked in this order: forty-nine men went in the governor's boat; the same amount went in a boat he gave to the accountant and the commissary; he gave the third to Captain Alonso del Castillo and Andrés Dorantes with forty-eight men; he gave another to two captains named Tél-

---

[1] In a Spanish expedition, one or more men were typically assigned the job of keeping track of how far the expedition walked every day. This was done by counting steps and then reckoning every 4,000 paces as one league. I do not know how common it was to refer to these men as "pilots," but they are who the author is referring to, not mariners. They were, sadly, very mistaken about the distance they had covered. 280 leagues equals 969 miles (1,550 km). I estimate that they have walked about 270 miles (169 km). If the expedition had traveled 280 leagues by this time, it would have already been in Texas. Pineda estimated the distance between the cape of Florida and Panuco, sailing along the coast, as 300 leagues. The sworn testimony of these "pilots" was, in effect, that the expedition had walked nearly the whole way to Panuco.

[2] Oviedo writes, "forty men, a few more or less, died in that place from disease." If the number of 300 men on the expedition given in 5:1 is precise, then by subtracting the 3 individuals who died in separate incidents (5:6, 7:5, and 7:10), the 10 from 8:5, and the 251 who remained after the boats were finished, that leaves 36 who died during the seven weeks of boatbuilding.

[3] Notice that Cabeza de Vaca writes most of this section in the first person plural, "we," but when mentioning the eating of the horses, he writes "they." He subsequently writes that he could not eat horse - see 12:4.

lez and Peñalosa,[1] with forty-seven men; he gave the other to the inspector and me, with forty-nine men.[2] After our clothing and supplies were brought aboard, the boats had no more than a span[3] left above the water. Besides this, we were so pressed together that we were unable to move. Necessity is so powerful that it brought us to venture out in this manner, putting ourselves into such a troubled sea, and without any knowledge of the art of navigation out of everyone who went.[4]

---

[1] These two men, Téllez and Peñalosa, are mentioned four times in La Relación, and they are always mentioned together. In the other three mentions, Peñalosa's name comes first.

[2] Oviedo gives a similar accounting of the boats, but in his, the second boat was assigned to "the purser and the friars." Also, the counts are different: in Cabeza de Vaca, the total number of people on the boats are 50, 51, 50, 49, and 51, for a sum of 251. In Oviedo, the boats carry 49, 49, 50, 50, and 50, for a sum of 248. Friar Suárez, who appeared numerous times in these first eight chapters of La Relación, is not mentioned after this. He, Bartolomé Fernández (see 4:6), Friar Juan De Palos (5:1), and Captain Valenzuela (5:4) are the only Narváez Expedition members who are mentioned by name during the exploration of Florida for whom Cabeza de Vaca does not state whether they survived to reach Texas. Suárez is the only one known to have survived Florida.

[3] Lit. *geme*, see 7:7.

[4] Yet there was one man, Álvaro Fernández, who Cabeza de Vaca describes in 13:4 as a sailor.

Chapter 9
Leaving the Bay of Horses

How we left the Bay of Horses

That bay we left from is named the Bay of Horses.[1] We went along those inlets for seven days, in waist-deep water, without seeing any sign of anything like a coast.[2] At the end of these [days], we came to an island that was close to the mainland.

---

[1] The affinity that men (and women) have for their horses is well-known in stories of the American West, but it is seen just as often in stories of the Spanish conquistadors. Bernal Díaz del Castillo, a chronicler of Cortés's exploits, remembered and wrote about individual horses that he and his fellow soldiers rode. It is fitting, and not surprising at all, that these Spaniards would commemorate this place by naming it after their faithful servants and companions, who made the ultimate sacrifice in their attempt to save themselves.

In 1539, some natives guided Captain Juan de Añasco of the De Soto Expedition to this location. They confirmed that ten of Narváez's party were killed there and showed Añasco where Narváez's men camped. Añasco saw a furnace surrounded by charcoal, horse watering troughs made from a hollowed-out tree trunk, and horse skulls. Añasco's party searched the area carefully for hidden or buried letters that Narváez's party may have left, but found none. Añasco erected markers at the site. The markers were not subsequently located, but the chronicles of De Soto's expedition confirm that the Bay of Horses was somewhere in Apalachee Bay.

[2] St. Mark's Bay is not the only place in the Apalachee Bay area that could be the Bay of Horses, but it fits the text very well. It is at the end of a river (7:11), it reaches 2½ miles (4 km) inland (7:12), and after reaching the sea and beginning to head west, one can meander through a maze of coves and islets for days without finding a place to land that has fresh water and wood for building a fire. In contrast, it would be hard for even the poorest of navigators to wander around Ochlockonee Bay for a

My boat went forward, and from it we saw five Indian canoes coming. When the Indians saw that we were going to them, they abandoned [the canoes] and left them in our hands. The other boats went on forward and set upon some houses on the same island. We found many mullets and their eggs, which were dry.[1] This was a very great help for the need that we were in. After taking them, we proceeded further. Two leagues* from there, we passed through a strait where the island met the mainland. We called it Saint Michael, because we made through it on his day.[2] Leaving it, we arrived on the coast where, with the five canoes I had taken from the Indians, we repaired the boats somewhat, making waist boards[3] of them and adding them so that they rose two palms above the water.[4]

---

full day, much less a week, without accidentally finding either deep water or an open coastline.

[1] Lit. *Liças i huevos de ellas, que eʃtaban ʃecas*, "lizas, and eggs of theirs, which were dry." *Liza* is the Latin name for the genus commonly called mullet. Mullet eggs (roe) are a popular delicacy in Florida – the eggs being more valued than the fish itself – and their season begins in late autumn.

[2] The feast day of St. Michael the Archangel is September 29. This agrees with Cabeza de Vaca's statement that it took seven days for them to reach this point from the Bay of Horses. The island could have been Piney Island. It would be reached by following the meanders of the coast for about 16 miles (26 km) from St. Mark's Bay. It is separated from the mainland by a channel a few hundred feet wide. About 4 miles (6.4 km) after passing it, one reaches Ochlockonee Bay, where the coastline becomes more solid and substantial.

[3] That is, boards attached to the waist, or middle, of a vessel.

[4] Cabeza de Vaca writes in 8:7 that the boats rose a span (*geme*), or about 7½ inches (19 cm), above the water. A palm is 3 to 4 inches, so two palms is about the same as a *jeme*. This would mean that after this

2 After this, we resumed traveling along the length of the coast toward the River of Palms. Our thirst and hunger were growing every day, because our supplies were very small and coming close to the end, and our water was finished, because the pouches we had made from the legs of our horses had become rotten and of no benefit. Sometimes we entered inlets and bays that reached very far inland; we found all of them shallow and dangerous. We made our way through them for thirty days. Sometimes we found Indian fishermen - poor and miserable people.

3 One night, at the end of these thirty days,[1] going along the coast in extreme need of water, we sensed a canoe coming. When we saw it, we waited for it to arrive. It did not want to show itself,[2] and although we called to it, it did not want to turn around or wait for us. Because it was night, we did not follow it, but went on our way. When dawn came, we saw a small island and went to it to see if we could find water, but our labor was in vain, for there was none. While we were anchored there, a very large storm overtook us. We were stopped there for six days without daring to go out to sea. As we had gone five days without drinking, our thirst

---

modification, the boats were at about the same level as before. Oviedo seems to have the right answer; he writes "the boats then rose up and were lifted two more palms out of the water."

[1] Cabeza de Vaca's count of the days from the launching of the boats to the day of his boat's landing is 50, but the dates he gives are 46 days apart. The cleanest way to resolve this discrepancy is to reckon this period of 30 days, during which nothing happens, as an approximation of the precise span of 26 days. That would make the current date October 18, 1528.

[2] Lit. *hacer cara*, "to show face."

was such that we were compelled to drink salt water. Some of us were so distressed by it that suddenly, five men died.[1]

4 I relate this briefly because I do not believe it is necessary to relate in particular the miseries and hardships* in which we saw ourselves. Moreover, considering the place where we were and the small hope we had for relief, each person can imagine what happened there. Seeing how our thirst grew and the water was killing us, although the storm had not ceased, we agreed to entrust ourselves to our Lord God and risk ourselves to the sea's danger rather than wait for the certainty of death by thirst. So, we left in the direction of the canoe we had seen the night we came there. On that day, we could see ourselves drowning many times, and were so lost that there was no one who did not believe that death was certain.

5 It pleased our Lord, who shows His favor in our times of greatest need, that at sunset[2] we turned a point of land where we found fair weather and a haven. Many canoes came out to us. The Indians in them came and spoke to us and, without waiting for us, turned around. The people were large and well-built, and carried neither arrows nor bows. We went, following them to their houses, which were near there in a tongue of water. We landed, and among the houses we saw many containers of water and a great quantity of cooked fish.[3] The lord of those lands offered all of it to the governor and, taking him with him, brought him to his house. Their houses were matted in a way that appeared to be fixed. After we entered the chief's house, he gave us much fish, and we

---

[1] When a person is dehydrated, drinking any amount of seawater, even a mouthful, is harmful. Cabeza de Vaca and some of the other men apparently believed that drinking it slowly or in small quantities is okay.

[2] October 25.

[3] Lit. *Pescado guisado*, which could be translated as "stewed fish" or "fish stew."

gave him our corn. They ate it in our presence and asked us for more, and we gave it. The governor gave him many items of barter.

6 While [we] were with the chief in his house, half an hour after sunset, the Indians suddenly struck us and those who were lying on the beach, very sick. [1] They also attacked the chief's house, where the governor was, and they wounded him in the face with a stone. Those [of us] who were with the chief seized him, but since those of his were so close by, he broke free, leaving a robe in their hands made of sable,[2] which I believe is the best that can be found in the world. They have an odor that is not unlike amber and musk that reaches so far, it seems like it is from a great number of them. We saw others there, but none were as such as these.

7 Those of us who happened to be there, seeing the governor wounded, laid him down in a boat. We had most of the men follow him to the boats, and we left about fifty of us on land to deal with the Indians. They attacked us three times that night with such vigor that each time, they made us retreat more than a stone's throw. None of us were left unhurt; I was hurt in the face. If they would have had more arrows (since only a few were found), they would have done much more damage, without a doubt. On the last occasion, Captains Dorantes,[3] Peñalosa, and

---

[1] Oviedo writes that three men were killed.

[2] Lit. *Martas Cebelinas*, or, in Latin, *Martes zibellina*, the sable. Sables are native to Russia and some of its neighbors. No species of marten is native to the Gulf coast. The animal with the pungent odor and fine fur that the author is describing was undoubtedly some other member of the weasel family, either the weasel itself or, very possibly, the mink.

[3] Here, Dorantes is referred to for the first time as a captain. I wonder whether his valor at this time, when the two commanders were wounded, along with the somewhat high status he brought to the expedition (see the footnote at 7:11) earned him a field promotion.

Téllez placed themselves in ambush with fifteen men and struck them in the rear, in such a manner as to make them flee, leaving us alone.

8 The morning of the next day, I destroyed more than thirty canoes, which helped us with a north wind,[1] for we had to stay there all day, very cold, not daring to go out onto the sea because of a great storm that was in it. When it passed, we went back out on the boats. We navigated for three days, with only a small amount of water to drink, and as the vessels we were carrying were also very few, we were finding ourselves in the same plight as before.

9 Continuing on our way,[2] we entered a swamp, and in it we saw a canoe of Indians coming. When we called to them, they came to us. The governor, to whose boat they had come, asked them for water. They offered to give him what our people could carry. A Greek Christian called Doroteo Teodoro (of whom I made mention above)[3] said he wanted to go with them. The governor and others tried hard to stop him, but were unable to. He wanted to go with them no matter what, and so he went, taking a Negro* with him. The Indians left two of their company as hostages. At night, the Indians returned bringing many vessels without water, and they did not bring the Christians that they had taken. Those that had stayed as hostages, when the others spoke to them, tried to jump into the water, but our men who were in the boat stopped them. So, the Indians in the canoe fled, leaving us very confused and sad for having lost those two Christians.[4]

---

[1] I.e., by burning them for heat.

[2] October 28.

[3] See 8:4.

[4] Cabeza de Vaca and his comrades do not appear to have considered the likelihood that Teodoro considered his chances of survival with the natives to be better than by staying with his fellow Christians, and forsook

---

the expedition by his own choice. In 1540, De Soto's men heard from natives that Teodoro had left the Narváez Expedition during a stop for water somewhere east of the Mississippi River, but they were given conflicting reports (or misunderstood what they heard) about where this occurred and whether he and his slave had been killed or were still alive. The two men lost here and the five who died from drinking seawater are the only losses out of the 251 men who boarded the boats that Cabeza de Vaca records until they land, but he also writes that two of the boats had about 80 men combined when they landed (14:2). If every boat landed with 40 men, that means there were about 44 deaths during the boat journey that Cabeza de Vaca does not mention. Oviedo has 248 men beginning the boat trip and records 3 or 4 additional deaths, making approximately 38 unrecorded deaths.

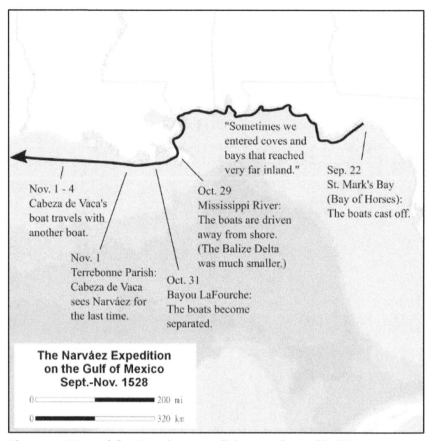

"Sometimes we entered coves and bays that reached very far inland."

Sep. 22
St. Mark's Bay
(Bay of Horses):
The boats cast off.

Nov. 1 - 4
Cabeza de Vaca's
boat travels with
another boat.

Oct. 29
Mississippi River:
The boats are driven
away from shore.
(The Balize Delta
was much smaller.)

Nov. 1
Terrebonne Parish:
Cabeza de Vaca
sees Narváez for
the last time.

Oct. 31
Bayou LaFourche:
The boats become
separated.

The Narváez Expedition
on the Gulf of Mexico
Sept.-Nov. 1528

0 — 200 mi
0 — 320 km

Figure 4 - Map of the Narváez Expedition on the Gulf of Mexico

Chapter 10
Trouble on the Sea

Of the Indians' skirmish against us

When morning came,[1] many canoes of Indians came to us, asking us for the two comrades who they had left in the boat as hostages. The governor said that he would give them if they brought the two Christians they had taken. With these people came five or six lords, who seemed to us to be more capable and composed, and have more authority than those we had seen previously, albeit not so large as those of whom we have related. They wore their hair loose and very long, and they were covered with mantles of marten, of the kind that we had taken earlier.[2] Some of them were made in a very strange manner, as there were knots on them made of patches of tawny skins,[3] which looked very good. They asked us to go with them and said they would give us the Christians, water, and many other things. Many canoes continued to help surround us, with the goal of controlling the mouth of that inlet. Because of this, because the country was very dangerous to stay in, we departed for the sea, where we stayed with them until noon. Because they did not want to give us the Christians, and for that reason we would not give them the Indians, they began to hurl stones with slings and throw staffs. They made threats of shooting arrows at us, although we saw but three or four bows among all of them.

---

[1] October 29, 1528.

[2] See 9:4.

[3] Lit. *en ellas havia vnos lacas de labors de vnas Pieles leonadas*, or "on them there were some knots (bows, ornaments, ties) of patchwork (embroidery, needlework) of lion-colored skins." *Leonadas* refers to the color of the skin, not the animal it came from.

2 During this conflict, the wind renewed, and they turned around and left us. We navigated that day until the hour of vespers,* when my boat, which was in front, discovered a point of land. On the other end of it was a very large river and an islet that made the point where I anchored to wait for the other boats. The governor did not want to come; instead he put into a bay very close by, in which there were many islets. We joined him there and took sweet water from the sea, because the river entered into the sea like a flood. We went onto that island to toast some corn* that we had brought, because we had eaten it raw for two days, but because we could not find firewood, we agreed to go to the river that was across the point, one league* from there. Going there, the current was such that it would not let us approach in any way. Instead, it separated us from the land, although we struggled and contended with it. The north [wind] that came from the land began to increase so much that it put us out to sea, without us being able to do anything. A half-league from where we were driven out, we sounded and found even with thirty fathoms,* we could not take the depth; we could not determine whether the current was the reason we could not take it.[1]

---

[1] Thirty *brazas* is about 165 to 180 feet. There is only one place on the Gulf coast where this could have happened: the Mississippi River. Its discharge is thrice as powerful as the next-strongest river on the Gulf coast between Apalachee Bay and Galveston Bay, and it pours directly into the sea, rather than emptying into a bay first. Along the rest of the Gulf coast, one can go 10 miles (16 km) from the shore and still be in less than 20 feet (6 m) of water, but at the mouth of the Mississippi, the depth reaches 100 feet (30 m) less than 7 miles (11 km) from land. The lowest part of the Mississippi River delta, called the Balize Delta or Bird's Foot Delta, formed over the past 250 years. Narváez's boats probably crossed the river at or somewhat north of the present-day town of Venice. The Narváez Expedition has just encountered the *Rio del Es-*

3 We navigated nevertheless for two days, struggling to reach land. At the end of them, a little before the sun was gone, we saw many smoke columns on the coast. Working to approach there, we found ourselves in three fathoms of water.[1] Because it was night, we did not dare to land, because we had seen so many smoke columns, we believed that could be the greater danger. We could not see, on account of the great darkness, what we ought to do, so we decided to wait until morning.

4 When dawn came,[2] each boat had found itself lost from the others. I found myself in thirty fathoms. Continuing on my way, I saw two boats at the hour of vespers. As I went to them, I saw that the first one I came to was the governor's. He asked me what it seemed to me we should do. I told him that he should re-group with the other boat that was ahead, and in no way leave it, and we would follow, all three boats together, the way God willed to carry us.[3] He responded that could not be done, because the

---

píritu Santo, or River of the Holy Spirit, which Alonso de Pineda discovered in 1519 and had been shown prominently on maps since then. Oddly, the men did not realize this, and believed they found Espíritu Santo when they reached Matagorda Bay.

[1] The boats are at a delta two days' travel west of the Mississippi River and are back in shallow water. This would be the Lafourche Delta in Lafourche Parish, Louisiana. Now that the boats are sailing day and night, simply trying to find land again, they are moving much faster than when the men were investigating every inlet, stopping for water, and camping at night.

[2] November 1.

[3] The natives attacked the Europeans at one recent encounter (9:6) and threatened them at their last encounter (10:1). The Europeans declined to land in Lafourche Parish because they feared the natives were too numerous (10:3). Cabeza de Vaca was undoubtedly thinking about the

boat was very far out to sea, and he wanted to reach land, and that if I wanted to follow him, the men on my boat had to take the oars and go to work, because with the strength of our arms it was possible to reach land. He was advised on this by a captain he had with him, who was named Pantoja,[1] telling him that if he did not reach land that day, that he would not reach it in six days,[2] and in that time, to die from hunger was inevitable. Seeing his determination, I took my oar, and everyone on my boat did the same. We rowed almost until sunset, but since the governor had with him the strongest and healthiest men of all, we could not keep up or follow him in any way. When I saw this, I asked him to give me a rope from his boat, so that I could follow him. He responded that it would not be a small thing to them if they alone could reach land that night. I said to him that since I saw little chance of our being able to follow him and do as he had ordered, to tell me what

---

greater safety the Europeans had in keeping as much of their army together as possible.

[1] Pantoja was the captain who went to Trinidad with Cabeza de Vaca in Chapter 1. Every time he appears in Cabeza de Vaca's narrative, it is in connection with something bad happening.

[2] Cabeza de Vaca does not report that he actually saw land on this occasion, and a sounding of 30 fathoms would mean he was quite far out. Nevertheless, Pantoja and/or Narváez sensed that they were within rowing distance of land. They had to have been off Terrebone Parish, which is some 40 miles west of Bayou Lafourche. The boats were apparently being steered by north winds (see 9:8, 10:2, 12:4, and 17:7) at this time, which would be expected as the jet stream moved south and brought winter weather to the Gulf coast. The Louisiana coastline is shaped so that once the boats passed Terrebone Parish, the land would curve away from them, meaning that without being able to sail northward, it would be impossible to reach the shore. (Also see Figure 4, "The Narváez Expedition on the Gulf of Mexico," on page 58.)

it was that he was ordering me to do. He answered that this was no time for some to give orders to others, that each one should do what seemed best to him to save his life, and that is what he intended to do. Saying this, he sheared off with his boat.[1]

5 Since I could not follow him, I went after the other boat, which was out at sea and which waited for me. Reaching it, I found that it was the one belonging to Captains Peñalosa and Téllez. We navigated together for four days, eating a ration of a half a handful of raw corn each day. At the end of these four days,[2] a storm came to us, and we lost [sight of] the other boat.[3] By the great mercy God showed for us through it all, we did not sink. In accordance with the weather, and it being winter, and very cold,[4] and suffering from hunger for so many days, with the injuries we

---

[1] This moment, even more than his arrest of Ayllón, his defeat by Cortés, and his foolish order in Florida to send his ships away, cements Narváez's place in history as a poor general. Gonzalo de Oviedo, who knew Pánfilo de Narváez personally, was referring to him when he wrote, "I have seen many who are valiant when they have the lance or the sword in hand. However, when deprived of weapons, they are very different individuals." He further commented on Narváez, "there are many captains who may know how to fight and how to command, but there are few who can govern an army."

[2] November 5.

[3] Lit. *que hiço perder la otra Barca*, "which made to lose the other boat." This makes it sound like the boat capsized in the storm and all the men on it drowned, especially given the author's next sentence, but 19:6 makes it clear that did not happen.

[4] Despite the Gulf coast's mild winter climate, freezing temperatures can arrive in Galveston in early December. When one considers that November 5 on the Julian calendar equals November 15 on the Gregorian calendar and takes the Little Ice Age and the earlier arrival of winter into account, it is easy to believe that the men on the boats felt like winter had already arrived.

sustained while at sea, the men began to become very dismayed the next day in such a way that when the sun went down, everyone who was in my boat had fallen down on top of each other, so close to death that few were conscious, and in that hour there were not five men standing.

6 When night came, only the mate[1] and I were left who were able to work the boat. Two hours into the night, the mate told me that I had to take charge of it, because he was in such a state that he believed he was going to die that night. So, I took the helm. After midnight, I went to see whether the mate was dead. He responded that he instead was better and that he would steer until morning. At that moment, I surely would much rather have tasted death than see so many people around me in such a condition.

7 After the mate took charge of the boat, I rested a little without much rest. There was nothing further from my mind than sleep. Around dawn, it seemed like I heard the sound of breakers, because the coast was low, it made a lot of sound. With this sudden surprise, I called to the mate, who responded that he thought we were close to land. We took a sounding and found we were in seven fathoms. He thought that we should stay on the water until daybreak. Therefore, I took an oar and rowed toward the shore, which we were a league from, and turned the stern seaward.

8 Near land, a wave took us and tossed the boat out of the water like a horseshoe in a game.[2] With the great blow from that,

---

[1] Lit. *Maestre*. The master of a Spanish vessel was below the captain in authority, but above the pilot and any other crew. Cabeza de Vaca was surely using the term loosely here. His second-in-command, Inspector Solís, must have either become incapacitated or lacked the ability to operate the boat.

[2] Lit. *echó la Barca fuera del Agua vn juego de herradura*, "threw the boat out of the water a game of horseshoe." As I explain in the preface of this book, most or all other translations of *La Relación* rework this

almost everyone in the boat who was like dead came to themselves. When they saw we were close to land, they began to slip out, crawling on their hands and feet. As they went out to some gullies on the shore, we made a fire and toasted our corn, and found rainwater.[1] With the warmth from the fire, the people came around and began to revive somewhat. The day that we landed was the sixth of the month of November.

phrase, changing it from a comparison with a game of horseshoes into an estimate of the distance the boat was thrown. I believe, though, that the author was referring to the *sensation* of being thrown up high and then crashing back down with a heavy thud, like a horseshoe in a game, and I believe the next phrase bears that interpretation out.

[1] Lit. *Agua de la que havia llovido*, "water of that which had rained."

Chapter 11
On an Island

Of that which happened to Lope de Oviedo with some Indians

After the men had eaten, I ordered Lope de Oviedo, who was the strongest and most robust of all, to go to some trees that were close by there, climb one of them, survey the land we were in, and collect some information about it. He did so and learned that we were on an island.[1] He saw that the land was rutted[2] in the manner of land where cattle walk, and it seemed to him that it was a land of Christians,[3] and he told us so. I ordered him to return and look very particularly to see if there were any trails that went through, and to do it without greatly increasing the danger that he could be in. He went, and chancing upon a footpath, followed it for nearly a half a league* and found some Indian huts that were empty because the Indians had gone out to the field. He took one of their pots, a little puppy, and a few mullets from them and came back to us.

---

[1] The Texas coast consists of some areas where the Gulf of Mexico washes up onto the mainland, and other areas where barrier islands and bays separate the mainland from the ocean. These barrier islands are narrow – typically a half a mile to two miles wide – and dozens of miles long. Some are true islands, while others are peninsulas. Depending on the height of the tree, a man in a tree can only see for about five miles over water and flat land, due to the curvature of the Earth. Lope de Oviedo could see that they were on one of these barrier landmasses, but there was no way he could see both ends of it to know whether it was a peninsula or a true island. Also see 15:5.

[2] Lit. *cabada*, "hollow, concave," from *cavar*, "to dig, to excavate."

[3] None of the native American tribes Spaniards had encountered to that point herded livestock, so signs of herding implied the presence of Europeans, i.e. "Christians."

2 It seemed to us that he was delayed, so I sent two other Christians to look for him and see what had happened to him. They chanced upon him close to there and saw three Indians with bows and arrows, coming to him and calling to him, and he likewise was calling to them by signs. So he came to where we were, and the Indians stayed back a little ways, seated on the same shore. After a half hour, a hundred more Indian archers joined them. They were so large now, or not, our fear made them appear to be giants. They were close to us, where the first three were. It was needless to think that there would be one among us who could defend himself, because it was difficult to find six who were able to raise themselves from the ground. The inspector[1] and I went over to them and called to them, and they came to us. We tried to assure them and assure ourselves as best as we could. We gave them beads and bells, and each one of them gave me an arrow as a sign of friendship. By signs they told us that they would return in the morning bringing food, because then they had none.

---

[1] Alonso de Solís, see 1:1.

Chapter 12
Losing the Boat

How the Indians brought food to us

The next day,[1] as the sun was coming out, which was the hour that the Indians had said, they came to us, as they had promised, and brought us a lot of fish and some roots that they eat, which are like nuts, some bigger or smaller, most of which are taken from below the water,[2] with great effort.* In the afternoon, they returned and brought us more fish and some of the same roots. They made their women and children come to see us, and so they returned rich in bells and beads that we gave them. They returned to visit us on other days with the same things as the other times.

2 As we saw that we were supplied with fish, roots, water, and the other things we asked for, we decided to apply ourselves to embarking and continuing on our way.[3] We raised the boat out of the sand in which it was lodged. It was necessary for us to remove all of our clothing for this, and we endured great difficulty

---

[1] November 7, 1528.

[2] Oviedo writes that these underwater roots were "like truffles."

[3] The author's statement in the previous paragraph that the natives visited them "on other days" makes it unclear how long they were there before they attempted to relaunch their boat. Based on subsequent events, I believe it is now on or about November 10, which would mean three additional days passed. As the reader will soon learn, this effort ends in failure and tragedy. In other instances in this narrative, when an undertaking has a similar outcome, Cabeza de Vaca walks us through the decision process, making a point of identifying the person who came up with the idea, and disclaiming any personal responsibility for it. I find the fact that he does not do that here to be revealing.

to cast it out on the water, because we were such that other, much lighter things sufficed to put us in it.[1]

3 And so, we embarked. At two crossbow shots[2] out at sea, such a great wave hit us that it soaked everyone. Since we were naked, and it was very cold, the oars dropped out of our hands. At the next blow that the sea gave us, the boat overturned. The inspector and two others clung to it to save themselves, but the reverse happened, and the boat took them down and drowned them.[3] As the coast is very rough, the sea threw everyone else in a heave, enveloped in waves and half-drowned, onto the coast of the same island, without losing more than the three who the boat

---

[1] I translated this phrase literally, hoping that, despite its vagueness, the reader would glean the author's meaning. I think Fanny Bandelier's translation has the right idea: "our condition was such that much lighter things would have given us trouble."

[2] A crossbow shot, or *tiro de bollesta*, is a Spanish idiom meaning "a long distance." It is always meant as a rough estimate, in much the same way that English speakers might use "a stone's throw" to mean "a short distance." Researching or estimating the length of a crossbow shot would be missing the point. Spanish writers often used "two crossbow shots" or, occasionally, three, to give a better idea of how long this great distance was.

[3] Unlike other Spanish soldiers who recounted their adventures, such as Bernál Díaz del Castillo and Pedro de Castañeda, Cabeza de Vaca never makes any personal observations about his comrades, as to what kind of men they were – proud or humble, generous or uncharitable, rash or thoughtful, etc. All we have to go on is what he says of their actions. I would like to know what Cabeza de Vaca thought about Alonso de Solís, who was usually by his side in Florida, who was with him throughout the harrowing ordeal on the Gulf of Mexico, who helped him make friends with the natives of this island, and who died under his command. The author's failure to characterize the people in his story, giving only their names and titles but telling the reader nothing of their essences, is, in my opinion, the biggest flaw of *La Relación*.

had taken down. Everyone else escaped harm, as naked as how we were born, and lost all that we carried. Although it was worth little, it was also worth much.[1]

4 Since it was November and it was very cold, and we were such that our bones could be counted with little difficulty, we were made into the figure of death itself. For myself, I know I can say that since the previous month of May I had not eaten anything but toasted corn,[2] and sometimes I found myself having to eat it raw, because although they killed the horses while the boats were being made,[3] I could never eat of them, and there were not ten times that I ate fish. I say this to explain the reasons why anyone could see why we were in such a state. On top of everything stated, a north wind arose, so that we were closer to death than to life. It pleased Our Lord that, while searching for the remnants of the fire that we had made, we found wood, with which we made large fires. And so we were asking Our Lord, crying many tears, for mercy and forgiveness of our sins. Each one of us took pity not only on himself, but everyone else who he saw in the same state.

5 At the hour of sunset, the Indians, believing that we had not gone, returned to look for us and bring us something to eat.

---

[1] It took me many readings to realize something which may be obvious to most. I shall spell it out for the benefit of those who, like myself, missed it: in order to avoid being out on the water in soaked-through clothing, the men removed their garments before launching the boat and laid them in it, expecting to get dressed again once they were underway. This is why, after the boat capsized, they were left without any clothing.

[2] Here we have an example of Cabeza de Vaca's tendency to exaggerate for effect. For the few days preceding this, he had roots to eat. He also had oysters at the Bay of Horses (7:11) and mullet eggs at a stop on the Gulf coast (9:1). He also adds, before completing his sentence, that he ate fish on several occasions.

[3] See 8:4.

When they saw us in such different attire from before,[1] and such a strange kind, they became so frightened that they turned back. I went over and called to them, and they came, very frightened. I made them to understand by signs how our boat had sunk and three of us had drowned. There, in their very presence, they saw two dead, and those who were left of us were going down that same path. The Indians, seeing the disaster that had come to us and the disaster we were in, with so much misfortune and misery, and with great pain and sadness at our plight, sat down among us and began to weep loudly and so sincerely that it could be heard far away. This lasted more than a half hour. Truly, seeing these men who were so crude and lacking in reason, like brutes, so pained for us increased my own emotions, and that of the others in the company, for what we had been through.

6 After all of the weeping had calmed down, I spoke to the Christians and asked them if they thought I should request the Indians to take us to their houses. Some of them who had been in New Spain answered that I should not speak about it because if they took us to their houses, they would sacrifice us to their idols.[2] Still, seeing that there was no other remedy, and that by any other course, death would be closer and surer, I did not heed

---

[1] We can suppose that the castaways made makeshift coverings out of grasses, leaves, or whatever other materials they could find.

[2] The Spaniards who visited the Yucatan Peninsula in 1517 discovered Mayan temples where humans were offered as sacrifices. A return visit in 1518 revealed that this barbaric practice was even more widespread among the Aztecs and their neighbors in the heart of the continent. The victims were frequently captured foreigners or enemies, but they also killed their own people, especially their children, in unbelievable numbers. The members of this expedition, who believed they were now near the lands where sacrifices were practiced (13:4) and had recently been "befriended" by natives only to be attacked once they were inside their homes (9:6), had good reasons to be afraid.

what they said, and asked the Indians to take us to their houses. They showed great pleasure at that. They had us wait for a moment, so that they could do that which we wanted. Later, thirty of them loaded themselves with firewood and went to their houses, which were far from there, and we waited with the others until almost night. Then they took hold of us and carried us with great swiftness to their houses. Because it was very cold, they had arranged to make four or five very large fires at intervals so that some would not die or faint. They warmed us at each one of them, and when they saw that we had gained some strength and warmth, they carried us to the next one so quickly that our feet hardly touched the ground. In this manner, we went to their houses, where we found that they had made a house for us, with many fires in it.

7 An hour after our arrival, they began to dance and have a great party, which went on all night. For us, though, there was no pleasure, party, or sleep, as we were waiting for when they were going to sacrifice us.

8 In the morning, they came to us to give us fish and roots. They gave us such good treatment that we were somewhat assured and lost some of our worry of sacrifices.

Chapter 13
More Survivors on the Island

How we knew of other Christians

This same day, I saw a trinket[1] on one of those Indians, and I knew that it was not one of those that we had given him. I asked where he had gotten it, and they answered by signs that some other men like us, who were behind[2] [them], had given it. Learning this, I sent two Christians and two Indians to guide them to those people. They happened upon them very close by, because they had also come looking for us, because the Indians that were staying with them had told them of us. They were Captains Andrés Dorantes and Alonso del Castillo,[3] with all the people of their boat. When they came to us, they were very frightened to see us in the state we were in. They were very grieved at having nothing to give us, since they had no other clothing except that they were wearing. They stayed there with us, and they related to us how their boat had capsized a league* and a half from there[4]

---

[1] Lit. *vn Refcate*, "an item of barter."

[2] Lit. *atrás*. One important thing to keep in mind when interpreting the castaways' route is that *atrás*, "behind," always refers to the direction they came from. In this case, that means toward Florida, or east.

[3] Note that Dorantes is not only a captain, the same as Castillo, but his name is placed ahead of Castillo's for the first time. I believe that this, along with other clues I have pointed out already, indicates a rise in his status or authority.

[4] About 5 miles (8 km). Recall that the camp the castaways are in is a half a league from where they landed and subsequently lost their boat (11:1). I take it that the native's camp was between the two boat landing sites, which would mean that on this long, narrow island, the boats landed some 2 leagues, or 7 miles (11 km) apart. There are other ways to figure this, but I believe this to be a reasonable one.

on the fifth of that same month, and they had escaped without losing anything.

2 All together, we agreed to repair their boat. Those of us who had the strength and inclination could go in it; the others would remain there until they recovered, then going as they were able along the coast, and that they wait there until God would take them with us to a land of Christians. So, we put ourselves to our plan.[1] Before we cast the boat into the water, Tavera, a gentleman of our company, died.

3 The boat that we thought would carry us was finished, but it could not stay afloat, and so it sank.[2]

---

[1] Lit. *como lo penfamos, afi nos pufimos en ello*, "as we thought, so we put ourselves in it."

[2] Lit. *no fe pudo foftener á si mifma, que luego fue hundida*, "it could not sustain itself, that then it was sunk." Oviedo adds, "because of the wood worms and other problems." Unlike with Cabeza de Vaca's boat, there is no mention of heavy waves or strong seas; the boat simply sank because it was unfit. Later, as part of a different discussion, Oviedo refers to "the inlet where they lost those boats." We know, however, that the boats were lost in different places that were up to 7 miles apart, and Cabeza de Vaca's site was by fierce waters that, on their arrival, tossed the boat up out of the water like a horseshoe in a game (10:8), and on their attempted departure, tumped it over and pulled it down (12:3). Oviedo was evidently mistaken in writing "those boats," but it still sounds like Castillo and Dorantes's boat was lost in an inlet, where the water was calm. This narrows down the possible locations of their landing substantially. I believe that Castillo's boat landed on the east end of a peninsula in Brazoria County known as Follet's Island, and that the inlet where the boat was lost was San Luis Pass, which separates Follet's Island and Galveston Island. Cabeza de Vaca's boat was lost some 7 miles or so west of San Luis Pass. There is a part of Follet's Island that is a little wider and higher than the rest of the peninsula about 5 miles west of San Luis Pass; perhaps Cabeza de Vaca's natives were camped there. I will comment more on this in subsequent chapters.

4 Because we were left in the state I have described - most of us naked - and the weather was so rough for walking and for swimming across rivers and inlets, nor were there any provisions or way to carry them, we determined to do what necessity asked, which was to winter there. We also agreed that four men, who were the strongest ones there, would go to Panuco, believing it was close to there,[1] and that if our Lord God would be served by taking them there, they would tell about those who remained on that island, and of our need and trouble.* These were very great swimmers: one they called Álvaro Fernández, a Portuguese carpenter and sailor;[2] the second was called Méndez; the third, Figueroa, who was a native of Toledo; the fourth, Astudillo, native of Zafra.[3] They took an Indian of the island[4] with them.

---

[1] The castaways are still over 500 miles (800 km) from Panuco. They have come a long, long way from Tampa Bay, but they are still so far from other Christians!

[2] Presumably, Fernández is the man Cabeza de Vaca referred to in 8:4 as "the only carpenter we had in our company." His statement that when the boats left the Bay of Horses they were "without any knowledge of the art of navigation out of everyone who went" (8:11) now sounds like one of his exaggerations.

[3] Lope de Oviedo, although he was "the strongest and most robust of all" (11:1) of Cabeza de Vaca's group, could not swim (16:7).

[4] According to Buckingham Smith, the words "of Auia" appear here in the first edition of *La Relación*. The name Auia does not appear anywhere in the second edition or in Oviedo. Oviedo refers once to an island "behind," i.e. east, of the one the castaways are presently on. Smith implies that Auia was the name of that island, which I believe to be present-day Galveston Island.

Chapter 14
The Natives of the Island of Misfortune

How the four Christians departed

A few days after these Christians left, such cold and stormy weather came that the Indians could not pull roots,[1] and the channels[2] in which they fished would not provide anything. Since the houses were such poor shelter,[3] the people began to die. Five Christians staying in the huts on the coast came to such an extreme that they ate each other until only one remained who, being alone, had no one to eat him. Their names were these: Sierra, Diego López, Corral, Palacios, Gonzalo Ruiz. The Indians were so disturbed by this - there was such a great scandal among them - that without a doubt if they had seen this at the beginning, they would have killed them, and all of us would have found ourselves in a lot of trouble.*[4]

---

[1] There are several other places in *La Relación* and Oviedo that refer to a turn in the weather all up and down the Gulf coast at about this same time, where a north wind brought in storms and freezing weather, and in the space of hours, an already cold season became even colder. This weather pattern is familiar to every Texan to this day, and it usually occurs between mid-December and early January. I believe in 1528, during the Little Ice Age, it occurred on November 12, which would have been November 22 on our calendar. I will comment on this again when the author brings it up again.

[2] Lit. *Cañales*, or channels for fishing, which were often filled with reeds or cane (*caña*), as opposed to channels for irrigation or navigation, which are *canales*.

[3] Lit. *eran tan defabrigadas*, "were so unsheltered."

[4] There are numerous reports from the 1700s and 1800s that natives who inhabited the Texas coast at that time practiced ritual cannibalism – specifically, that they cut off pieces of a captive enemy's flesh and ate it

2 Finally, in a very little time, of eighty men of our both parties who arrived there,[1] only fifteen were left. After these died,[2] the Indians of the country had a sickness of the stomach from which half of them died. They believed that we were those who were killing them.[3] Taking it as a certainty, they decided among themselves to kill those of us who remained. But when they came to put it into effect, an Indian who kept me told them not to believe that we were the ones killing them, because if we had such power, we would have exempted ourselves, and so many of us would not have died (since they saw who had died) without being

---

before his eyes. Besides the obvious terroristic effect, it is said that the natives believed this imparted the victim's power or virtue to the eater and/or it denied the victim of an afterlife. Cabeza de Vaca never mentions cannibalism of this sort among the natives of the Island of Misfortune, but he also mentions no wars or captive enemies during his time there. His statement here that the natives would have been shocked to see Spaniards eating the dead bodies of their comrades has sometimes been used to doubt the later reports of cannibalism among their descendants. I believe, however, that the differences between the two sets of circumstances are too great to make any sort of comparison: the Spaniards were comrades, not enemies; they were dead, not prisoners of war; they were being eaten for sustenance, not as a ritual. Additionally, these natives were not entirely innocent of eating their own dead – see 14:6.

[1] This is the only information we have about how many members of the Narváez Expedition of the 251 who departed from the Bay of Horses made it to Texas alive. If two boats had 80 men between them, then presumably the five boats had around 200 altogether.

[2] Not the 15 who were left, but the 65 who died.

[3] They probably were. The native populations of the Americas were decimated by diseases brought over by Europeans, who carried them in their systems, but also had some level of immunity owing to generations of exposure.

able to cure ourselves, and that now but very few of us remained, none of whom had done any harm or damage, and it was better to leave us alone. Our Lord willed that the others followed this counsel and opinion, and so their plan was obstructed.

3 We gave this island the name "Island of Misfortune."[1] The people we saw there were large and well-formed.[2] They have no other weapons than arrows and bows, with which they are extremely adept. The men have one nipple pierced from one side to the other; there are some who have both. They place a cane as long as two and a half palms and as thick as two fingers through the hole they make. They also have their lower lip pierced, and they put a piece of cane as thin as half a finger through it. The women do a lot of work.[3]

4 The habitation of this island is from October until the end of February. The sustenance is the roots I have told of, harvested from below the water in November and December. They have channels for fishing, which have more fish at this time than any other.[4] From then on, they eat the roots. At the end of February, they go to other places to look for their sustenance, because the roots are beginning to sprout then, and are no good.

---

[1] Lit. *Isla de Malhado. Malhado* is a compound of *mal,* a common adjective meaning "bad," "evil," etc. and *hado,* a noun which means "fate" or "destiny." Other translations render it as "Ill-fate," "Bad Luck," or other such variations, or they leave it untranslated as "Malhado." All of these are valid, but I wanted to express it as a single English word, and "misfortune" seemed to fit the bill.

[2] See the footnotes to 15:6 for a discussion of the identity of these natives.

[3] Lit. *son para mucho trabajo,* "are for much work."

[4] Lit. *no tienen más Peces de para efte tiempo,* "they do not have more fish than for this time."

5 Of all the people in the world, they love their children the most and give them the best treatment. When it happens that one of their children should die, the parents and relatives and the whole village cry for it. The weeping lasts for a complete year, in which every day, in the morning, before sunrise, the parents begin to cry first, and after this the whole village. They do the same thing at midday and nightfall. When a year of weeping has passed, they pay their respects to the dead, and they wash and clean themselves of all the paint they wear. They mourn all of their dead this way, except for the elderly, of whom they make no occasion, because they say that they have had their time and they are of no use except to occupy the ground and take sustenance from the children.

6 Their custom is to bury the dead, other than those who are healers,[1] whom they burn. While the fire burns, all of them dance and make a very large celebration, and they make powder of the bones. After a year, when they pay their respects, everyone partakes[2] in them, and they give the relatives the powder of the bones to drink, in water.

---

[1] Lit. *Fíficos*. In modern Spanish, *físico* means "physique" or "physicist," but in earlier centuries, it meant "physician." The English word, "physician," has taken on much more of a professsional, technical connotation than it had in the 1500s, however, so I chose to translate it as "healer."

[2] Lit. *quando ſe hacen ſus Honras, todos ſe jaſan en ellas*, "when they make their honors, all [present-tense verb] in them." The word *jasar* does not exist in Spanish. Bandelier, taking the mystery verb to be a misspelling of *sajar*, "to scarify," renders it as "they scarify themselves." However, the object of the verb, *ellas*, is in the feminine form, meaning it can only refer to *honras* (respects), not *todos* (everyone). I think the author is simply saying that after a year, everyone partakes in a ceremony. When spoken out loud, *se jasan* sounds like *se hacen*, which would mean the same thing. Smith translates the phrase the same way I do,

7 Each one has one recognized wife. The healers are men with more liberty; they can have two or three, and among these there is very good friendship and harmony. When it happens that someone gives his daughter to marry,[1] the man who takes her for a wife, from the day that he marries her, everything that he kills hunting or fishing, the woman takes all of it to her father's house, without daring to touch or eat anything of it. It is taken from the father-in-law's house to him to eat. In all of this time, neither the father-in-law nor the mother-in-law may enter his house, nor does he enter theirs, nor the wife's siblings. If they should happen to meet somewhere, they each turn away the length of a crossbow shot[2] from the other. As they are parting, they turn their heads down and put their eyes toward the ground, because they believe it a bad thing to see or speak to them. The women have the freedom to communicate and converse with their in-laws and relatives. This custom exists from the island to more than fifty leagues inland.

8 There is another custom, which is that when some child or sibling dies, those of his house do not gather food for three months, leaving themselves to die of hunger, and their relatives and neighbors provide for them to have something to eat. And since, in the time we were there, so many of their people died, there was very great hunger in most of the houses, due to their observance of their customs and ceremonies - those who searched had to work very hard - and also because the weather was so rough, they could find but very little.

---

except for his habit of gratuitously changing the tense of Cabeza de Vaca's verbs, resulting in "every one taking part in them."

[1] Lit. *caſa ſu Hija*, "marries his daughter."

[2] See the footnotes to 12:3.

9 Because of this, the Indians who kept me[1] left the island, and went on canoes to the mainland, where there were some bays that had many oysters.[2] For three months of the year, they eat nothing else, and they drink very bad water. There is a great lack of firewood, and the mosquitos are in very great abundance. Their houses are built out of mats over many oyster shells. They sleep over them on hides, which they only have by chance. We stayed there until the end of April, when we went to the seashore, where we ate blackberries[3] all month, during which time they never ceased to have their ceremonial dances* and celebrations.

---

[1] As Cabeza de Vaca will explain in 16:2, he joined a different group of Indians, who evidently lived primarily on the mainland and visited Malhado seasonally. The first group of natives also crossed over to the mainland with the seasons, but apparently they stayed on the island most of the year.

[2] The bay between Follet's Island and the mainland has long been known as Oyster Bay. Oysters thrive in brackish water and low-salinity saltwater. Prior to the invention of modern oyster farming, eastern Brazoria County was one of the top oyster-producing areas on all of the Gulf coast. The author's description of the mainland adjacent to Follet's Island - that of treeless, mosquito-infested wetlands with brackish ponds – is just as accurate today as it was 500 years ago.

[3] These are actually dewberries, a close relative of the blackberry. They still grow all over Brazoria County, including Follet's Island, in the spring.

Chapter 15
Becoming Healers

Of what happened to us on the Island of Misfortune

On that island, which I have discussed, they wanted to make healers[1] of us without examining us or asking us for our credentials, because they cure illnesses by blowing on the sick, and with that puff and their hands, they remove the sickness from a person. They ordered us to do the same thing, thereby serving some purpose to them. We laughed at them, saying that it was a joke and that we did not know how to heal. And so they took our food from us until we did what they told us to. Seeing our obstinacy, one Indian said to me that I did not know what I said in saying that I did not want to take advantage of what he knew, since the rocks and other things that grew in the fields have power. [He said that] he, with a hot stone, placed on the stomach, healed and removed pain, and that we were surely men who possessed greater virtue and power. In the end, we saw ourselves in such a necessity that we had to do it, without fear that anyone would punish us for it.[2]

2 This is the manner in which they cure a person: when they feel sick, they call a doctor.[3] After being cured, they give him not only all that they possess, but they look for things for their relatives to give him. What the doctor does is cut a few scars where the pain is, and they suck around them. They cauterize

---

[1] Lit. *Fiſicos*, see 14:6.

[2] That is, the castaways had been reluctant to attempt to cure the natives because they expected to be punished if their attempts to cure were ineffective. By this point, however, they saw less risk in trying to cure and failing than in refusing to try.

3 Lit. *Médico*, which differs from *Fiſico*, which I translate as "healer."

with fire, a thing which is considered very beneficial by them. (I have experimented with it, and it worked well for me.) After this, they blow on the spot that hurts them, and with this, they believe that the malady has left them.

3 The manner with which we cured was to make the sign of the Cross* over them, blow on them, recite an Our Father and a Hail Mary, and pray as best as we could to our Lord God to give them health and inspire them to give us some good treatment. Our Lord God willed, in His mercy, that all those for whom we entreated, after we made the sign of the Cross over them, said to the others that they were sound and well. For this reason, they treated us well and stopped eating so that they could give food to us. They also gave us hides and other small things.

4 The hunger that went through there was so extreme that many times, I went three days without eating anything at all, and they were also [like this], and it seemed impossible to me for life to go on, although later on, I saw myself in other, greater states of hunger and need, as I will relate later.

5 The Indians who kept Alonso del Castillo, Andrés Dorantes, and the others who were still left alive, who were of another language and another bloodline, had gone to another part of the mainland to eat oysters. They stayed there until the first day of the month of April and then returned to the island, which was almost two leagues* from there, where the water is widest. The island is a half a league across and five in length.[1]

---

[1] I have explained in footnotes to 13:3 and 14:9 some of my reasons why I believe the Island of Misfortune is Follet's Island in Brazoria County. The dimensions given in this paragraph support this theory. Cabeza de Vaca says Malhado was 5 leagues long and ½ league wide. This comes to 17 miles (28 km) long and 1¾ miles (2¾ km) wide. Only two landmasses on the Texas coast come close to these dimensions: Follet's Island and the Bolivar Peninsula. In contrast, the traditional candidate, Galveston Island, is 30 miles long. The theory that Malhado is Follet's

6 All of the people in this country go nude; only the women wear on their bodies some covering made of a wool that grows on the trees.[1] The girls cover themselves with deer skins. They are a very liberal people with regard to [giving] what they have to others. There is no lord among them. All who are of the same lineage stay together. Two manners of language inhabit them. The first are called Capoques, and the others Han.[2] They have a custom

---

Island was first advanced in 1918 by Harbert Davenport and Joseph K. Wells. It has since been adopted by many historians, but not all. Many encyclopedias, almanacs, historical markers, and other authorities still promote the long-held view that it is Galveston.

[1] Spanish moss is neither native to Spain nor a member of the moss phylum. It hangs from the branches of trees in warm, humid climates throughout the Western Hemisphere. It is especially associated with the southeastern U.S., where it thrives on oak and cypress trees. Natives commonly called it "tree hair." The name "Spanish moss" came from French explorers and settlers who compared it to the beards that most Spaniards wore.

[2] Cabeza de Vaca has stated that the natives of the Island of Misfortune were tall (11:2), pierced their nipples and lips with cane (14:3), went nude, and wore paint (14:5). He also mentioned that they possessed dogs (11:1). These characteristics were shared by the natives who lived on the Texas coast in the 1600s through 1800s, which were known as Karankawa. There were five known clans of Karankawa in the 1800s. The easternmost clan, which lived from about the Colorado River to Galveston Bay, was called the Cocos. Davenport and Wells, along with many others, believe the Cocos and the Capoques to be one and the same. The Han, who spoke a different language, are associated with the Akokisa clan of the Atakapa tribe, which inhabited the coast from Galveston Bay east. The Atakapa had a physical and cultural resemblance to the Karankawa, and the Cocos were known to be on friendly terms with the Atakapa. Davenport and Wells also classify the Cocos as "the least barbarous of the Karankawan Indians," a description that is borne out in

when they know each other and see each other from time to time, before they speak, they spend a half hour crying. After this is over, the one who is being visited rises first and gives all that he has to the other, and after a little while, he leaves with it. Sometimes, after receiving it, they leave without speaking a word. They have other strange customs, but I have related the most important and notable ones in passing forward and relating what else happened to us.

the way the Narváez Expedition castaways were treated as they moved further west.

Chapter 16
A Group Leaves the Island

How the Christians left the Isla de Malhado

After Dorantes and Castillo returned to the island,[1] they gathered together all of the Christians, who were scattered. They found fourteen in all. I, as I have said, was in another place on the mainland, where my Indians had taken me and where a great illness had come over me. In other circumstances,[2] I would have had a hope of surviving, but that was enough to totally remove [that hope] from me. When the Christians learned this, they gave an Indian the marten mantle that we had taken from the chief, as we stated earlier,[3] so that they could come to where I was and see me. So, twelve came to me, because two of them were so feeble that they did not dare to bring them with them. The names of those who came were: Alonso del Castillo, Andrés Dorantes, Diego Dorantes, Valdivieso,[4] Estrada, Tostado, Chaves, Gutiérrez, a cleric[5] from Asturias, Diego de Huelva, Estevanico the Negro,*[1]

---

[1] According to 15:5, the date is April 1, 1529, although I consider all dates given by the author between now and the time he emerges from the wilderness seven years later to be approximations.

[2] Lit. *iá que alguna otra cofa*, "now that some other case."

[3] See 9:6.

[4] According to Oviedo, his full name was Pedro de Valdivieso, and, like Diego Dorantes, he was Andrés Dorantes's cousin.

[5] Lit. *Clerigo*, also see 5:1. In 1:1, Cabeza de Vaca writes that five Franciscan friars (*Frailes*) went on the expedition. In 5:1, he writes that two friars and three clerics stayed in Florida after Narváez sent the ships away. At least one of the friars was put on Accountant Enríquez's boat in 8:7, and in 17:5 and 17:7, Cabeza de Vaca refers to that boat as the one belonging to "the accountant and the friars." Thus, it is difficult to dis-

and Benítez.[2] As they came to the mainland, they found another one of ours, who was called Francisco de León,[3] a total of thirteen

---

cern whether or not this cleric or clergyman from the province of Asturias, who was not on Enríquez's boat, was one of the five Franciscans originally mentioned. If he was, he had less authority in the order than Friars Suárez and Palos. Apparently, neither Cabeza de Vaca nor the other survivors knew this man's name; possibly because they only addressed him as "father" or by some other religious title.

[1] The fourth recurring character of the narrative is finally introduced. He was from Azemmour, Morocco, which the Portuguese occupied from 1513 to 1541. He went on the Narváez Expedition as Andrés Dorantes's slave – a fact that neither Cabeza de Vaca nor Oviedo ever mention, but we can take as certain because of a letter that Viceroy Mendoza wrote to King Charles saying that he "bought" him from Dorantes. His name is written in Barcia's source text as *Estebanico*. The common convention in English literature is to spell his name as "Estevanico." His name is written without any accent marks, so the stress is on the fourth syllable – the "i." (Those who add an accent mark over the "a," to make it "Estevánico," do so without the authority of the texts.) The "-ico" ending is a common Spanish diminutive suffix, and could mean that he was but a lad in 1527, when the expedition began. In documents related to the Coronado Expedition, when he was 10 to 12 years older, he is called *Esteban*.

[2] According to Oviedo, one member of the group was "a young boy." I choose to believe that this young boy was Benítez, the only member of the group whose name is listed after the slave's.

[3] Oviedo accounts for Dorantes's group of twelve plus the two who had to stay on the island (Alaniz and Lope de Oviedo), and then writes, "Cabeza de Vaca and another Christian were farther inland, and these two men could not be recovered to go with the group." Oviedo subsequently states that at the second river Dorantes's group crossed, which would have been the Brazos, they found another Christian. I take León to be both the man who was with Cabeza de Vaca on the mainland and the straggler who joined Dorantes's group at the Brazos River.

along the coast. After they had passed through, the Indians who kept me advised me of it, and how Hierónimo de Alaniz and Lope de Oviedo[1] remained on the island. My sickness hindered me, so that I could not follow or see them.

2 I had to stay with these same Indians of the island more than a year,[2] and for the hard work they gave me to do and the poor way they treated me, I decided to flee from them and go to those who dwell in the forests on the mainland[3] - they are called "those of Charruco." I was unable to bear the life I had with these others, because, among many other hardships,* I had to gather the roots to eat from the ground below the water, from among the reeds, where they were deep in the soil. My fingers were so worn out from this that touching one straw made them bleed. The reeds would cut me in many places, because many of them were broken and I had to go among them in the clothing that I have said I wore.[4] This is why I put myself to the task of going over to the

---

[1] In case the reader has forgotten, Alaniz was the scribe who supported Cabeza de Vaca at the contentious officers' meeting in Florida (4:9). Oviedo was the robust man who Cabeza de Vaca sent to scout the Island of Misfortune (11:1).

[2] Chapter 16 of *La Relación* is an oddity, for it compresses more than four years' worth of events into a few paragraphs, and most of those consist of either complaining or boasting and are lacking in real information. Furthermore, most of the information the author provides is contradicted either by his own words, by the timeline, or by Oviedo. Cabeza de Vaca was on the Island of Misfortune at least till mid-November 1528, and by April 1, 1529, he had already left. That is 4½ months maximum, not "more than a year."

[3] The low-lying areas of the upper Gulf coast of Texas just above the tidal wetlands are heavily wooded with live oaks, pines, and many other varieties of trees.

[4] The author never described his clothing, other than calling it "different" and "strange" (12:5).

others. It was somewhat better for me with them, because I made myself into a merchant. I made the most use of that office that I knew how, and for this they gave me food and treated me well and entreated me to go from one place to another to get things that they needed, for the reason that they bring war continually, therefore there is not much travel or trade.

3 And so, with my wares and merchandise, I journeyed inland as far as I wished, and I extended forty or fifty leagues* along the coast.[1] The main part of my trade was in the shells and bodies of sea snails and a shell with which they cut a fruit that is like beans, which they use for curing and in their dances and celebrations - this is the most precious thing that they have - and beads from the sea and other things. This was what I carried across the land, and in barter and exchange for it, I brought hides, red ochre[2] - with which they rub and dye their faces and hair - flint for arrow points, glue and hard canes for making them, and some tassels which they make from deer hair, which they dye until they are red. This office was good to me, because while going about it I had the liberty to go where I wanted, and I was not obligated to

---

[1] I.e. 138 to 173 miles (221 to 277 km). It is doubtful that he went more than about 20 leagues, which would have taken him to the east side of Matagorda Bay. The events described later in this chapter certainly imply that he never went as far as the Guadalupe River. (For one thing, every other member of the expedition who went that far was enslaved, killed, or both.) If he had traveled 40 to 50 leagues, he would have crossed the Nueces River and been well on his way to the Rio Grande.

[2] Some interpreters believe this means Cabeza de Vaca may have traveled as far as the redlands of east Texas, in the vicinity of present-day San Augustine, where the soil has a deep, rusty color. That is possible, but it means he would have discovered Galveston Bay, a bay that is even larger than Matagorda Bay and dwarfs Tampa Bay; crossed the Trinity River, and met the Caddo, a friendly and, compared to the natives of the coast, advanced tribe. He does not describe any of these things.

anything, and was not a slave. Wherever I went, they treated me well and gave me food in consideration for my wares. The most important reason for going about this is that I was trying to find out where I might be going later.

4 I was very well-known among them. They greatly enjoyed when they saw me and when I brought them that which they needed. Those who did not know me desired and took measures to see me because of my fame.

5 It would take a long time to relate all of the hardships, dangers, and hungers I endured during this time, along with storms and cold, many of them overtaking me alone and in the field. Through the great mercy of our Lord God, I escaped. Because of this, I did not attempt to perform the office in the winter, for that was the season in which they stayed in their huts and dwellings, and did not protect or assist themselves.

6 The time I spent in this country alone among them was almost six years.[1] I was naked, like all of them went about. The reason for staying so long was so I could take a Christian who was on the island with me, called Lope de Oviedo. (The other companion, Alaniz, who had remained with him when Alonso del Castillo and Andrés Dorantes left with all of the others, died later.[2]) In order to take him from there, I went over to the island every year and proposed to him that we go in the most skillful way we could in search of Christians, and each year, he put me off, saying that we would go the following year.

---

[1] It was actually 4 to 4½ years: from late 1528 or early 1529 to early 1533.

[2] Lit. *murió luego*, "died later." The sentence that follows this one makes it sound like Lope de Oviedo was the only Christian on the Island of Misfortune for several years, thus implying that Alaniz died soon after Dorantes's group left. With this in mind, many translators alter Cabeza de Vaca's wording here to read "died soon" or "soon died."

7 Finally, I got him out in the end. I took him across the inlet and four rivers that were on the coast,[1] because he did not know how to swim. And so we went forward with some Indians until we came to an inlet that is one league across and is deep everywhere. From what we saw of it, it seemed to us to be the one called *del Espíritu Santo*.[2]

8 On the other side of it, we saw some Indians, who came to meet those who were with us. They told us how further on, there were three men like us, and they told us their names. When asked about the others,[3] they replied that all were dead of cold

---

[1] Cabeza de Vaca and Lope de Oviedo probably left the Island of Misfortune in early 1533, perhaps March. Gonzalo de Oviedo has information about the four rivers that helps identify them. Davenport and Wells write that their identification as Oyster Creek, the Brazos River, the San Bernard River, and Caney Creek is "beyond dispute." I agree as far as Cabeza de Vaca and Lope de Oviedo's journey go, but I believe the first river in the case of Dorantes's party was Bastrop Bayou.

[2] The inlet is Cavallo Pass, between Matagorda Island and the Matagorda Peninsula. Because of a man-made ship channel built in 1966 and a change in the outflow of the Colorado River, Cavallo Pass is now much more narrow and shallow than it used to be. *Espíritu Santo*, or "Holy Spirit," was the name given by explorer Alonso Álvaro de Pineda in 1519 to the Mississippi River. The members of the Narváez Expedition knew they would be crossing *Espíritu Santo* as they traveled on the Gulf from Florida to Panuco; they never realized it was the river that pushed their boats away from the coast on October 29, 1528. The name Espiritu Santo was later applied to several bodies of water in the Matagorda Bay area before ultimately becoming fixed to the bay that separates Matagorda Island from the mainland.

[3] Cabeza de Vaca is now about 125 miles (200 km), or 36 leagues, from the mainland across from the Island of Misfortune. If he had spent his time traveling 40 or 50 leagues down the coast, as he wrote, and if he was as famous and well-liked as he wrote, he would not just now be

and hunger, and how the Indians of further on had killed Diego Dorantes, Valdivieso, and Diego de Huelva for their own amusement, because they had gone from one house to another.[1] The other Indians, their neighbors, who now had Captain Dorantes, had killed Esquivel and Méndez because of a dream that they had dreamt.[2] We asked them how the ones who were alive were doing; they told us that they were treated very poorly, as the boys and some other Indians who were lazy and ill-behaved kicked them, struck them on the face, and hit them with sticks many times, and that was the life that they lived with them.[3] We asked them to inform us about the land further on and the sustenance that was in it. They responded that it was very thinly inhabited,[4] there was nothing to eat in it, and [people] died of cold because they had no hides or any covering. They also told us that if we wanted to see those three Christians, who were two days from there, the Indians

---

learning about the fates of his comrades, who preceded him there by four years or more.

[1] See my notes on 18:2 for more on the deaths of these three men. As Oviedo describes it, the phrase "for their own amusement" is consistent with some of the tortures the natives inflicted upon them, but not concerning their deaths.

[2] Oviedo agrees that Esquivel, whose story is told in Chapter 17, was killed because of a dream, but Cabeza de Vaca himself gives a contradictory account of Méndez's death in 17:6. That account, and not this one, is probably correct. The natives who held Dorantes and killed Esquivel were the Mariames or Mareames (18:3).

[3] Oviedo attributes these tortures not to the natives who currently held the survivors, but to another group they lived with previously and managed to escape from. It was those very cruel natives who killed Valdivieso and Huelva.

[4] Lit. *pobre de Gente*, "poor of people."

who had them would come to eat nuts[1] a league from there, on the bank of the river.[2] So that we could see what they had told us of the poor treatment of the others was true, while we were staying with them, they beat my companion and struck him with sticks. I also endured my share of it. They threw many balls of mud at us and held their arrows to our hearts each day, saying that they wanted to kill us like the others did our companions. Fearing this, Lope de Oviedo, my companion, said that he wanted to return with some of the Indian women who had crossed the inlet with us and had stayed behind somewhat. I contended greatly with him not to do it, and tried everything,[3] but in no way could I make him stay. So, he returned and left me alone with those Indians, who were called Quevenes.[4] The others who he went with were called Deaguanes.[1]

---

[1] In Spanish, *nueces*, the generic word for "nuts," also translates to "walnuts," which are the most common type of nut in Spain. Oviedo makes it clear that these nuts were not walnuts. They were, without question, pecans, which are native to Texas and thrive in areas that are well-watered, have good drainage, and experience mild winters. The pecan is the official Texas state tree.

[2] Interpreters of Cabeza de Vaca now almost uniformly take this "river of nuts" to be the Guadalupe. Alex D. Krieger writes, "It is likely ... that the pecan groves they visited were along the lower reaches of the San Antonio and Guadalupe River." The San Antonio River pours into the Guadalupe River about seven miles (11 km) above San Antonio Bay. Oviedo alludes to this confluence when he writes, "they hunt mice between those rivers." The events related in this paragraph probably took place on the mainland of present-day Calhoun County, which is between Matagorda Bay and the Guadalupe River.

[3] Lit. *pasé muchas cofas*, "I passed many things."

[4] The Quevenes are mentioned a few more times in *La Relación*. No physical description is given of them, and little is said of their culture, but they dwelt in the heart of the territory occupied by the 18th and 19th-

century Karankawa. The phonetic similarity between the name "Quevene" and the tribe later known as Cujane, Cojane, or Kohani, which inhabited the same area, is compelling.

[1] We know little of the Deaguanes except that they occupied the coast between the Capoques and Han and the Quevenes, and they were at war with the Quevenes. They may be the same tribe that Oviedo states helped Dorantes's party at the last river they crossed before reaching *Espíritu Santo,* which I take to be Caney Creek in Matagorda County. In Chapter 24, the author recalls a skirmish between the Queneves and Deaguanes that occurred when he was with the latter, but whether it occurred on this occasion or on one of his previous visits to the area, he does not say.

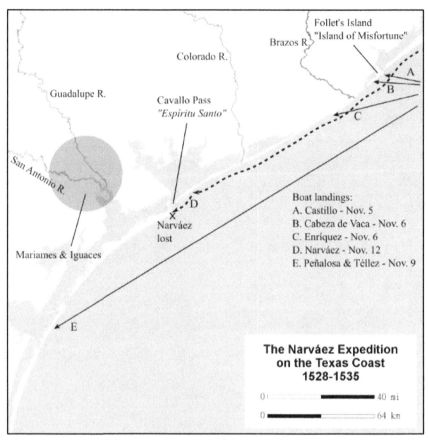

Figure 5 - Map of the Narváez Expedition on the Texas Coast

Chapter 17
A Happy Reunion

How the Indians came and brought Andrés Dorantes,

Castillo, and Estevanico

Two days after Lope de Oviedo had gone, the Indians who had Alonso del Castillo and Andrés Dorantes came to the same place that they had told us about to eat those nuts on which they subsist, grinding some grains with them, two months of the year, without eating another thing. Even at that, they do not have them every year, because they grow one and not another.[1] They are the size of those of Galicia,[2] and the trees are very large, and there are a large number of them.

2 An Indian advised me that the Christians had arrived, and that if I wanted to see them, I should sneak away and hide on the edge of a forest which he pointed out to me, because he and his relatives had come to see those Indians, and they would take me with them to where the Christians were. I trusted them and decided to do it, because they had a different language than that of my Indians. Putting myself to the task, they went the next day, and they found me in the place that he had pointed out, and so I went with them.

3 When I came near to where they were lodging, Andrés Dorantes came out to see who it was, because the Indians had also said how a Christian would be coming. When he saw me, he was very frightened, because he had believed me to be dead for many days, and the Indians had told him so. We gave many thanks to God for being reunited. This day was one of the happi-

---

[1] Pecan trees are notorious for producing abundantly some years and barely at all other years.

[2] Galicia is a province of Spain.

est[1] that we had in all of our days. Coming to where Castillo was, they asked me where I was going. I told them that I intended to travel to a land of Christians, and that I went on this trail on this search. Andrés Dorantes responded that for many days, he had urged Castillo and Estevanico to go forward, but they did not dare to do so because they did not know how to swim, and they were very afraid of the rivers and inlets through which they had to pass, of which that land had many. Still, as it had pleased our Lord God to protect me among so many hardships* and illnesses and finally brought me into their company, they decided to flee, as I would take them across the rivers and inlets that we encountered. They advised me to in no way give the Indians to understand, nor that they would know from me, that I wanted to go onward, because then they would kill me. For this reason, it was necessary that I stay with them six months, at which time those Indians went to another country to eat tunas.*[2] (This is a fruit

---

[1] Lit. *vno de los de maior placer*, "one of those of most pleasure."

[2] Here the author introduces a contradiction into the timeline. The season for tunas was August and September. The Mariames and Iguaces may have begun their annual migration to the prickly pear fields in July, or perhaps even in June, as Oviedo indicates that they generally stopped along the way to hunt deer. After the tunas were exhausted in late September or October, they would go back to the Guadalupe River to pick pecans, which ripen and drop in November. If the author arrived at the river and met the other survivors when the natives came to eat nuts, as both he and Gonzalo de Oviedo state, the meeting had to have been in or around November 1532. However, if the plan to escape has to wait six months, when the natives go eat tunas, Cabeza de Vaca had to have met them later than that. Cabeza de Vaca restates twice in *La Relación* (18:10, 19:1) that the natives began leaving for the tuna country six months after his arrival. This would place his arrival in December, January, or February at the latest. That would also mean Cabeza de Vaca and Lope de Oviedo left the Island of Misfortune during the peak of win-

that is the size of eggs. They are black and bright red and taste very good.[1] They eat them three months of the year, in which they do not eat anything else.) At the time when they gather them, other Indians from beyond come to them, bringing bows to barter and exchange with them. When those departed, we would flee from ours with them, and return with them.

4 With this decided, I stayed there. They gave me as a slave to an Indian with whom Dorantes stayed. This one was cross-eyed,[2] as was his wife and one of his children, and another that kept in his company; all of them were cross-eyed. These are called

---

ter, which does not make sense. I doubt that they left after November or before March.

Then there is the matter of Cabeza de Vaca's statement that he was alone for "almost six years" (16:6). Gonzalo de Oviedo writes that Cabeza de Vaca and Dorantes were reunited five years after Dorantes's party left the island. These statements would have the reunion taking place between November 1533 and April 1534, but I do not see how it could have been later than March 1533. I believe that either Cabeza de Vaca and his Joint Report co-authors misremembered the occasion of why the Mariames and Iguaces were at the River of Nuts together when Cabeza de Vaca arrived, the interval of six months between his arrival and the departure for the tuna fields is incorrect, or both.

[1] Tunas are the fruit of the prickly pear cactus. For more information, see the glossary at the end of this book.

[2] Lit. *tuerto*. This can also mean "one-eyed," "lazy-eyed," or "blind in one eye." More generally, *tuerto* refers to things that are wrong or contrary. Other European explorers to the Americas observed widespread eye problems among the natives. The trait of being cross-eyed may have even been considered desirable in some cultures; for example, Mayan art often depicts faces with crossed eyes. Studies have shown that, even today, Native American populations experience a higher than average occurrence of eye problems, including crossed eyes and "lazy" eyes.

Mariames. Castillo was with others, their neighbors, called Iguaces.

5 Staying here, they related what happened after they left
the Island of Misfortune. Along the coast, they found the boat belonging to the accountant and the friars on its side.[1] Continuing,
passing some rivers - four very large ones, with strong currents -
the boats in which they crossed were carried off, and four of them
drowned. They went further until they crossed an inlet, which
they crossed with much trouble.[2] Fifteen leagues further, they
found another.[3] By the time they arrived there, another two of
their company had died[4] in the sixty leagues* that they had trav-

---

[1] Oviedo documents the movements of Dorantes and Castillo's party
with significantly more detail than Cabeza de Vaca presents here. The
boat assigned to Alonso Enríquez and the friars was at or near the third
river between Galveston Bay and Matagorda Bay, which I and most interpreters take to be the San Bernard River in Brazoria County. This location is about 25 miles west of San Luis Pass. I believe the boat landed
there on November 6, 1528, the same day Cabeza de Vaca's boat landed
on Follet's Island. The boat was apparently a total loss, because the people who came on it abandoned it, and Dorantes's party did not attempt
to use it.

[2] Oviedo writes, "they suspected that it must be the river of *Espíritu
Santo.*" This was Cavallo Pass. Oviedo states that they crossed it in a ca-
noe they found and repaired. I estimate that Dorantes's party crossed
Cavallo Pass on the eighth day after they left the Island of Misfortune, or
April 9, 1529.

[3] This would be Cedar Bayou, which separates Matagorda Island in Calhoun County from St. Joseph Island in Aransas County. Oviedo places it
12 leagues from *Espíritu Santo*, not 15. The actual distance from Cavallo
Pass to Cedar Bayou is 35 miles (56 km), or 10 leagues. They probably
reached this point on or around April 12.

[4] Going by the list of names Cabeza de Vaca gives in 16:1, the first six
men of Dorantes's party to die were Estrada, Tostado, Chavez, Gutiérrez,
Benítez, and Francisco de León. Oviedo does not use any of their names,

eled,[1] and the same was going to happen to those who were left.[2] On the whole trail, they had not eaten anything but crabs[3] and seaweed.[4] When they came to this last inlet, they said that they found Indians in it who were eating blackberries. When they saw the Christians, they went away to the other end. While [the Christians] were trying and looking for a way to cross the inlet, an Indian and a Christian crossed over to them. When they arrived,

---

but according to his accounting, two of them, not including León, drowned while trying to cross the second river – the Brazos – on rafts. Two more died "of hunger and fatigue" between the fourth river (Caney Creek) and Cavallo Pass. Two more died of hunger in the Cedar Bayou area. These last two, however, died some days *after* the events that are described next.

[1] It is about 130 miles (208 km), or 38 leagues, from San Luis Pass to Cedar Bayou. As we see, Cabeza de Vaca tends to overestimate travel distances, and the greater the distance, the greater the degree of error.

[2] Lit. *todos los que quedaban eſtaban para lo miſmo*, "all those who remained were for the same."

[3] Lit. *Cangrejos*. In early editions, I translated this as "crawfish," which are more properly called *cangrejos de río*, or "river crabs." These were most likely hermit crabs or Atlantic ghost crabs (*Ocypode quadrata*), which are plentiful on Texas beaches, but are small and not good food. Oviedo aptly describes them as "shellfish that were mostly shell."

[4] Lit. *Yerva Pedrera*, "quarry herb" or "rock grass." Oviedo adds, "It is the same plant they use in Spain to make glass." This note is helpful. Spain was a leading exporter of *barilla*, a variety of seaweed that was the primary source of soda ash, a key component of glass. *Barilla* is frequently translated as "kelp," but these are actually two different, albeit overlapping, groups of plants. The plant the Narváez Expedition survivors found on the Gulf coast was definitely not *barilla* and may or may not have been kelp, but it was certainly seaweed.

they recognized that [the Christian] was Figueroa, one of the four who we had sent ahead from the Island of Misfortune.[1]

6 [Figueroa] related for them there how he and his companions had come to that place, where two of them and an Indian had died - all three of cold and hunger, because they had come and stayed in the worst weather in the world.[2] He told them that the Indians had taken him and Méndez. While staying with them, Méndez had fled, going as best as he could in the direction of Panuco, and that the Indians had gone after him and had killed him.[3] While staying with these Indians, [Figueroa] learned from them that a Christian staying with the Mariames had passed over from the other side. He had been found with those called Quevenes. This Christian was Hernando de Esquivel, a native of Badajoz. He came in the commissary's company. [Figueroa] learned from Esquivel what had finally happened[4] to the governor, the accountant, and the others.[5]

---

[1] See 13:4.

[2] Remember 14:1, "A few days after these Christians left, such cold and stormy weather came that the Indians could not pull roots..." Figueroa's journey from San Luis Pass to Cedar Bayou is not documented either here or in Oviedo, but I estimate that the frigid weather arrived on the night of November 12-13, 1528 and that Figueroa and his companions crossed Cavallo Pass on November 13 at the earliest. Álvaro Fernández, Astudillo, and their native guide died on Matagorda Island. Figueroa and Méndez reached Cedar Bayou on November 16 at the earliest.

[3] Compare to 16:8, where Cabeza de Vaca states that the Mariames killed Méndez because of a dream. I believe the account given here to be the correct one. The natives who killed Méndez and took Figueroa captive may have been the Guaycones (see 26:1).

[4] The text reads *parado*, but this is a misprint; the correct word would be *pasado* (or *pafado*, in the text's archaic style).

[5] There is a story within a story within a story here, and it can be slightly confusing to follow. Andrés Dorantes is telling Cabeza de Vaca what be-

7 He told him that the accountant and the friars had been thrown out of their boat on the rivers.[1] Going along the coast, the governor's boat came to land, with its people. [Narváez] went with his boat until they came to that large bay, and there he returned to take the people and pass over to the other side and returned for the accountant, the friars, and all the others.[2] When they were disembarked, the governor had revoked the authority that he had

---

came of him and his companions, who left him on the Island of Misfortune on April 1, 1529. Dorantes's story includes a conversation he had with Figueroa, one of the four strong swimmers who left the island in November 1528. Figueroa's account to Dorantes included a conversation he had not long ago with Esquivel, the last survivor of Governor Narváez and Accountant Enríquez's party.

[1] Lit. *havian echado al través su Barca entre los Rios*, "had been thrown across their boat among the rivers."

[2] Here we learn that Narváez's boat was still in good condition and he was still using it to skim the Gulf coast westward in hopes of reaching Panuco, in the same manner that all five of the boats had been doing prior to the disaster at the Mississippi River. I assume from this that Narváez was able to reach land at Terrebonne Parish, Louisiana, on November 1, 1528, the last time Cabeza de Vaca saw him (10:4). I place his meeting with Enríquez and the other boat as occurring on the Matagorda Peninsula, near Cavallo Pass, on November 12. If these points are correct, he crossed the Sabine River, which is the Louisiana-Texas state line, on either November 7 or 8. He probably spent the night of November 9 somewhere on Galveston Island and passed Follet's Island on November 10 without knowing some members of his expedition were there. Some route interpreters assert that the castaways did not walk down the Matagorda Peninsula, but instead walked around the north side of Matagorda Bay. The fact that Narváez happened to find Enríquez's party while sailing along the coast is one of many indications the text gives that they did, in fact, stay on the sea coast.

given to the accountant as his lieutenant[1] and put in charge a captain that he had brought with him, who was called Pantoja. The governor did not want to go on land that night, and he remained on his boat. A mate and a page who was sick stayed with him.[2] There was no water or anything to eat on the boat. At midnight, a north wind came that was so rough, it carried the boat out to sea without anyone seeing it,[3] because it had nothing for an anchor but a rock, and they knew nothing more of him.[4]

8 Seeing this, the people who remained on land went along the coast. As they found themselves so greatly impeded by water, they made rafts with much difficulty, and passed in them to the other side.[5] Going further, they came to a point of a forest at the

---

[1] That is, the lieutenant governor, the person who had the authority to act as governor in his absence and to succeed him in the event of his death. A Spanish governor typically had the authority to designate his own lieutenant governor. Also see the footnote at the end of this chapter.

[2] Oviedo writes, "The Governor was not only very weak and sick, but he was totally leprous." The mate's name was Anton Pérez, and the page's name was Campo.

[3] I take this north wind to be the one that brought in the cold and miserable weather Cabeza de Vaca mentions several times, and the date to be the night of November 12-13.

[4] Narváez's announcement of his successor, which Oviedo does not include in his version of the story, now seems eerily coincidental, but Narváez, being ill, may have felt it prudent to put his affairs in order. The observation that there was no food or water on the boat is meant to assure us that Narváez did not take the boat deliberately. As Oviedo succinctly and poetically comments here, "one must conclude that the sea swallowed them up."

[5] Oviedo states that they went "inland," and I believe that to be the case. These castaways, who have lost their boat and their governor, and now have winter upon them, have decided to stop trying to reach Panuco for now and instead dig in for the winter on the mainland.

edge of the water, and they found Indians,[1] who, when they saw them, put their dwellings into their canoes and passed over to the other part of the coast. The Christians, in view of the season, because it was the month of November, stopped to stay in these woods, because they found water, firewood, some crabs, and seafood, yet they began to die little by little of cold and hunger. Furthermore, Pantoja, who had remained as lieutenant, treated them poorly. Sotomayor, the brother of Vasco Porcallo[2] of the island of Cuba, who had come on the fleet as field master,[3] was unable to bear it. He quarreled with him and hit him with a stick, so that Pantoja fell dead.

9 And so this was their end, and those who died, the others made jerky out of them. The last one to die was Sotomayor. Esquivel made jerky of him, and eating of him, held on until the first of March,[4] when one of the Indians who had fled came to see if they were dead, and took Esquivel with him. Being in the custody of this Indian,[5] Figueroa spoke to him and learned from him all

---

[1] These were Quevenes, as per 17:6.

[2] According to a legal document from 1526 in which his name appears, his full name was Alonso de Sotomayor. Also see 1:3.

[3] The *Maeſtre de Campo* was usually a very high-ranking officer, but it may have been nothing more than an important-sounding title in Sotomayor's case, for he was not part of the meeting Narváez had with his officers in Florida (4:6), was not put in charge of one of the boats, and was not even mentioned before now.

[4] Of 1529.

[5] 17:6 describes Esquivel as a Christian who was "staying with the Mariames" but who had been found with the Quevenes. This paragraph states that Esquivel was with the Indian who found him when he spoke with Figueroa. 18:1 implies that he went to the Mariames after speaking with Figueroa. I believe that is correct, and the statement in 17:6 that he was "staying with the Mariames" refers to a later time, not when he met with Figueroa.

that we have related, and he entreated that he go with him, to both go in the direction of Panuco. Esquivel did not want to do this, saying that he had learned from the friars that Panuco was behind them.[1] So, he remained there, and Figueroa went to the coast to where he had been previously.[2]

---

[1] The friars convinced Esquivel that Panuco was to their northeast, not their southwest. This is baffling, because both Friars Suarez and Palos had previously been to New Spain and had firsthand knowledge of what the country looked like. The castaways have been on the coast for a week or more and have not seen one mountain or palm tree. The people who came on Narváez's boat, who saw the entire length of the Texas coast up to that point, would know beyond any doubt that they had not passed the River of Palms or Panuco, yet the friars still believed they had. This had to have been the source of some heated arguments.

[2] The natives who were holding Figueroa, who I believe were the Guaycones, evidently brought him over to the Quevenes' territory for the specific purpose of speaking with Esquivel, who was taken captive on March 1. I suppose that the natives wanted to learn if there were any other foreigners in their vicinity, and if so how many, where they were, etc.

Chapter 18
The Mariames and Iguaces

Of the account that Esquivel gave

Figueroa gave all of this account of the narrative that Esquivel had made known to him. And so, hand in hand, it came to me. Through it, one can see and know the end of the whole fleet and the particular events that happened to each one of the others. [Figueroa] also said that if the Christians spent some time walking through there, they might be able to meet Esquivel, because he knew that he had fled from that Indian with whom he was staying to others who were their neighbors, who were called the Mareames. As [Figueroa] finished speaking,[1] he and the Asturian wanted to go to other Indians further on, but when the Indians who were keeping them heard about it, they came over to them and clubbed them many times. They disrobed the Asturian and passed an arrow through his arm.[2]

---

[1] Lit. *Y como acabo de decir*, "And as I finish saying." The difference between *acabo*, "I finish," and *acabó*, "he finished," is an accent mark. The source text does not have one, but in context, this appears to be a misprint.

[2] Here, the author is still relating events that were related to him by Andrés Dorantes. Gonzalo de Oviedo, who had the Joint Report co-authored by Dorantes as his source, tells the story more clearly, but even still there is some confusion, because, among other reasons, Oviedo never gives the names of the native tribes in his narrative. After Figueroa finished telling his story to Dorantes's party, he, the Asturian, and "a young boy who could swim" went with the native – who I believe to be of the Guaycones – to get some food. The boy came back to Dorantes's group with some fish, but the Asturian stayed with Figueroa. A couple of weeks later, a member of Dorantes's party saw these two again. They had left the tribe I take to be the Guaycones, had been beaten and

2 In the end, the Christians fled and escaped and remained with those Indians.[1] They ended up being taken as slaves, although no slaves, or men of any sort, were ever as mistreated as they were while serving them, because of the six who were there, not content with giving them many beatings, whipping them, and pulling their beards for their own amusement, for only going from one house to another, they killed three of those who I told above: Diego Dorantes, Valdivieso, and Diego de Huelva,[2] and the other three who remained expected to meet the same end.[3]

3 Unable to bear[4] this life, Andrés Dorantes fled and went over to the Mareames, who were those to whom Esquivel had gone.[5] They related to him what had happened to Esquivel there,

_____

stripped, and were on their way to Panuco. Cabeza de Vaca mentions them again in 22:9.

[1] Drawing again from Oviedo: after the Asturian left, Dorantes's group at Cedar Bayou was down to eight. They were taken in, probably as slaves, by a tribe on the mainland for a few days, but those natives threw them out in two separate groups. They went back to the coast and tried to resume their march to Panuco. Two died. Diego Dorantes was enslaved by one group, which I again believe to be the Guaycones. The other five made it across Aransas Pass and were captured by the cruel tribe who I believe were the Quitoles. By then it was late April or early May 1529.

[2] According to Oviedo, the Indians killed Valdivieso "because he wanted to leave" and Huelva "because he changed from one lodging to another." Oviedo implies that both of these men were killed soon after their arrival. A different group of natives killed Diego Dorantes "at the end of two years which he served them," (which would appear to be around May 1531) but he does not give the reason for it, as none of the survivors witnessed his death.

[3] Lit. *esperaban parar en esto mismo*, "expected to end in this same."

[4] Lit. *por no sufrir*, "for not to suffer."

[5] Lit. *parado*, see the footnotes to 17:6.

and how staying there, he desired to flee because a woman had dreamed that he would kill her son, and the Indians went after him and killed him. They showed Andrés Dorantes his sword, rosary,[1] book,[2] and other things of his. They have this as one of their customs, which is that they kill their own children because of dreams.

4 When daughters are born, they leave them for the dogs to eat, and they throw them out. The reason why they do this is – according to what they said - because everyone in the land is their enemy, and they are continually at war with them. If it should happen that they give their daughters in marriage, their enemies could multiply so much that they might subjugate them and take them as slaves. For this reason, they prefer to kill them, rather than that they bear those who would be their enemy. We asked them why they do not wed them among themselves. They said that among them, it was a bad thing to wed them to their relatives, and it was better to kill them than give them to either their relatives or their enemies. Only they and the others, their neighbors who are called the Iguaces, follow this custom; no one else in their land keeps it.[3]

5 When they are to be married, they buy women from their enemies. The price each one gives for his is one bow - the best that can be had - with two arrows. If it happens that he does not

---

[1] Lit. *cuentas*, "beads," from *contar*, "to count." A rosary is a string of beads used for keeping count in a prayer.

[2] That is, prayer book.

[3] The Mariames are one of the best-documented tribes in *La Relación*, but their identity is a mystery; none of the tribes that inhabited the Guadalupe River area in the 1700s are a good match with either them or the Iguaces. Perhaps being at constant war with all of their neighbors, killing all of their daughters as a matter of custom, killing their sons when so inspired by dreams, and depending on their mortal enemies for wives were not effective means of perpetuating the tribe's existence.

have a bow, a net up to one fathom* wide and one long. They kill their children and buy another's. Marriage lasts no longer than as much as they are content; they undo marriage over trifles.[1]

6 Dorantes was with these, then fled after a few days. Castillo and Estevanico went into the mainland to the Iguaces. [2]

7 All of these people are archers and well-built, although not as large as those who we left behind. They wear the nipple and lip pierced. Their principal sustenance is two or three kinds of roots, and they look for them throughout the country. They are very bad, and cause gas in those who eat them. [3] It takes two days to roast them, and many of them are bitter. In addition, pulling

---

[1] Lit. *con vna Higa*, "with an *higa*." *Higa* has many meanings, most of them slang or idiomatic, but it generally means something of no value, something that is ridiculed or despised. It can mean something deserving of a rude gesture, or the gesture itself.

[2] Between here and Paragraph 3, Cabeza de Vaca's explanation of the movements of Dorantes, Castillo, and Estevanico is muddy. Oviedo's account, while still messy, is a little clearer. In April or May 1529, all three, plus Valdivieso and Huelva, became captives of the tribe who I believe to be the Quitoles. They killed Valdivieso and Huelva. In May 1530, Dorantes fled to the Iguaces, leaving Castillo and Estevanico behind. In mid-August 1530, Estevanico fled to the Iguaces. He was only with Dorantes for a short time before Dorantes fled to the Mariames (Mareames) to learn that they had killed Esquivel. Castillo fled to the Iguaces about 18 months later, or around April 1532. The fact that Oviedo has nothing to say about the 18 months Castillo was alone with the most cruel tribe any of the castaways encountered is one of the main reasons I believe Castillo's contributions to the Joint Report were minimal.

[3] Lit. *hinchan los Hombres que las comen*, "inflate the men that eat them."

them is hard work.* Those people are so hungry[1] that they cannot get by without them, and they walk two or three leagues* searching for them. Sometimes they kill some deer, and at times they catch some fish, but this is so little, and their hunger is so great, that they eat spiders, ant eggs, grubs, newts, salamanders, snakes, and vipers that kill the men that they bite.[2] They eat earth, wood, and all that they are able to - deer dung, and other things that I am leaving out. I surely believe that if there were rocks in that country, they would eat them. They keep the bones of the fish that they eat, and of the snakes and other things, to grind all of them later and eat their powder.

8 Among these, the men do not carry loads or any heavy thing, but the women and old men carry them, as they are the people for whom they have the least regard.[3] They do not have as much love for their children as those who we discussed above.[4] There are some among them who practice sin against nature. The women work much and very hard. Out of the twenty-four hours that are in day and night, they do not have six hours of rest. They pass the rest of the night stirring their ovens to dry those roots that they eat. At dawn they begin to dig and carry firewood and water for their houses and arrange the other things that they have to have. Most of these [Indians] are great thieves, for although

---

[1] Lit. *Es tanta la hambre, que aquellas Gentes tienen*, "Is such the hunger, that those people have."

[2] There are four varieties of venomous snakes native to the United States: rattlesnakes, copperheads, cottonmouths, and coral snakes. All four can be found on the upper Gulf coast of Texas. The big, nasty-tempered cottonmouth or "water moccasin" is the only one that swims and is the one most likely to be found in coastal lowlands.

[3] Lit. *es la Gente que ellos en menos tienen*. "is the people that they have in least."

[4] I.e., the natives of the Island of Misfortune, discussed in Chapter 14.

they are very liberal with each other, when one turns his head, his own son or father takes all that he can. They lie very much and are great drunks; they drink a certain thing for this. They are so used to running that they can run from morning until night, following a deer, without resting or tiring. They kill many of them in this way, because they follow them until they tire, and sometimes they take them alive. Their houses are of mats placed over four arches. They carry them on their backs and move every two or three days to look for food; they sow nothing than can be of any use.

9 They are a very joyful people; though they are very hungry, this does not stop them from dancing or having their celebrations and ceremonial dances.* For them, the best time that these have is when they eat tunas,* because then they are not hungry, and they pass all of their time dancing, and they eat of them night and day. The whole time that they last, they squeeze them, open them, and set them out to dry. After they are dry, they put them in some baskets, like figs, and keep them to eat along the trail for their return. They grind the rinds and make them into powder. Many times when we were with them, it would happen that we would go three or four days without eating, because they do not have [anything]; they, to cheer us up, would tell us to not be sad, for soon there would be tunas, and we would eat much, and drink their juice, and we would have very large bellies, and would be very content and merry, and without any hunger. From the time that they would say this to us until there were tunas to eat would be five or six months.

10 Finally, having waited those six months, when it was time, we went to eat tunas.

11 We found a very great quantity of three kinds of mosquitos in the country. They are very bad and bothersome, and they gave us great anguish for most of the summer. To defend ourselves, we made many fires of rotten, wet wood all around the community, so that they made smoke but did not burn. This de-

fense gave us another hardship, because at night we could do nothing but weep because of the smoke it sent into our eyes. On top of this, the great heat of the many fires caused us to leave and sleep on the coast. If at some time we were able to sleep, they would come to us and club us to return and kindle the fires.

12 Those from further inland use another remedy for this that is even more unbearable than this one that I explained, which is to go around with burning sticks in their hands, setting fire to the plains and forests that they come to, so that the mosquitos flee, and also to draw out the lizards and other similar things from below the ground so they can eat them. They also usually kill deer by encircling them with many fires. They also use this to drive the animals from the pasture, so out of necessity they have to go looking for it where [the Indians] want. Because of this, they never situate their houses except where there is water and firewood. Sometimes they load themselves with these provisions and go to look for deer, which quite commonly are where there is neither water nor wood. On the day they arrive, they kill deer and anything else they can. They use up all their water and firewood cooking their food and with the fires they make to defend against the mosquitos. They wait another day to get something to take for the road. When they leave, the mosquitos have been such that they appear to have the infirmity of Saint Lazarus.[1] They satisfy their hunger in this manner two or three times a year, at such a great cost, as I have said. From having been through it, I can affirm that no hardship or suffering in the world equals this.

---

[1] In Luke 16:19-31, Jesus tells the parable of a beggar named Lazarus, who was "covered with sores." In John 11, Jesus raises one of his followers, Lazarus of Bethany, from the dead. This second Lazarus is the one Catholics refer to as "St. Lazarus." The Bible never suggests that these two men were the same person, but many Christians, including Cabeza de Vaca, have conflated them.

13 In this country, there are many deer and other birds and animals than those that I have related so far. Cattle come as far as here.[1] I have seen them three times and eaten them. It appears to me that they will be the size of those of Spain. They have small horns, like Moorish [cattle], and very long, wooly hair, like a rug. Some are brown, and others black. It seems to me that they have better and fattier meat than those from over here. From those that are not large, the Indians make blankets to cover themselves with, and from the bigger ones, they make shoes and shields.[2] These [cows] come from the north, from the land further on, up to the coast of Florida. They are found in all of the country for over four hundred leagues, and in all of this way, through the valleys in which they come, the people who live there go down and subsist on them, and a great quantity of hides are found inland.

---

[1] Lit. *Alcançan aqui vacas*, "cows reach here." I believe this means the country the author is describing is on the edge of a natural cattle (or bison) range.

[2] This is the earliest written description of the American bison.

Chapter 19
The Plan to Escape

How the Indians separated us

Whether the six months were complete that I stayed with the Christians, waiting to put our plan we had made into effect, the Indians went for tunas.*[1] From there to where they picked them was almost thirty leagues.*[2] Right when we were about to flee, the Indians with whom we were and the others quarreled over a woman, and they hit and beat and wounded each

---

[1] Cabeza de Vaca writes that the tunas were eaten for three months (17:3). He further states that the natives were in the tuna fields in September (19:3), and that around the middle of the month, they were dwindling (20:1). Oviedo writes in one place that the tunas lasted for 1½ or 2 months. In another place, he writes that tunas ripen in August and are ripe for 50 or 60 days. It would seem, then, that tuna season lasted from late July or early August to late September or early October. Oviedo also states that these natives hunted deer on their way to the prickly pear fields and implies that they may have begun their migration in early summer. The departure the author is referring to, then, might have been in either June or July of 1533. Whether or not this was actually six months after Cabeza de Vaca arrived is another matter, which I discuss at length in the footnotes of 17:3.

[2] This is about 100 miles (160 km). Oviedo states the distance as "more than forty leagues forward, toward Panuco." The castaways conspired to escape during the tuna harvest not only because their captors would be mingling with other tribes at that time, but because they would be escaping at a place that was significantly closer to their destination than their regular dwellings on the River of Nuts. It is about 60 miles (96 km), or 17 leagues, from the Guadalupe River to the Nueces, and about 200 miles (320 km) to the Rio Grande, so even if the two writer's estimates are too large, which they often are, it seems clear that the prickly pears were between these two rivers.

other, and in the great furor that they made, each one took up his house and went his own way. It was necessary, therefore, that all of the Christians who were there also separated, and there was no way for us to get together for another year.[1]

2 In this time, I had a very bad life, as much as from the great hunger as from the bad treatment that I received from the Indians. It was such that I had to flee three times from my masters. Each time, they went to search for me diligently in order to kill me, but our Lord God, in His mercy, willed to protect me and save me from them.

3 When the time of tunas came around,[2] we returned to that same place to get together. We had already planned to flee and chose the day. That very day, the Indians separated us, and each one went his own way. I told the other comrades that I would wait for them in the tunas until the full moon. This day was the first day of September and the first day of the moon.[3] I advised them that if they did not come as planned at that time, I would go alone and leave them. And so, we parted, each one going with his Indians. I remained with mine until the thirteenth of the moon,[4] and I had decided to flee to other Indians with the full

---

[1] Oviedo seems to state that there were aborted escape attempts during two successive tuna harvests – one, involving a disturbance, which occurred the season before Cabeza de Vaca joined the other three castaways, and one after he joined, which fell apart for unspecified reasons. I am inclined to believe there was a single attempt and that it happened the way Cabeza de Vaca describes it.

[2] Summer of 1534.

[3] I.e., the new moon. The new moon in September 1534 was on the 8th. Since it had presumably been almost six years since the author had seen a calendar, I take it that his recollection of the phase of the moon was superior to his estimation of the date, and conclude that the date was September 8.

[4] September 20.

moon. On the thirteenth day of the month, Andrés Dorantes and Estevanico came to where I was, and they told me how they had left Castillo with other Indians who were called Anagados,[1] who were close to there.[2] They had endured many hardships* and had been lost. The next day, our Indians moved on to where Castillo was, and were going to join those who kept him, to make friends with each other, because until then they had been at war. In this way, we recovered Castillo.

4 The whole time that we ate tunas, we were thirsty. For relief of this, we drank the juice of the tunas, extracting it in a hole we made in the ground. When it was full, we drank of it until we were satisfied. It is sweet and the color of must.[3] [The Indians] make it this way for lack of other vessels. There are many kinds of tunas, and among them there are some very good ones, although they all were good in my opinion, as hunger never gave me a moment to choose or to reflect on which ones were the best. All of the rest of the people drink rainwater collected from various places because, although there are rivers, since they never stay settled, they never have known or marked places.

5 Throughout the land, there are many large and beautiful meadows, with very good pastures for cattle. It seems to me that it would be good land, and very productive, if it were worked and

---

[1] According to Smith, the first edition of *La Relación* reads "Lanegados."

[2] Oviedo writes that Dorantes escaped to other natives (the Anagados) first, then Castillo and Estevanico joined him. They saw some smoke columns at a distance and believed that was where Cabeza de Vaca was. Dorantes and Estevanico went to investigate, leaving Castillo behind to assure the natives that they were coming back.

[3] Must is fresh-squeezed grape juice that has not had the solid material – skins, seeds, and stems – filtered out. It is darker and sweeter than filtered grape juice.

inhabited by people of reason. We did not see mountains in all of it as long as we were there.[1]

    6 Those Indians told us that there were others further, called Camones, who live toward the coast, and who had killed all of the people who came in Peñalosa and Téllez's boat. They were so weak, that although they were being killed, they could not defend themselves, and so they finished them off.[2] They showed us some of their clothing and weapons and said that the boat was there, on its side. This is the fifth boat that was lost. We already told how the governor's was carried away by the sea, and the accountant and friars' was seen capsized on the coast. Esquivel told us of their end.[3] The two in which Castillo, Dorantes and I were, we have already told how they both sank at the Island of Misfortune.

---

[1] The terrain of south Texas within 100 miles (160 km) of the Gulf is flat and ranges from nearly level to perfectly level.

[2] Based on information the author gives in 26:1 about the relative locations of the native tribes, and other information he and Oviedo give about the dwellings of the tribes, I figure that the Camones had to have been in the vicinity of Baffin Bay in Kleberg and/or Kenedy County and were certainly no farther north than Corpus Christi Bay. I estimate that the boat landed on November 9, 1528 (also see Figure 5 on page 98). The facts that the castaways are just now hearing about this boat and the Anagados are showing them artifacts from it supports the theory that they are now in the level coastal plains between the Nueces River and the Rio Grande. Davenport and Wells place the tuna field where the castaways escaped in south Duval County, near the boundary with Jim Wells County (also see Figure 7, "Map of the Journey of the Four Ragged Castaways," on page 198).

[3] That is, Esquivel told Figueroa, who told Dorantes, who told Cabeza de Vaca.

Chapter 20
Accepted by the Avavares

Of how we fled

Two days from after we had been moved,[1] we commended ourselves to our Lord God and fled, trusting that, although it was
late and the tunas were dwindling, with the fruits that remained
in the field, we would be able to cover a good part of the country.
As we went on our way that day, completely afraid that the Indians would follow us,[2] we saw some smoke [columns].[3] Going to-
wards them, we reached that place after vespers.* There we saw
an Indian who fled as he saw us coming to him, not wanting to
wait for us. We sent the Negro* after him, and as he saw him
coming alone, he waited for him. The Negro told him that we
were going in search of that people who had made that smoke.[4]
He responded that there were houses close to there, and that he
would guide us there. And so, we followed him, and he ran to give
notice that we were on our way. When the sun set, we saw the
houses. Two crossbow shots[5] before we reached them, we found
four Indians who were waiting for us, and they received us well.

---

[1] If the author remembered the date correctly in 19:3, then this would be
September 16, 1534, but if we assume that his memory of the phases of
the moon is correct, which I believe is more likely, it is September 23,
the day after the full moon.

[2] Even though the castaways had escaped their captors and were staying
with others now, they undoubtedly worried about being recaptured,
treated as slaves, tortured, and/or killed by any natives they stayed with
and thought it best to leave abruptly and unnoticed.

[3] Lit. *unos humos*, "some smokes."

[4] Lit. "those smokes."

[5] Or, "a very long distance," see 12:3.

We told them in the language of the Mariames that we were looking for them. They indicated that they accepted our company, and
so they took us to their houses. Dorantes and the Negro were
placed in the house of one healer,[1] and Castillo and I in the house
of another. These speak another language and are called Avavares. They are those who used to bring bows to ours and trade
with them. Although they were of another nation and language,
they understood the language of those with who we had been before, and they had arrived with their houses that very day.

2 Then the villagers offered us many tunas, because they
had already heard of us and how we had cured, and of the won-
ders that our Lord had worked through us. Even if there had been
no others, I was greatly gratified that there were ways opened for
us through such an uninhabited country, and for giving us people
in places where at many times there were none, and saving us
from such perils, and not permitting us to die, and sustaining us
through such hunger, and putting in those people's hearts to treat
us well, as we will relate further.

---

[1] Lit. *Fiſico*, see 14:6.

Chapter 21
Cabeza de Vaca Gets Lost

How here we cured some suffering ones

That same night that we arrived,[1] some Indians came to Castillo and told him that they were very sick in their heads, entreating him to cure them. After he made the sign of the Cross* and commended them to God, at that moment the Indians said that all of the illness had left them. They went to their houses and brought many tunas* and a piece of venison - something that we did not know what it was.[2] As this became publicized among them, many other sick came that night for him to heal them, and each one brought a piece of venison. There were so many that we did not know where to put the meat. We gave many thanks to God because every day His mercy and favors grew. After the cures were finished, they began to dance and make their ceremonial dances* and celebrations until the sun came out the next day.

2 The celebration over our arrival lasted three days. At the end of them, we asked them about the land further on, about the people we may find in it, and what sustenance there is in it. They responded that there are many tunas throughout the whole land, except that they were gone now, and that no people were there, because they had all gone to their homes, all the tunas having been gathered. They said that the country was very cold and there were very few skins in it. In view of this, with the winter and cold

---

[1] September 23, 1534. According to Oviedo, it was October.

[2] The castaways may not have known that they were given venison, but they knew what venison was. Deer, deerskins, and venison are mentioned throughout *La Relación*. The natives in Florida gave Alonso Enríquez venison (3:1) ; the Mariames hunted deer (18:7, 18:12).

temperatures already moving in, we decided to spend it with these [Indians].

3 At the end of five days from our arrival, they left to look for more tunas where other people of other nations and languages were. We walked five days[1] with very great hunger, because there were no tunas nor any other fruit on the way. We came to a river, where we set up our houses. After they were set up, we went to look for a fruit of certain trees, which is like peas.[2] Since there are not any trails in this whole country, I stayed too long looking for [the fruit]. The people returned and left me alone. Going to look for them that night, I became lost. It pleased God that I found a burning tree, and I spent that cold night by its fire. In the morning,[3] I loaded myself with firewood, took two firebrands, and went back to looking for [the Indians]. I walked this way five days, always with my fire and load of wood, because if the fire died on me in a place where there was no firewood - as in many parts there is none - I would have the means of making other firebrands and not be left without fire, because I had no other remedy from the cold, as I was going about as naked as I was born.

4 At night, I had this solution, which is that I went to the brush in the woods that were close to the rivers, and stopped in them before the sun set. I made a pit in the ground and threw a lot of firewood - which comes from the many trees - into it. There is a very great quantity of it there, and I collected a lot of firewood

---

[1] Lit. *jornadas*. In this context, *jornada* means "a day's journey."

[2] Lit. *hieros*. This appears to be an alternate spelling of *yero*, the Spanish name for a pea plant species called bitter vetch. The Texas ebony tree, a member of the pea family, produces seed pods that resemble those of other pea plants. Its native habitat is the coast of Tamaulipas and south Texas. Davenport and Wells place this location in northeast Hidalgo County and identify the river as the Arroyo Colorado.

[3] October 3.

from that which had fallen and dried up from the trees. Around the circumference of that hole, I made four fires in a cross, and I took charge and was careful to rebuild the fire from time to time. I made bundles of the long straw that was around there and covered myself with them in that pit. In this manner, I sheltered myself from the cold of the night. One of those [nights] the fire fell onto the straw with which I was covered, and while I was sleeping in the pit, it began to burn very rapidly. I got out with great speed; nevertheless it left a mark on my hair[1] of the danger that I was in.

5 In all this time, I did not eat a mouthful, neither did I find anything that could be eaten. As I was going with bare feet, much blood ran from them. God had mercy on me that in all of this time, there was no north wind, because in that event, there would have been no way for me to live.

6 At the end of five days,[2] I arrived at the bank of a river, where I found my Indians, who, along with the Christians, had reckoned me as dead. They believed all along that a viper had bitten me. They all had great pleasure in seeing me, especially the Christians. They told me that they had until then been going about very hungry, and this was the reason that they had not searched for me. That night they gave me the tunas that they had. We left there the next day and went to where we found many tunas, with which we all satisfied our great hunger. We gave many thanks to our Lord, because His aid never failed us.

---

[1] Lit. *señal en los cabellos*, "sign (mark, signal) on the hair (of the head or face)." I take this to mean that the author received an injury that changed his appearance, such as a scar, discoloration, or bald spot in the area of his scalp or beard.

[2] October 7.

Chapter 22
Life with the Avavares and Their Neighbors

How they brought us other sick ones the next day

The morning of the next day,[1] many Indians there came and brought five sick people, who were crippled and very ill. They came in search of Castillo, so he could cure them, and each one of the sick offered his bow and arrows. He received them, and at sunset he made the sign of the Cross* and commended them to our Lord God. All of us entreated Him in the best way we could to bring them health. And He saw that there was no other remedy by which those people would help us and to get us out of such a miserable life, and He acted so mercifully, that when the morning came, all of them awoke so well and sound, and were so hearty, as if they had never had any illness. This caused very great admiration among them, which moved us to give many thanks to our Lord, that we more fully knew His goodness and had a firm faith that He would save us and bring us to where we would be able to serve Him. For myself, I can say that I always had faith in His mercy, that He would take me from that captivity, and I always told my companions so.

2 As the Indians were going and taking away their healthy Indians, we departed to where there were others eating tunas.* These are called Cutalches and Malicones,[2] which are other languages. Alongside them, there were others who were called Coayos[3] and Susolas. In another place, others called Atayos, and

---

[1] October 9, 1534.

[2] These tribes' names are spelled Cutalchiches and Maliacones elsewhere in *La Relación*.

[3] I take these to be same as the Comos, who are named in Chapter 26 as neighbors of all of the other tribes mentioned in this paragraph.

these were at war with the Susolas, with whom they exchanged arrow shots every day.

3 As nothing was spoken of in the whole country but the mysteries that our Lord God worked through us, they came from many places to seek us so that we would cure them. At the end of two days from their arrival, some Indians of the Susolas came to us and asked Castillo to go and cure a wounded person and some sick people. They said that one of their people was at the very end. Castillo was a very timid physician, especially when the cures were very worrisome and dangerous; he believed that his sins would interfere so that the cures would not succeed every time. The Indians told me to go and cure them, because they liked me, and they remembered that I had cured them at the nut groves. They had given me nuts and hides for that - this had happened when I was coming to join the Christians.[1] So, I had, to go with them, and Dorantes and Estevanico went with me.[2]

4 When I came close to the huts that they had, I saw that the sick one that we came to cure was dead, because there were many people around him, crying, and his house torn down, which is the sign that the owner was dead. And so, when I arrived, I found the Indian with his eyes turned, without any pulse, and

---

[1] "At the nut groves" literally reads *en las Nueces*, "in the nuts." In giving his account of his journey from the Island of Misfortune to the River of Nuts in Chapters 16, and 17, the author does not mention any healings.

[2] Why did Castillo stay behind? On another occasion, the four men left one of themselves behind to assure their hosts they were coming back, but that does not seem to be the case here, because some of the Avavares went with them. Was Castillo so worried about his sins interfering with the cure that he thought he should not even go? Did he think he and his comrades were crossing a line by trying to "cure" a man who was at the point of death? Was he jealous that the natives turned to Cabeza de Vaca? Was there an argument? There is so much the author does not tell us about what happened on a personal level between these men.

with all of the signs of death. It seemed that way to me, and Dorantes said the same. I removed a mat that was on top of him, which was covering him, and as best I could, I requested our Lord to be served by giving health to that one and to all the others who were in need. After I made the sign of the Cross and blew many times, they brought me a bow and gave it to me, and a basket of ground tunas, and they took me to cure many others who were ill from drowsiness.[1] They gave me two more baskets of tunas, which I gave to our Indians, who had come with us. With this done, we returned to our lodgings.

5 Our Indians, to whom I gave the tunas, stayed there. At night, they returned to their houses and said that the one who was dead and who I had cured in their presence had awoken well and had been walking, eating, and speaking with them, and that all who had been cured were left healthy and very happy. This caused very great admiration and awe, and nothing else was spoken of in the whole country. All those to whom this fame reached came to us seeking for us to cure them and make the sign of the Cross over their children. When the Indians who were in the company of ours, who were the Cutalchiches, had to go to their country, they offered us all of the tunas they had for their journey before they parted, without leaving any for themselves. They also gave us flints as large as a palm and a half, with which they cut, and are a very highly valued thing among them. They implored us to re-

---

[1] Lit. *malos de modorra*, "ill from drowsiness." I believe the fact that some of the ailments these natives suffered from consisted simply of feeling drowsy is a hint that many of them just wanted to be cured by the visitors. As subsequent chapters will show, there were benefits for a village to have such renowned healers in its midst, and every cure they performed enhanced their reputations. That being said, I do not intend to imply that none of the natives Cabeza de Vaca and his companions encountered were ill, nor do I intend to imply that none of the ones they ministered to were restored to health.

member them and pray to God that they would always be well. We promised it to them, and with this, they parted, the most content men in the world, having given us all the best that they had.

6 We stayed with those Avavares Indians eight months.[1] (This is the count we made of the moons.) In all this time, [people] came from many parts to seek us, and they said that truly we were children of the sun. Until then, Dorantes and the Negro* had not cured, but because of the heavy demands on us,[2] as they were coming from many places to seek us, we all came to be doctors. I, however, was the most well-known for being bold and daring to undertake any cure. Never did we cure anyone who did not tell us that he became well, and they had such confidence that if we healed someone they would be cured, that they believed that as long as we stayed there, none of them had to die.

7 These [Indians] and those further behind us told us a very strange thing, and by the account that they represented to us, it seemed that it had been fifteen or sixteen years since it had happened. They said that in that country a man went about who

----

[1] As noted in the footnotes to 21:1, the castaways arrived at the Avavares' village, by my calculations, on September 23, 1534. They remained in the prickly pear fields for five days, then they traveled for five days to their winter home, arriving there on October 3. Depending on whether the eight months began on September 23 or October 3, they ended from late May to early June. In 36:4, Cabeza de Vaca states that the castaways traveled for ten months. Their journey appears to have ended in April 1536, which confirms a start date of around June 1535. This start date is also confirmed by various seasonal clues given in the following chapters, as I will show. Oviedo gives the interval that the castaways stayed with the Avavares as October to August, which does not seem to be right.

[2] Lit. *por la mucha importunidad que teniamos*, "for the great importunity that we had."

they called "Bad Thing." He was small of stature and had a beard,[1] although they were never able to see his face clearly. When he came to the house where they stayed, their hair would stand on end, and they trembled. Later, a piece of burning wood would appear at the door of the house. Next, that man would enter and take whichever of them he wanted and give them three large cuts on their sides with a very sharp flint, as big as a hand and two palms in length. He would insert his hand into the cuts and remove the entrails, and cut an entrail more or less [the size] of a palm, and he threw that cut one into the coals. Next, he gave [the person] three cuts on the arm. He made the second one inside the elbow[2] and disjointed it. After a little while, he returned it to normal and he put his hands over the wounds, and they told us that they would later be healed. He would often appear among them when they danced, in a woman's clothing sometimes, and other times as a man. When he wanted to, he took a hut or house and would toss it up high, and a moment later he would fall with it in a very great crash. They also told us that many times, they would give him food, which he never ever ate. They asked him

---

[1] Pre-Columbian American natives normally had sparse facial and body hair, so beards were rare among them. The implication here is that Bad Thing was a foreigner. In 1519, sixteen years before Cabeza de Vaca heard this story, A Spanish explorer, Alonso Álvarez de Pineda, sailed along the entire coast of the Gulf of Mexico. It is unknown whether Pineda or his men landed anywhere in present-day Texas. I will leave it to the reader to imagine whether there could be any connection between Pineda and Bad Thing. There are already too many myths about Pineda's role in Texas history, and I do not want to start another one, but at the same time, I would be remiss in not pointing out the coincidence in dates.

[2] Lit. *por la ſangradura*, from *sangrar*, "to bleed." The *sangradura*, when used as an anatomical term, is the part of the arm that was usually bled, i.e., the inside of the elbow.

where he was going and where his home was, and that he showed them a fissure in the ground and said his home was down there.

8 We laughed a lot at these things that they told us, making fun of them. When they saw that we did not believe it, they brought many of those who they said he had taken, and we saw the marks from the cuts that he had made in the places and in the manner that they related. We told them that he was an evil one, and in the best way we could, we gave them to understand that if they believed in our Lord God and became Christians like us, they would no longer fear that one, nor would he dare to come and do those things, and they would be certain that as long as we were staying in the country, he would not dare to appear in it. They were very eased by this, and lost a great part of the fear that they had.

9 These Indians told us that they had seen the Asturian and Figueroa with others who stayed further on the coast, who we called "of the figs."[1]

---

[1] The fact that the Avavares had first-hand knowledge about natives who lived on the coast is another sign that their winter home was not too far from the Gulf of Mexico. If it was in Hidalgo County, as Davenport and Wells theorize, then Figueroa and the Asturian may have made it as far south on the coast as Cameron County, or even into Mexico, since they were "further on the coast." The texts do not tell us whether or not these two Christians were slaves of the Fig-Indians, but considering how common slavery was among the other coast-dwelling tribes, that seems likely. These two men who were determined to make it to Panuco at all costs never made it.

The origin of the name "of the figs" is unknown. The castaways never reported seeing either figs or these natives, so how would they come up with this name? I believe that whatever name the Avavares called the natives simply may have sounded like *higos*, the Spanish word for "figs," to the castaways.

10 All of these people do not know the seasons by the sun or the moon, nor do they keep count of the month and year, but they understand and know the different seasons when the fruits come and mature, the time that the fish die, and the appearance of the stars, in which they are very skilled and practiced. We were always treated well with these, although whatever we ate, we dug, and we carried our own loads of water and firewood. Their houses and sustenance are like those from earlier, although they are much more hungry, because they are not near any[1] corn,* acorns, or nuts. We always went about undressed, like them, and at night we covered ourselves with deer skins.

11 Of the eight months that we stayed with them, we suffered from much hunger for six, for they are not near fish either. At the end of this time, the tunas began to ripen.[2] Without them being aware, we left to others who were staying further ahead, called Maliacones. These, where the Negro and I went, were a day's journey away. At the end of the three days, I sent [him] to bring Castillo and Dorantes, and they came. We left together with the Indians, who went to eat a little fruit of some trees, which they subsist on ten or twelve days, during which the tunas appear. There they joined with these other Indians who are called Arbadaos. We found them very sick, thin, and swollen; so much that we were very amazed at them. The Indians with whom we had come returned by the same trail. We told them that we wanted to stay with those; they showed grief over this. So, we stayed with those in the field, close to their houses.

---

[1] Lit. *no alcançan*, "they do not reach."

[2] The author repeats a point made in 22:6 that the castaways stayed with the Avavares for eight months, which would be approximately until late May or early June of 1535. Tunas take a few months to ripen. One would see the process beginning in mid-spring, when the green fruit begins to turn yellow-orange. The color deepens until the tunas are ready to pick in July and August.

12 When they saw us, they came together, after having spoken among themselves, and each one of them took his own [of us] by the hand and took us to their houses. We suffered more hunger with these than with the others, for we ate nothing all day but two handfuls of that fruit, which was green and had so much milk that it burned our mouths. With the lack of water, it gave much thirst to anyone who ate it. Since our hunger was so great, we bought two dogs from them and, in exchange, gave them some nets and other things, and a hide with which I covered myself. I have already told how we went about naked through all of this land. Not being accustomed to it, we shed our skins two times a year, like snakes. With the sun and the air making very large blisters[1] on our chests and backs, we were in very great pain because of the very large loads that we carried, which were very heavy, and which had ropes that cut into our arms.

13 The country is so rough and so closed that many times when we made firewood in the woods, when we finished gathering it, we were bleeding in many places from the thorns and bushes that we came up against, which cut us wherever they touched us. Sometimes after making it, after it costing me much blood, I could not gather it, either on my back or by dragging it. When I found myself in these hardships,* I had no other remedy or consolation but to think about the Passion of our Savior, Jesus Christ, and of the blood that He spilled for me, and to consider how much greater was His torment, from the thorns He endured, than those from which I suffered.

14 I contracted with these Indians, making combs, bows, and arrows for them, and we made mats from reeds, as these are

---

[1] Lit. *empeines*. According to dictionaries, the most common translations of *empeine* are "groin," "instep," and "hoof," but it can also mean "ringworm," "tetter," and "cotton flower." It appears that the author has these latter meanings in mind and is describing the pustules and blisters that form with second-degree sunburn.

the things for which they have the greatest need. Although they know how to make them, they do not want to do any work when they could be searching for something to eat. When they are engaged in this, they experience very great hunger. Other times, they told me to scrape and soften skins. The greatest luxury I experienced was the day that they gave me some to scrape, because I scraped thoroughly and ate the scrapings. That sustained me for two or three days. Also, with these and those we had left behind, when it happened that they gave us a piece of meat, we ate it raw, because if we grilled it, the first Indian who came by would take it and eat it. We thought that it was not good to take this chance, and also we were not to give ourselves the trouble of eating it grilled, and we also could not endure as raw. [1] This is the life we had there, and we earned that little sustenance with the barter that we made with our hands.

---

[1] Lit. *no eftabamos tales, que nos dabamos pena comerlo afado, i no lo podiamos tambien pafar como crudo*, "we were not such that we gave pain to us to eat it grilled, and we could not also pass as raw." The meaning of this phrase is unclear. Bandelier edits it to read, "neither were we particular to go to any trouble in order to have it broiled and might just as well eat it raw." Smith interprets it as "besides we were in such condition it would have given us pain to eat it roasted, and we could not have digested it so well as raw." Bandelier's version seems more logical to me.

Chapter 23
A Village with Fifty Houses

How we departed after having eaten the dogs

After we ate the dogs, we felt that we had the will to be able to go ahead. Commending ourselves to our Lord God to guide us, we took our leave of those Indians, and they set us on the path to others of their language who were close to there. While going on our way, it rained, and we walked in water that whole day.[1] Furthermore, we lost the trail and came to a stop in a very large forest. We ate many tuna* leaves[2] and roasted them that night in an oven that we made. It gave off so much heat that in the morning, they were ready to eat. After we had eaten them, we commended ourselves to God and departed, and found the trail that we had lost.

2 Past the woods, we found more Indian houses. Upon arriving there, we saw two women and some children, who were scared and went into the woods. They fled at the sight of us and went to call to the Indians who were in the woods. They came, and they stopped to look at us through some trees. We called to them, and they approached in great fear. After having spoken to them, they told us that they were very hungry, and there were many of their own houses close to there, and they said that they would take us to them.

3 That night, we arrived at a place where there were fifty houses. They were scared to see us and showed great fear. After

---

[1] Oviedo writes, "That day they walked five or six leagues without finding anything to eat."

[2] That is, prickly pear cactus pads, or *nopales* in Spanish. Unlike the fruit, the pads of prickly pears are unappetizing when eaten raw. Exposing them to fire also burns off the needles.

they became somewhat less afraid of us,[1] they approached us and reached their hands to our faces and bodies. Next, they brought their own hands to their faces and bodies.[2] We stayed there that night. When morning came, they brought their sick to us, requesting that we bless* them.[3] They gave us from what they had to eat, which were baskets of tunas and grilled green tunas.[4] For the good treatment that they gave us, and because they gave us that which they had, gladly and of free will, and they were content with being left without anything to eat from giving it to us, we stayed with them several days.[5] When we were there, others came from further on. When they wanted to depart, we said to the first ones that we wanted to go with those. They were very grieved, and begged us very earnestly not to go. At the end, we said goodbye to

---

[1] Lit. *foſegados de noſotros*, "calmed of us."

[2] This means that the natives wanted the castaways to touch them. Oviedo writes, "By signs, they explained to the Christians that should they rub and stroke them, they could cure them."

[3] Lit. *ſantiguaſemos*. This is the from same word, *santiguar*, that I usually translate as "make the sign of the Cross." As stated in the glossary, this can refer to both the hand motion Catholics make when making a blessing and to the blessing itself. In this instance, I am using it in its more generic sense, as I wish to avoid describing the natives' beliefs and behaviors in language that is distinctly Catholic or Christian.

[4] The season must now be where there are some ripe tunas, but not enough to satisfy the natives' hunger, so they are also subsisting on unripe tunas and cactus pads, cooking them so as to make them more palatable. Perhaps it is early July. Oviedo mentions the passage of eight days between now and when the castaways left the Avavares, but there is probably some time unaccounted for.

[5] Oviedo writes that the castaways stayed in this village for 15 days, and by the end of this time, they felt stronger and "became themselves again."

them, and left them crying at our departure, because it grieved them a great deal.

Chapter 24
The Indians' Customs Regarding Disputes and Warfare
Of the customs of the Indians of that country

Since the Island of Misfortune, all the Indians of this land that we saw have the custom[1] that from the day that the women know they are pregnant, they do not sleep together until two years have passed since the children have been born. They nurse until they are of the age of twelve years, at which they are then at the age that they know how to search for food. We asked them why they raise them so; they said that it is because of the great hunger that exists in the land, it often occurs, as we saw, that two or three days go by without eating - sometimes four - and for this reason, they are left to nurse, so that they would not die during the times of hunger, and although some escaped, they would be left very delicate and weak.

2 In the event that some of them become sick, they leave them to die in those fields if he is not a child. All the rest, if they cannot go with them, are left behind, except if they are a son or brother; they are taken and carried on their backs.

3 All of them have a custom to leave their wives[2] when there is disagreement among them, and to turn around and marry whoever they want. This is among the youths; those who have

---

[1] Here, Cabeza de Vaca takes a break from the narrative to relate some general information about the natives. As this sentence indicates, the information given here applies over a larger area than just his current location. For the most part, he seems to be discussing the natives of Texas, but in a few places, it seems like he may be remembering things about the natives of Florida or other parts of the Gulf coast that he visited. This informational section consists of Chapters 24 through 26.

[2] Lit. *Mujeres*. *Mujer* usually means "woman," but in many contexts, such as here, it means "wife."

children remain with their wives and do not leave them. In some villages, when [the men] quarrel and have disputes with each other, they strike and beat [each other] until they are very tired, and then they separate. Sometimes the women go between them and separate them, but men do not go in and separate them. Regardless of their passion,[1] they do not use either bows or arrows. From the time that they have fought and settled the matter, they take their houses and wives and go to live in the fields apart from the others until their anger has passed. When they are calmed down and without ire, they return to their village, and from there forward, they are friends as if nothing had happened between them. There is no need for anyone to make pacts,[2] because they make them in this manner. If those who argue are unmarried, they each go to their neighbors. Even if they are their enemies, they receive them well and are very relaxed with them and give to them from what they have in such a way that when their anger has passed, they return to their village wealthy.

4 All of this people are warlike and have such cunning about protecting themselves from their enemies, as if they had been born in Italy and in constant war. When they are in a place where their enemies can offend them, they set down their houses

---

[1] Lit. *por ninguna paſion que tengan*, "for no passion that they have."

[2] Lit. *que nadie haga las amiſtades*, "that no one makes the friendships." The author is pointing out that disputes are settled without using any kind of arbitrator, judge, or authority figure. The natives of Florida had chiefs and lords, but except for the privileges enjoyed by healers, Cabeza de Vaca never mentions or hints at any social organization among the natives of Texas beyond the basic expectations regarding sex, age, and marital status. As he writes in 15:6, "there is no lord among them." I will note that a dispute-resolution system that lacks an impartial mediator, and requires the aggrieved parties to work their out differences between themselves, tends to favor whichever party is stronger, rather than the one who is in the right.

at the edge of the roughest and thickest woods that they find there, and together, they make a pit, and in this they sleep. All of the men of war are covered with brushwood, and they make their loopholes, and they are so covered and concealed, yet although [their enemies] are nearby, they do not see them. They make a very narrow trail and enter the middle of the forest, and there they make a place for the women and children to sleep. When night comes, they burn fires in their houses so that if there were spies, they would believe that [the men] are in them, and before dawn, they would return to burn the same fires, and in case the enemies came to engage the same houses, those who are in the pit leave them and do much damage from the ditches, without those outside seeing them nor able to find them.

5 When there are no woods in which they can hide themselves in this manner and make their ambushes, they settle down on the part of the plain that seems the best, surround themselves with trenches covered with brushwood, and make their loopholes, with which they shoot arrows at the Indians. They make these defenses[1] for the night. While I was those of Aguenes,[2] they were not warned. Their enemies came at midnight and attacked them,

---

[1] Lit. *reparos*. This word usually means "repairs," but it can be used to refer to preventative measures as well as corrective ones. Bandelier mistranslates it as "parapets," possibly because of the outward similarity of that word to *reparos*.

[2] Lit. "*los de Aguenes*." These were the same natives the author calls Deaguanes in 16:8 and Doguenes in 26:1. Cabeza de Vaca and Lope de Oviedo traveled with the Deaguanes in early 1533. Cabeza de Vaca did not write of any such skirmish, but he did note that they were enemies with the Quevenes. Since these natives lived in between the Island of Misfortune and the bay of *Espíritu Santo*, Cabeza de Vaca may have spent time with them during the years he supposedly was an itinerant merchant, and this incident could have occurred during one of those visits.

killed three, and hurt many others in such a way that they fled to their houses through the woods ahead. Once they felt that the others had gone, they returned and recovered all of the arrows that the others had shot, and followed them as covertly as they could. They were there that night, at the houses, without being detected, and at the quarter of dawn, they attacked and killed five. Many others were wounded. They made them flee and leave their houses and bows, and all their belongings. In a short time, the women of those who are called Quevenes came, and they reached an understanding with them and made friends with them, although sometimes they are the cause of the war. All of these people, when they have particular enmities, when they are not of one family, kill by night with traps and inflict great cruelties upon each other.

Chapter 25
How the Indians Fight

How the Indians are ready with a weapon

These people are the most ready with a weapon of all I have seen in the world, because if they fear their enemies, they are awake all night with their bows and a dozen arrows near them. He who sleeps tests his bow, and if he does not find it in order, he gets up to fix it. Often, they leave their houses down on the ground, so as not to be seen, to look and spy in all places to sense what is there. If they sense something, all of them are in the field with their bows and arrows on the spot. They so remain until daybreak, running from one place to another, when they see that it is necessary or they believe that their enemies can be there. When the day comes, they loosen their bows until they leave to hunt.

2 Their bowstrings are deer sinews. The manner in which they fight is crouched to the ground. While they shoot, they go about talking and always jumping from one spot to another, watching for the arrows of their enemies, such that they are generally able to receive very little damage from crossbows and arquebuses.[1] Rather, the Indians mock them, because these arms are worthless against them in open fields, where the Indians jump about; they are good in narrow and watery places. Most of all, horses are what can subdue them, and are what the Indians fear universally.[2]

---

[1] The arquebus was the first form of shoulder-fired long gun, preceding the musket.

[2] The Narváez Expedition brought neither crossbows, arquebuses, nor horses to Texas, so the author must be drawing from his experiences with the natives of Florida. The Gentleman of Elvas, who was with Her-

3 Whoever fights against them must be very wise that [the Indians] do not sense weakness or greed for what they have. During war, one must treat them very badly, because if they are aware of any fear or greed, these are people who know the time to avenge themselves, and to take strength from the fear of their foes. When they have shot arrows in war and spent their ammunition, they each go their own way, even though some are many,[1] and the others few; this is their custom.

4 Often, the arrows pass all the way through, and they do not die of the wounds if the bowels or the heart are not touched; rather, they heal quickly. They see and hear better and have more acute senses, I believe, than all of the people in the world. They are great sufferers of hunger, thirst, and cold, as they are more accustomed to it and used to it than others. I wished to state this because, besides that all men desire to know the customs and practices as others, those who go to see them at some time would be wise to their customs and tricks, as there is usually some benefit in similar cases.

---

nando de Soto in Florida in 1539, wrote, "They are never quiet but always running and crossing from one side to another so that the crossbows or the arquebuses cannot be aimed at them; and before a crossbowman can fire a shot, an Indian can shoot three or four arrows, and very seldom does he miss what he shoots at."

[1] Lit. *los unos fean muchos,* "the ones are many."

Chapter 26
The Indians' Drinking Ceremony and Other Customs
Of the nations and languages

I also want to mention their nations and languages, which are from the Island of Misfortune to the last ones.[1] On the Island of Misfortune there are two languages, some called Caoques and others called Han.[2] On the mainland, facing the island, there are others who are called "of Chorruco";[3] they take the name of the woods where they live. Further on the sea coast, others dwell who are called Doguenes,[4] and facing them, others by the name of Mendica.[5] Even further on the coast are the Quevenes,[1] and facing

---

[1] In a footnote to his translation, Buckingham Smith states that these "last ones" were identified in the first edition as the *Cuchendados*. I have included alternate spellings of other tribe names from Smith's edition in these footnotes and indicated them with *italics*. See Figure 6, "Map of the Native Tribes of Coastal Texas," on page 158 for a visual depiction of the information given here.

[2] Also see 15:6. Cabeza de Vaca says the Capoques (Caoques, *Cahoques*) and Han were different tribes with different languages, but otherwise, he does not distinguish them from each other. They inhabited the coast of Brazoria County and also, probably, Galveston Island.

[3] Also see 16:2. "Those of Chorruco" (Charruco) lived in wooded areas inland from the Capoques and Han, so probably on the mainland of Brazoria County and possibly Galveston, Fort Bend, and/or Harris Counties.

[4] Also see 16:8 and 24:5. The Deaguanes (Los de Aguenes, Doguenes) inhabited the coast on the east side of Matagorda Bay, probably in Brazoria and Matagorda Counties.

[5] The Mendica are not mentioned elsewhere in *La Relación*, so nothing whatsoever is known of them. Based purely on this one reference, I as-

them, further within the mainland, the Mariames.² Going further along the coast are others who are called Guaycones,³ and facing them, within the mainland, the Yguaces.⁴ At the end of these are others who are called Atayos,⁵ and in back of these, others, Acu-

---

sume they lived in Brazoria, Matagorda, Fort Bend, and/or Wharton Counties.

¹ Also see 16:8, 17:6, and 24:5. The Quevenes inhabited the west side of Matagorda Bay, in Calhoun County, definitely on the mainland and possibly also on Matagorda Island.

² See Chapters 17 and 18. The Mariames (Mareames) inhabited the mainland interior to the Quevenes, which would be Calhoun and Victoria Counties. If their territory extended across the Guadalupe River, which seems probable, it also included parts of Goliad and Refugio Counties Every year, the Mariames migrated to the prickly pear fields of south Texas.

³ Since the Guaycones' area of habitation was down the coast from the Quevenes, it probably included St. Joseph Island and the mainland of Aransas County. This is the only place in *La Relación* where this tribe is mentioned by name, but they were presumably involved in some of the events that occurred to the "strong swimmers" and Dorantes's party that are related in Chapters 17 and 18.

⁴ Also see 17:4 and 18:4-6. The Iguaces (Yguaces, *Yguazes*) are mentioned several times in *La Relación*, always in connection with their neighbors to the east, the Mariames. Their habitation probably included Refugio, Goliad, and Victoria Counties.

⁵ Also see 22:2. This list names two tribes as inland neighbors of the Guaycones. The Atayos must have been southwest of the Iguaces, so perhaps they lived in San Patricio, Bee, and/or Refugio Counties. They are mentioned in 22:2 as one of the tribes who visited the castaways when they were living with the Avavares, who were conclusively a south Texas tribe.

badaos.[1] There are many on the path ahead of these. Others called Quitoles[2] live on the coast, and facing these, within the mainland, the Avavares. The Maliacones are joined with these, and others, Cutalchiches, and others who are called Susolas, and others who are called Comos,[3] and further on the coast are the Camoles.[4]

---

[1] They are not mentioned anywhere else. We only know they were "in back of" the Atayos, who were inland from the Guaycones and next to the Iguaces. If I had to make a guess, I would say they lived in Live Oak, San Patricio, Nueces, and/or Jim Wells Counties.

[2] The author returns to the coast, giving the name of the tribe that lived down the coast from the Guaycones. I take the habitation of the Quitoles (*Quitoks*) to be the area around Aransas Pass, probably including Mustang Island in Nueces County, and perhaps parts of San Patricio and Aransas Counties as well. I believe the Quitoles are the tribe referred to in 18:2 that inflicted the worst tortures on Andrés Dorantes, Castillo, and Estevanico and who killed Valdivieso and Huelva (but not Diego Dorantes, if Oviedo is to be believed.)

[3] These five tribes – the Avavares (*Chavavares*), Maliacones (Malicones), Cutalchiches (Cutalches, *Cultalchulches*), Susolas, and Comos (Coayos) are listed as living inland from the Quitoles, who I believe inhabited the Aransas Pass and Mustang Island area. The last four tribes all visited the four castaways when they were with the Avavares in 1533 and 1534 (see Chapter 22). I believe it is safe to say that the range of these tribes included parts or all of Nueces, Jim Wells, Live Oak, Duval, and Kleberg Counties at a minimum. The Avavares, and perhaps the others, may have ranged as far south as Hidalgo County. We have little information about the internal arrangement of these five tribes with respect to each other, but we do know that the Susolas fought daily with the Atayos (22:2), who lived further north, so they may have been the most north-dwelling of them.

[4] Also see 19:6. The Camones (Camoles) lived down the coast from the Quitoles, who lived down the coast from the Guaycones, who lived down the coast from the Quevenes, who lived on the west side of Matagorda Bay. This may put the Camones' habitation on N. Padre Island, in the

Further on the same coast, others who we call "those of the figs."[1] All of these people have homes and villages and diverse tongues. Among these there is a language in which they call men to look here, "*arre acá*",[2] and dogs, "*xó.*"

2 In all of the country, they get drunk with a smoke, and they give all they have for it.

3 They also drink another thing that they collect from the leaves of trees, similar to oak, toasting it in some bowls over the fire. After they have toasted them, they fill the bowl with water, and so hold it over the fire. When it has boiled two times, they pour it into a pot and it is cooled with half of a gourd.* When there is a lot of foam, they drink it as hot as they can stand, and from when they take it from the bowl until they drink it, they shout, saying "Who wants to drink?" When the women hear these voices, they stop without daring to move - although they may be heavily loaded, they do not dare to do anything. In the event that

---

area of Baffin Bay in Kleberg and/or Kenedy Counties. This location is corroborated by the fact that the Anagados, a tribe that apparently lived near the prickly pear fields where the four castaways escaped, visited them on at least one occasion between 1528 and 1533.

[1] Also see 22:9. The *de los Higos* lived even further down the coast. Their habitation was certainly south of Corpus Christi Bay and probably south of Baffin Bay, in either Kenedy, Willacy, or Cameron County, or perhaps even in Mexico. Cabeza de Vaca's knowledge of the Fig-Indians is very limited; there may have even been one or more tribes in between them and the Camones.

[2] "Look here" is *mire acá* in Spanish. I believe the author included this sample of native speech because of its coincidental similarity to the same phrase in Spanish.

one of them moves, they dishonor[1] her and beat her, and with very great anger, they spill the water that they have to drink, and he who has drunk it heaves it out, which they do effortlessly[2] and without any pain. The reason they gave for this custom, they said, is that when they want to drink that water, if the women move from where they hear the shouts, that a bad thing enters the body through that water, and in a short time, makes them die. All the time that the water is cooking, the pot has to be covered, and in the event it is uncovered and some woman passes by, they spill it, and do not drink more of that water. It is yellow and is drunken three days without food, and each day, each of them drinks an *arroba*[3] and a half of it.[4]

---

[1] Lit. *deshonrar*, "dishonor." This word is sometimes used as a euphemism for "rape." Whether that is what the author meant to imply here, I cannot say.

[2] Lit. *mui ligeramente*, "very lightly (casually)."

[3] The *arroba* was a Spanish and Portuguese unit of measure of weight and volume. Estimates of its size vary, but it was certainly multiple gallons. 1½ *arrobas* may be around 5 gallons (19 liters).

[4] The author is describing the "black drink" ritual practiced by a number of native American tribes. The black drink was a tea made from the leaves of the yaupon holly. Elements of the ceremony described here that have been corroborated in other accounts include its method of preparation, the exclusion of females, drinking it in large quantities, spilling it, fasting, and vomiting. Yaupon holly has no emetic properties, so historians are unsure whether the natives mixed an emetic herb into the drink, or whether the vomiting was simply the result of drinking it in such large volumes, but the association between yaupon holly and vomiting is so strong that the plant was given the Latin name, *Ilex vomitoria*. Yaupon holly grows natively in the woodlands of the southeastern United States, so the black drink ritual is most associated with the natives of that region, as opposed to the dry plains of south Texas. Cabeza de Vaca may have witnessed the ritual while in Florida, in the Galveston

4 When the women are with their custom, they do not look for any food except for themselves, because no other person eats what they bring.

5 In the time that I was with them, I saw a diabolical thing, which is that I saw a man married to another. These were some effeminate, impotent men,[1] and they went about dressed as women and performing the duties of women.[2] They pull the bow and carry very great loads. We saw many of them among them - effeminate, as I said. They are burlier[3] than other men, and taller. They bear very great loads.

Bay area, or the Matagorda Bay area. In an account parallel to the one Cabeza de Vaca gives in 18:1 about the natives who held Figueroa and the Asturian cleric on what I interpret to be St. Joseph Island in Aransas County, Oviedo writes of the natives "going nearby to gather a certain leaf which they had the custom of picking. From it they make a special beverage, which they drink as hot as they are able to stand."

[1] Lit. *hombres amarionados impotentes*. *Amarionado* is an obsolete form of *amaricado*, "effeminate." The author's observation that these men were bigger than others indicates they were eunuchs who were castrated before puberty.

[2] Lit. *hacen oficio de Mugeres*, "doing [the] office of women."

[3] Lit. *mas membrudo*, "stronger, more robust, stouter."

Chapter 27
The Mesquite Eaters at the Large River

Of how we moved and went well-received

After we parted from those who we left crying, we went with others to their houses.[1] Those who stayed in them received us well and brought their children so that we could touch their hands, and they gave us much mesquite[2] flour. This mesquite is a fruit that when it is in the tree is very bitter, and is in the manner of carobs. They eat it with dirt, and with it, it is sweet and good to eat. The manner they prepare it is this: they make a pit in the soil, to whatever depth each one pleases, and after they cast the fruit in this pit, they grind it with a stick as thick as a leg and a fathom* and a half long[3] until it is very ground. In addition to the dirt that sticks to it in the pit, they take fistfuls and throw it into the pit and take another turn grinding. After that, they put it in a wooden bowl, like a basket, and add enough water to cover it, in such a way that there is water on the top. He who ground it tests it, and

---

[1] Here the author returns to the narrative at the point where he departed from it, at the end of Chapter 23. I believe it is mid-July 1535.

[2] Lit. "*Mezquiquez.*" The usual Spanish spelling of "mesquite" is *mesquite*. Mesquite trees are native to the Rio Grande region of Texas. They produce seed pods that are very similar in appearance to that of the carob or locust bean tree found in Mediterranean regions. The pods bloom in early summer and are harvested until they drop from the tree in early autumn. They contain seeds surrounded by husks, but it is the pods themselves that are eaten. The husks are woody, and the seeds, besides being indigestible, are hard enough to break a tooth. The mesquite's natural range was extended much further north by the cattle drives of the late 1800s, due to cows dropping seeds along the trails in their dung.

[3] About 8 to 9 feet (2½ to 2¾ m).

if it seems to him that it is not sweet, he asks for dirt and mixes it in. He does this until he finds it sweet. They sit all around, and each one sticks his hand in and takes out what he can. They throw the pips in that basket, add water as before, and squeeze the juice and water that they produce. They put the pips and hulls in a hide, and in this fashion take three or four times in grinding it. Those who are in this banquet, which is very large for them, are left with very large bellies from the dirt and water that they have drunk.

2 Of this, the Indians made a very great party for us, and held very grand dances and ceremonies* among them the whole time that we were there. When we slept at night, six men looked after each one of us at the door of the hut where we stayed, so that no one would dare to enter within until the sun came out.[1]

3 When we wanted to part from them, some women from others who live further on came there. Informed by them where their houses where, we departed from there, although they begged us much to remain with them that day, because the houses where we were going were far, there was no trail to them, those women came tired, and if we rested another day, they would go with us and guide us. With that, we said goodbye. A little ways out, the women who had come followed us with others from the same village. As there were no trails in that country, we became lost. We went four leagues, * and at the end of them, we came to drink at a spring where we found the women who had followed us. They told us about the trouble* they had gone through to catch up with us.

---

[1] This sentence ("When we slept …") is omitted in Buckingham Smith's translation. Smith used the first edition of *La Relación* for his source, but he noted the differences between it and the second edition in various places. He made no such note here.

4 We departed from there, taking them as guides. When it was already evening, we passed a river that had water up to our chests. It may have been as wide as the one of Seville, and ran very strong.[1]

5 At sunset we arrived at a hundred Indian houses.[2] Before we arrived, all of the people who were in them came out. They received us with shouts, such as if they were frightened, slapping their thighs hard with their palms.[3] They carried gourds* with holes in them and rocks inside. This is the thing of great celebra-

---

[1] Lit. mucho, "much." The river of Seville is the Guadalquivir, which has its mouth at San Lucar de Barrameda. It is the only great navigable river of Spain, and it made Seville the center of Spanish trade in the 16th century. The character of this river in Seville was altered substantially in the 20th century, but at the point where the alterations began, it is nearly 1,000 feet (330 m) wide. Some Cabeza de Vaca route interpreters have claimed that the great river the castaways crossed in this paragraph was one in Texas's interior, such as the Colorado or the Frio, but I agree with Davenport and Wells' assertion that the evidence it is the Rio Grande is "overwhelming." They place the castaways' crossing at the present-day town of Penitas, about 8 miles east of the Hidalgo-Starr County line. Alex D. Krieger, who has the castaways on a more westerly track all the way through south Texas, has them crossing the Rio Grande at Falcon Lake on the Starr-Zapata County line. Krieger's interpretation is probably the most widely-accepted right now, but I prefer Davenport and Wells', because they considered the characteristics of the terrain and flora when making out their route, while Krieger was more focused on travel times and distances, which I believe the castaways were more liable to remember incorrectly.

[2] Oviedo writes that the castaways walked "eight or nine leagues," which is about 30 miles (48 km), that day, which seems to have started at the mesquite-eaters' village, although Oviedo does not mention mesquite here.

[3] Lit. *dando en los muslos grandes palmadas*, "giving (or hitting) on their thighs great slaps."

tion - they do not take them out except to dance or to cure, and no one dares to hold them but them. They said that those gourds had power and came from Heaven,* because they are not of that land, and they do not know where they are found, except that the rivers bring them when the floods come.[1]

6 These [people] were so worried and anxious to be the first to come and touch us that they squeezed us so hard that they nearly killed us,[2] and they carried us to their houses without letting our feet touch the ground. So many were in charge of us and in such a manner that pressed against us that we stayed put in the houses that they made for us, and we did not consent in any way that night for them to make more celebrations with us. They passed that whole night among themselves in ceremonies and dances.

7 The morning of the next day, they brought all of the people of that village to us for us to touch them and bless* them, as we had done to the others with whom we had stayed. After doing this, they gave many arrows to the women of the other village who had come with theirs.

8 We departed from there the next day. All of the people of the village went with us. When we came to other Indians, we were received well, like those of the past, and they gave us of what they had and the deer that had died that day. We saw a new custom among these - it is that those were with us took the bow, arrows, shoes, and beads, if they had any, from those who came to be cured. After having taken them, they placed them before us, so

---

[1] Several months and several hundreds of miles later, the castaways would encounter, for the first time since leaving Florida, natives who grew gourds (see 30:10). Those natives lived on the Rio Grande in present-day west Texas.

[2] Oviedo writes that the castaways worried about their eyes being poked out by the fingers being frantically waved in front of their faces.

that we would cure them. Those who were cured were very content, saying they were well. [1]

9 And so, we parted from those and went to others, who received us very well, and brought us their sick. Upon making the sign of the Cross over them, they said they were well, and he who was not healed believed that we could heal him. With that which the others who we cured told them, they held so many festivities and dances that they did not let us sleep.

---

[1] Oviedo writes that this village was a league and a half, or about 5 miles (8 km) from the previous one. It had about 70 or 80 huts. The natives fed the castaways "prickly pears in great quantities" and 28 loaves of bread made from mesquite flour. He does not mention deer. Despite the discrepancies between the two accounts, it does appear to be the same village, for Oviedo describes the "new custom" in much the same language.

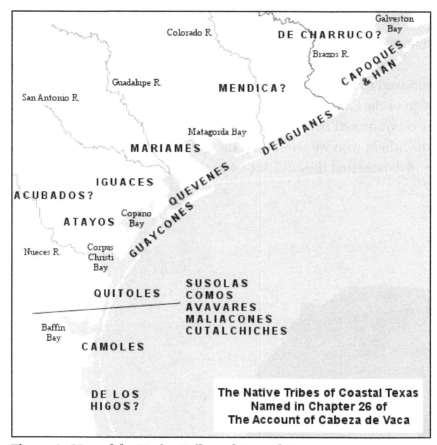

Figure 6 - Map of the Native Tribes of Coastal Texas

Chapter 28
The Custom of Robbery

Of another new custom

Parting from these, we went to many other houses, and from here another new custom began, and it is that, receiving us very well, that those who went with us began to behave so poorly that they took their property and sacked their houses, without leaving anything else. We were very grieved by this, to see the poor treatment of those who had received us so well, and we also worried that it would be a cause of some altercation or scandal among them, but it was not for us to remedy it, nor to dare to chastise those who had done this. We had to bear it, then, until we had more authority over them. Also, the same Indians who lost their possessions, understanding our sadness, consoled us, saying that they did not receive sorrow from it; that they were so pleased at having seen us that they gave their possessions for a good use, and that further on they would be paid by others who were very rich.

2 We had very great difficulty* on this whole trail because of the many people who followed us. We could not flee from them, although we tried, because the urgency they had to come and touch us was very great. The annoyance of them over this was so much that three hours passed that we could not finish with those who left us.

3 The next day, they brought all the people of the village to us. The majority of them have one clouded eye,[1] and others of

---

[1] Lit. *Tuertos de Nubes*, "one-eyed from clouds," i.e. they had cataracts. Oviedo describes it as "film on that eyeball." Also see the footnote to 17:4.

them are blind from the same cause,[1] by which we were appalled.[2] They are very well-built, with very good faces - whiter than all others who we had seen there.[3]

[4] We began to see mountains here, and it seemed that they came from the direction of the North Sea.* From the account that the Indians gave us of them, we believe that they are fifteen leagues* from the sea.[4] We parted from here with these Indians

---

[1] Lit. *de ellas mismas*, "of those same [clouds]."

[2] Lit. *eſpantados*, "frightened, terrified."

[3] Oviedo locates this village six leagues, or about 21 miles (33 km) from the one Cabeza de Vaca describes in 27:8, and says it was about the same size, i.e. 70 or 80 huts. He has the castaways at this village the day after the one in 27:8, omitting the village Cabeza de Vaca describes in 27:9.

[4] The fact that the castaways saw mountains for the first time a few days after crossing a great river near the coast should be conclusive in and of itself that the river was the Rio Grande, for the only mountain range along the Gulf coast is the Sierra Madre Oriental, and the first large river north of it is the Rio Grande. These mountains "come from" the North Sea, i.e. the Atlantic Ocean (see the glossary), in the sense that they approach the Gulf of Mexico at their south end. (Most people would probably have written that they "reach" or "extend to" the sea rather than "come from" it, but that is purely a matter of semantics.) Davenport and Wells have the castaways now at mountains they call the Pamoranes, which lie south of the Rio Conchos in the state of Tamaulipas, near the boundary with Nuevo Leon and about 100 miles (160 km) south of the Rio Grande. If these are the mountains mentioned, then Cabeza de Vaca's reckoning of the distance was quite accurate, for they are just a little over 50 miles (80 km), or 14½ leagues, from the Gulf. Krieger identifies them as the Cerralvo mountains in Nuevo Leon, northeast of Monterrey. These mountains are some 150 miles (240 km), or 43 leagues, from the coast. By attempting to make the distances work better in Texas, Krieger created a discrepancy in Mexico. This is one of several reasons why I consider Davenport and Wells' work to be superior.

up to these mountains that we describe.[1] They took us to where some of their relatives were, because they did not want to take us except where their relatives inhabited, and they did not want for their enemies to enjoy the benefit, as they saw it, of seeing us.

5 When we arrived, those who went with us sacked the others, and as they knew the custom, before we arrived, they hid some things. After we were received with much celebration and joy, they took out that which they had hidden and presented it to us; this was beads, red ochre, and some little pouches of silver. We, following the custom, gave it then to the Indians who came with us. When we had given it to them, they began their dances and celebrations and sent for others of another village that was near there, for them to come and see us. All of them came in the afternoon and brought us beads, bows, and other little things, which we also distributed.

6 The next day, when we wanted to depart, all of the people wanted to take us to other friends of theirs who were staying on a point of the mountains, and they said that there were many houses and people there, and that they would give us many things.[2] But since it was out of our way, we did not wish to go to them, and we took the plain by the mountains, which we believed were not far from the coast. All of the people of [the coast] are very bad, and we thought it best to cross the country, because the people who are further inland are better conditioned, and treated us better, and we believed for certain that we would find the country more populated and with superior sustenance. Finally, we did this because, by crossing the country, we would see many

---

[1] Oviedo writes that they went another five leagues, or 17 miles (27 km) to a river at the foot of the mountains, to a village of 40 or 50 huts.

[2] Oviedo writes, "These people tried hard to take these men toward the sea, since there they intended to compensate themselves for that which had been taken by the other Indians."

of its particulars, because if our Lord God was served to bring out some of us and take us to a land of Christians, he would be able to give news and an account of it.[1]

---

[1] The author is justifying a major change of plan and direction here. Reading between the lines, this means he felt it was necessary to defend this decision from critics and second-guessers. Ever since the Narváez Expedition was stuck at the Bay of Horses, the men had been trying to make it to Panuco, the northernmost Spanish settlement on the Gulf of Mexico. At the above moment, they had covered over two-thirds of the required distance since leaving the Island of Misfortune and were less than 200 miles (320 km) from their goal. They could have been back in Spanish civilization in less than a month if they had simply kept going forward. Instead, they decided to cross the country, adding 1,500 miles (2,400 km) and another nine months to their journey. The first defense he gives for this decision is that "all of the people of the coast are very bad." Except for the friendly natives of the Island of Malhado and their neighbors, the Deaguanes, all of the rest of the natives along the coast did in fact kill, enslave, and/or inflict physical abuse on the castaways. Even those of Malhado came close to slaughtering them at one point (14:2). The four castaways had also learned somewhat recently about the massacre of the men of Peñalosa and Téllez's boat at a location on the coast that was not far from where they had just come. In contrast, the natives of the interior treated them like "children of the sun." When they saw that following the plain below the mountains was going to push them toward the coast, they feared the worst and decided to change course. I find the other answers the author gives for wanting to change directions to be dubious. He said he believed the interior of the country would be better-populated and have more sustenance, but the natives, whose guidance he had always relied upon, told him the opposite. His claim that he wanted to explore just for exploration's sake after being lost for seven years sounds most insincere. I find it notable that in a story filled with gross miscalculations, bad decisions, and tragic outcomes, Cabeza de Vaca does not at any point confess, "I made a bad decision," or "I miscalculated." These moments in his narrative where he

7 As the Indians saw that we were determined not to go to where they had directed us, they told us that there were no people where we wanted to go, nor tunas* or anything else to eat, and they begged us to stay there that day, which we did. They then sent two Indians to look for people on the way that we wanted to go, and we departed the next day, bringing many of them with us. The women went loaded with water,[1] and our authority was so great among them that no one dared to drink without our permission.

8 Two leagues from there, we came across the Indians who had gone to look for people. They said that they found no one. The Indians were grieved at that and resumed entreating us to go by way of the mountains. We did not want to do it, and they, upon seeing our determination, said goodbye to us, although with much sadness. They turned back down the river to their houses, and we proceeded up the river. After a while, we came across two women carrying loads. When they saw us, they stopped, unloaded themselves, and brought us from what they were carrying, which was corn* meal. They told us that further on that river, we would find houses, many tunas, and more of that meal. And so we said goodbye to them, because they went to the others where we had left.

9 We walked until sunset and arrived at a village of about twenty houses, where they received us weeping and with great sadness, because they already knew that wherever we arrived, all were sacked and robbed by those who accompanied us. As they

---

stops to explain the reason behind a decision, then, ought to be read with a hearty dose of skepticism.

[1] Oviedo writes, "This was necessary as there was a lack of it, and moreover, it was very hot." Both Cabeza de Vaca and Oviedo describe the passage of only a few days from the village north of the large river where the castaways ate the dogs (23:1) to here, so it may still be July. If some days have been omitted, it may be early August.

saw that we were alone, they lost their fear and gave us tunas, and nothing else. We stayed there that night. At dawn, the Indians we had left the previous day set upon their houses, and as [those of the village] had taken themselves to be safe, and were unprepared, they took all they had, without there being any place to hide anything. They wept much at this. The robbers, to console them, told them that we were children of the sun, and that we had the power to heal the sick and to kill them, and other lies even bigger than these, which they know to make when they feel it better suits them. They told them that they brought us with great reverence, and they must take care not to anger us in any way, and that they were to give us all that they had, and to try to take us to where there were many people, and when they arrived, they would rob them and sack that which the others had, because so was the custom.

Chapter 29
In a Land of Plenty

Of how they rob each other

A fter making them well-informed and instructed what they
had to do, they returned, and left us with those [Indians]
which, keeping in mind that what the others had said to them,
began to treat us with the same fear and reverence as the others.
We journeyed with them for three days,[1] and they took us to
where there were many people. Before we arrived, they announced of our coming, and said about us all the others had indicated. They added much more, because all of these Indian-folk
are great story-tellers and very deceitful, especially when they
have something at stake.[2]

2 When we arrived close to the houses, all of the people
came out to receive us with much pleasure and celebration.
Among other things, two of their healers[3] gave us two gourds.*
From here, we began to carry gourds with us. We added this ceremony, which is very great to them, to our authority. Those who
had accompanied us sacked the houses, but as there were many
and they were few, they could not carry all they took, and they left
more than half of it lost.

---

[1] Lit. *fuimos con ellos tres jornadas*, "we went with them three days'
journey."

[2] Lit. *grandes amigos de Novelas, i mui mentirofos, maiormente donde
pretenden algun interefe*, "great friends of novels, and very lying, principally when they claim an interest."

[3] Lit. *Fiſicos*. See 14:6.

3 From here, following the skirt of the mountains, we turned inland for more than fifty leagues,*¹ and at the end of them, we found forty houses. Among other things that they gave us, Andrés Dorantes had a large, thick copper bell,² on which a face was represented. They showed that they regarded this highly, and they said that they had obtained it from others, their neighbors. Upon asking them where it had come from, they told us that they had brought it from the north, and that there was much there, and it was held in great esteem. We understood that wherever it had come from, there was a foundry and [metal] was cast in molds.

---

¹ 173 miles (277 km). After deciding to change their direction and go inland (28:7), the castaways walked four days (28:9, 29:1) to the village where they obtained the gourds. This means they have followed the base of the Sierra Madre Oriental for some 200 miles (320 km) or more and are probability in the vicinity of Monterrey, Nuevo Leon. I believe it must be around early September, more or less. Oviedo puts the distance as 80 leagues, or 277 miles (443 km), and states that they were traveling "directly north." To follow the base, or "skirt," of the Sierra Madre Oriental, they would have gone roughly north-northwest. They knew they needed to cross the mountains, but were obviously looking for the best place to do it.

² Lit. *Cascabel*. This is not like a church bell, but the type of bell one places around the neck of an animal, such as a cat or cow. It can also mean a rattlesnake's rattle or the round knob at the end of a cannon. Oviedo writes that the metal was "brass," a word that historically could refer to any kind of copper alloy, including bronze, and indicated a more advanced stage of civilization than copper did. Francisco Coronado wrote that during his expedition into the American Southwest and Midwest in 1541, the only metal he found was copper, with which the natives made *cascabeles*.

4 And with this, we departed the next day and crossed through a mountain seven leagues long.[1] Its stones were iron slags. In the evening, we arrived at many houses that were located on the bank of a very beautiful river. The lords of the houses came out to halfway on the road and received us with their children on their backs. They gave us many pouches of fool's gold[2] and ground antimony[3] (they smear this on their faces). They gave us many beads and many cowhide robes and loaded all who came with us with everything they had. They ate tunas* and pine nuts; there are small pines in that country, and their cones are like small eggs, but their nuts are better than those of Castile, because

---

[1] 24 miles (39 km). The castaways are crossing the Sierra Madre Oriental, probably at or somewhere north of Monclova. Oviedo writes, "the Christians moved off for the mountains toward the west, or where the sun sets." This means they began walking toward the next mountain range, the Sierra Madre Occidental.

[2] Lit. *Margagita*. Some translations take this to be a misspelling of *margarita*, or "margarite," a mineral of the mica group. It is actually, however, an alternate spelling of *margajita*, which translates as "marcasite." In Cabeza de Vaca's time, marcasite was iron pyrite, not the similar mineral now known as marcasite. Bandelier inexplicably translates it as "silver."

[3] Lit. *Alcohol molido*, "ground alcohol." The Spanish word *alcohol* usually means the same thing it means in English. This usage, however, obviously refers to a substance that can be ground, not a liquid. That substance is antimony. "Alcohol" comes from the Arabic *al-kohl*. "*Kohl*" is an Arabian cosmetic made from ground stibnite, or antimony sulfide, that was applied on the eyelids and around the eyes to darken them. In Spanish, an animal, such as a cow, that has dark fur around its eyes is an *alcoholado*. Some kohl was made from lead or galena (*alquifol* in Spanish). It is possible that the substance was actually powdered lead or powdered galena and the author misidentified it as antimony.

they have very thin husks.¹ When they are green, they grind them and make them into balls and eat them that way. If they are dry, they grind them with husks and eat them as meal. Those who received us there, upon having touched us, returned running to their houses, then turned around to us. They never ceased running, going and coming. They brought us many things for the trail in this manner.

5 They brought a man to me here, and they told me that a long time ago, he had been wounded by an arrow in the right side of his back, and the arrowhead was over his heart. He said that it gave him much pain, and that he was always sick because of it. I touched him and felt the arrowhead and saw that it had passed through the cartilage. With a knife I had, I opened his chest up to that place and saw that the point had passed through and was very bad to remove. I resumed cutting and inserted the tip of the knife, and with great effort,* I finally removed it. It was very long. Using my experience in medicine, I made two stiches with a deer bone, and making them, I was bled upon, and I stopped the blood with [hair] scraped from a hide.² When the point had been re-

---

¹ This is the papershell pinyon (*Pinus remota*), which is native to southwest Texas and northeast Mexico. This pinyon variety was not recognized as a distinct species until 1979. It was confirmed to grow in the vicinity of Monclova in 1996. Prior to this discovery, many route interpreters mistakenly believed the castaways were describing the ordinary pinyon (*Pinus edulis*), which is native to New Mexico and far west Texas, but not Mexico, and has a thicker husk than the aptly-named papershell variety. According to several web sites, pine cones are harvested in late August and early September and then the cones are dried for three weeks before the nuts are ready to eat. That schedule matches with my estimate that the castaways were at this location in the second half of September.

² Lit. *raspa de vn Cuero*, "raspa of a hide." *Raspa* has a multitude of meanings, including the spine of a fish, the hairy fibers attached to

moved, they asked me for it, and I gave it, and the whole village came to see it, and sent it further inland so that those who were there could see it. They had many dances and celebrations over this, as they usually do.

6 The next day, I cut the Indian's two stiches, and he was well. It did not seem that the wound that was made there was less than a line of the palm of the hand, and he said that he felt no pain and had no problems. This cure gave us such standing among them throughout the whole land, as much as they were able to and knew how to value and praise.

7 We showed them that bell that we had brought. They told us that in that place where it had come from, many sheets of that [metal] were buried, that it was a thing that they esteemed greatly, and there were fixed[1] houses there. We believe that this is [on] the South Sea,* for we have always heard that sea is more rich than that of the north.[2]

---

grains like wheat and corn, a bunch of grapes, a fruit rind, and a piece of dust that sticks to the end of an ink pen. It is a form of the verb *raspar*, "to scrape." Smith translates it as "hair from a skin," and I believe that is right – the author took a wad of hair that had been scraped off of a hide and applied it like we would use a cotton ball. Bandelier cuts this sentence short, ending it with "I made two stiches with a deer bone."

[1] Lit. *de afiento*, "seated."

[2] In the parts of North America that had been explored prior to the Narváez Expedition leaving Cuba – Panama, Honduras, southern Mexico, etc. – the width of the continent, the distance from the Atlantic to the Pacific Oceans, was never more than 300 miles (480 km). The castaways probably calculated that they had gone about that far inland and must be approaching the "South Sea." Even at the time Cabeza de Vaca wrote his first edition of *La Relación* in 1540, the Pacific Ocean coastline of the U.S. and Mexico had not been mapped, and explorers and cartographers assumed the continent was not nearly as wide as it actually is. The Span-

8 At this, we departed and walked among so many kinds of people and of so many different tongues that there is not enough memory to be able to relate. They always sacked each other, and in that, those who lost as well as those who gained were left very content. We carried so much company that we could in no way derive any worth from them. Through those valleys where we went, each one of them carried a club as large as three palms, and they all went in a wing, and when a hare (which there are plenty of there[1]) came out, they closed in on it, and so many clubs fell down over it that it was a thing to marvel. In this manner, they made it move from one to the other, that to me, seeing it was the most beautiful hunt that can be imagined, because many times they [the hares] came up to their hands. When we stopped at night, they had given us so many that each one of us carried eight or ten loads of them.

9 Those who carried bows did not seem to be in front of us; rather, they went separately into the mountains to look for deer. When they came at night, they brought five or six deer for each one of us, and parrots, quail, and other game. Finally, that people put everything they found and killed before us, without daring to touch anything unless we blessed* it first, although they would die of hunger. That was their custom after walking with us.

10 The women brought many mats, with which they made houses for us - a separate one for each, with all of his company.[2]

---

iards believed the Pacific coast was "richer" than the Atlantic coast mostly because the Pacific coast was the "other side of the pasture," where the grass is always greener.

[1] Lit. *que por alli havia hartas*, "that for there was stuffed." *Harta* is a form of the verb *hartar*, which means to be fed up with something (or tired of it, oversatisfied, stuffed, etc.).

[2] Lit. *Gente conoſcida*, "known people." This phrase could also be translated as "acquaintances." It stands to reason that many of the people fol-

When this was done, we ordered that they roast those deer, hares, and all that they had taken. They also did this very quickly in some ovens that they had made for this. We took a little of all of it, and we gave the rest to the principal of the people who came with us,[1] ordering that he distribute it among all. Each one came to us with his own part[2] for us to blow on it and make the sign of

---

lowing the children of the sun would have a favorite, or that if the four castaways walked with some distance separating them, each one would have a subset of the natives in his wake, and they would claim him as "theirs," or vice-versa. Also see 22:2, "each one of them took his own [of us] by the hand and took us to their houses." Several commentators have speculated that by this time, the castaways had harems, and this is why, rather than putting all of four men in one hut, separate huts were built for each castaway and his "acquaintances," with watchmen posted outside all night (see 27:2). Even though this is speculation, there is a foundation to it. After the castaways reached Mexico, Estevanico was sent back out on another expedition. Pedro de Castañeda writes that the natives who followed Estevanico and carried his things gave him a "large quantity of turquoises" and "some beautiful women," and that he was killed by a different group of natives in another country who were offended by his requests for more turquoises and women. There are other reports given of the reason for Estevanico's killing, however, and Cabeza de Vaca and his companions did not and would not admit to promiscuity in their accounts of their journey, so we should also be willing to entertain the possibility that these "acquaintances" were platonic admirers. Also note that, as the epilogue will relate, when Cabeza de Vaca became a provincial governor, he forbade his colonists from taking native girls from their homes, even when their fathers offered them.

[1] Cabeza de Vaca does not mention chiefs or lords among the natives of northern Mexico. These "principals" may have been people who were responsible for dealing with the children of the sun on behalf of the tribe, rather than people with decision-making authority.

[2] Lit. *la parte que le cabía*, "the part that fit him."

the Cross over it; they did not dare to eat of it by any other manner. Many times, we brought three or four thousand persons with us, and it was a great labor* for us that for each one, we had to blow on and bless that which he had to eat and drink. They asked our permission for many other things that they wanted to do, so one can see how much of a nuisance it was for us to receive them. The women brought us tunas,[1] spiders, worms, and whatever they could, because although they would die of hunger, they ate nothing without giving it to us.

    11 Going with these, we crossed a great river, which came from the north.[2] Crossing some thirty leagues of plains, we found many people who came far from there to receive us, and came out to the trail of where we had to go. They received us in the manner of those of earlier.

---

[1] This is the last mention of tunas in the narrative. It is autumn.

[2] The only river between Monclova and the Rio Grande is the Rio Sabinas. Apparently, the castaways have been traveling mostly north-northwest or even straight north. They are making little progress in crossing over the Sierra Madre Oriental, but are instead following the contours of the ridges.

Chapter 30
The People of the Cows

Of how the custom of receiving us changed

From here, there was another manner of receiving us, with regard to the plunder, because those who came out to the trails to bring something to those who came with us were not robbed, but after we entered their houses, those same ones offered us that which they had, and the houses with them. We gave them to the principals to divide among them, and those who were left dispossessed always followed us to where many people thrived in order to recoup their loss. They told them to be careful and not to hide anything that they had, because it could not be done without us knowing, and we would make it so that everyone would die, because the sun would tell us so. They put such fear in them that the first few days that we stayed with them, they were always trembling, and did not dare to speak or lift their eyes toward the sky.*

2 These guided us for more than fifty leagues* of desert[1] and very rugged mountains. As it was so dry, there was no game in them, and we endured great hunger because of this. Finally, [they guided us] to a very large river; the water came up to our chests. From there, many of the people who we brought suffered from the great hunger and hardship* that had taken place in those mountains, which were extremely acrid[2] and troublesome.

---

[1] Lit. *defpoblado*, "deserted."

[2] Lit. *agras*. This is an outdated spelling of *agrias*, which means "acrid" or "sour." As it is commonly used in describing the tart flavor of citrus fruits, it could also reasonably be translated as "acidic." More generally, it means a bitter impression left by anything, including harsh words. Smith interprets it as "sterile"; Bandelier as "barren." While it is possible these are what the author meant, I think it is also possible that he meant it in the more general sense that he found the country distasteful. As

3 These same ones took us to some plains at the end of the mountains, where [others] came from very far away to receive us. They received us like those earlier, and gave so much of their estates to those who came with us that they left half of it for being unable to carry it. We said to the Indians that had given it to take it back and carry it so that it would not be lost there. They responded that in no way would they do that, because it was not their custom to take something back once they had offered it. So, not valuing it as anything, they left it all to be lost.

4 We told these that we wanted to go toward the sunset. They responded to us that the people over there were very distant. We ordered them to send there and make it known that we were going there. They excused themselves of this as best as they could, because those were their enemies, and they did not want us to go to them. But, they did not dare to do differently, and so they sent two women - one of their own, and one that they had taken captive. They sent these because the women are able to negotiate even though there is war.[1] We followed them, and we stopped in a place where it had been agreed that we would wait. We waited five days, and the Indians said that they must not have found people. We told them to take us northward; they responded in the same manner, saying that there were no people there, except very far away, and that there was nothing to eat and no water to be found. Through all of this, we insisted and told them that we wanted to go there, and they still excused themselves as best as they could.

5 We became angry at this, and I went out one night to sleep in the field, apart from them, but then they came to where I was, and they stayed awake all night, very fearful, speaking to me

---

always, when the author's meaning is vague, I think it is better to convey that vagueness than to feed a specific interpretation to the reader.

[1] See also 24:5 – "although they are sometimes the cause of the war."

and telling me how scared they were, begging us not to be angry any longer, and even though they knew they would die on the trail, they would take us to where we wanted to go. We still feigned being angry so that their fear would not leave them,[1] and then a strange thing happened, which was that many of them became sick that very day, and the following day, eight men died. Through all the land where this became known, they had such fear of us that it seemed that they were worried they would die from looking at us. They begged us not to be angry with them and that we would not wish death upon more of them, and they knew for certain that we killed them simply by willing it. In truth, the sorrow we received from this could not have been greater, because beyond seeing those who died, we feared that all would die or that they would leave us by ourselves out of fear, and that all of the other people from there forward, seeing what had happened to them, would do the same. We prayed to our Lord God for His aid, and so all those who had been sick began to become well.

6 We saw something that was of great wonder: the parents, siblings, and wives of those who died had great pain on seeing them in that [dying] state,[2] and after they died, they showed no feeling, neither did we see them cry, talk to each other, or make any other indication, neither did they dare to go over to them until we ordered them to take them and bury them.

---

[1] Instead of the preceding sentences, Oviedo writes, "Then Andrés Dorantes said to an Indian of his that he should tell the others that they were probably going to die, because of this which they did not want to do."

[2] Lit. *en aquel eſtado*, "in that state." Undoubtedly, the author meant the state of being *near* death.

7 In more than fifteen days that we stayed with them,[1] we never saw them speak to each other,[2] nor did we see them laugh or any infants cry, except, because one cried, they took it very far from there and cut it with some sharp mouse teeth from its shoulders almost to its legs. I, seeing this cruelty and angry about it, asked them why they did this. They responded that it was to punish it because it had cried before me. All of these fears that they had of us were placed upon all of the new ones who came to meet us, with the result that they gave us all that they had, because they knew that we did not take anything and we had to give all of it to them.[3]

8 This was the most submissive people that we found in this land, and in the best condition; they were generally very well-built.

9 With the afflicted recovering, and we had already been there three days, the women who we had sent out returned, saying that they had found very few people, and that everyone had gone after the cows,[4] as it was the season for them.[5] We ordered those who had been sick to stay there, and those who had been well would go with us.[6] After a two-day journey, those same two

---

[1] I believe it has to be the second half of October 1535 now. Also see my footnote in Paragraph 9.

[2] Oviedo adds, "they never saw one of these natives laugh, cry, or show any other emotional change. This was even though the parents of some died; others lost their wives and children; and still others lost their husbands."

[3] See the footnotes to Paragraph 14.

[4] All "cows" referred to in this chapter were probably bison; see 18:13.

[5] Oviedo states that the season for tunas was over, meaning it must be October or later.

[6] Oviedo writes, "and that twenty or thirty of those natives who were healthy should continue with them."

women would go with two of us to gather people and bring them to the trail for them to meet us.

10 With this, all those who were the healthiest split off with us the next morning, and after a three-day journey we stopped. The following day, Alonso del Castillo[1] left with Estevanico the Negro,* taking the two women as guides. The one of those who was a captive took them to a river that ran through some mountains where there was a town in which her father lived. These were the first houses we saw that had the appearance and form of [houses].[2] Castillo and Estevanico arrived here. After having spoken with the Indians, at the end of three days Castillo came to where he had left us, and he brought five or six of those Indians. He told of how he had found houses that were fixed, with people, and that this people ate beans and gourds,* and that he had seen corn.* This cheered us up more than anything in the world,[3] and we gave infinite thanks for it to our Lord. He said that the Negro would come with all the people of the houses to wait on the road nearby, and for this reason, we departed.

11 When we had walked a league and a half, we ran into the Negro and the people who had come out to receive us, and they gave us beans, many gourds to eat and for carrying water, cowhide robes, and other things. Since these people and those who had come with us were enemies, and did not understand

---

[1] Oviedo adds that Castillo "was the most fit."

[2] Lit. *de ello*, "of it."

[3] The castaways had not seen any of these since leaving Florida, except for the gourds that some natives said came from Heaven and some corn meal that was obtained through trade. Their presence as crops indicated that these natives, or others in the area, were advanced enough to understand and practice agriculture. The castaways were overjoyed to see this tincture of civilization, along with the houses that looked like houses, after seven years of living in the Stone Age.

each other, we took leave of the first ones,[1] giving them all that that had been given to us.

12 We went with these, and six leagues from there, when night was already coming, we came to their houses, where they made many celebrations with us. We stayed here one day, and we left the following one.

13 We took some of them with us to other fixed houses, where they ate the same as those. From here on, we found a new custom: those who knew of our coming did not go out and receive us on the trails, like the others had done, but we found them in their houses, and they had made others for us. They were all seated, and all had their faces turned to the wall, their heads lowered, and their hair put over their eyes. Their belongings were put in a pile in the middle of the house. From here on, they began to give us many leather robes; they had nothing that they did not give us.

14 These people had the best bodies that we saw, were the most lively and skilled, and best understood us and responded to what we asked them. We called them "of the cows," because the majority of them that die are close to there, and because they go up that river more than fifty leagues to kill many of them.[2] This

---

[1] Lit. *los primeros*, "the first ones." The author meant this as those they met first - those who accompanied them to that spot. Both Smith and Bandelier invert this to "the latter," referring to their sequence in the author's discussion.

[2] 50 leagues is 173 miles (277 km). In 1541, the Coronado Expedition encountered natives who were hunting bison in the High Plains region of Texas, between Amarillo and Lubbock, some 350 miles from where the Four Ragged Castaways are now. The chroniclers of the expedition wrote that these natives remembered seeing "four others like us many days before," and offered the Spaniards "a pile of tanned skins and other things." These natives were dismayed when Coronado allowed his men to take all of the skins, "because they thought that the strangers were not

people go about completely naked, in the manner of those who we first found. The women go about covered with some deer hides - and a few men, especially those who are old, who do not serve in war.[1] It is a very populated country.[2]

15 We asked them why they did not plant corn. They responded that it was so as not to lose what they planted, because

---

going to take anything, but would bless them as Cabeza de Vaca and Dorantes had done."

[1] Lit. *que no firven para la Guerra,* "that do not serve for the war." This could also be translated as "that are not useful for war."

[2] Oviedo states that there were "four groups of settlements" at this location. In 1581, about 45 years later, a small expedition found some villages at the confluence of the Rio Conchos and the Rio Grande, at what is now present-day Presidio, Texas and Ojinaga, Chihuaua. The Spaniards called the place *La Junta* ("the junction"). The natives at La Junta grew squash and beans and were described as "handsome" and "very friendly." A chronicler wrote, "We asked them if any men like us had passed through there. By the descriptions they gave, we realized clearly that the leader must have been Alvar Núñez Cabeza de Vaca, because, according to his narrative, he had come by way of these people." The following year, Spanish explorer Antonio de Espejo visited La Junta. He found five villages of natives who lived in "permanent" pueblos, had "flat roofed" houses, and raised corn, beans, and gourds. They had "buffalo hides, very well tanned," and settled the Rio Grande above the Conchos "for a distance of twelve days' journey." Espejo wrote that the natives "told us, and gave us to understand through interpreters, that three Christians and a Negro had passed through their land." There is near-universal agreement among historians that La Junta was the village of the "cow people." This establishes a key waypoint for interpreting the route taken by the Four Ragged Castaways. Based on information found in preceding and succeeding chapters about their journey, I believe the castaways visited La Junta in late October or early November 1535.

there had been a lack of water[1] for two successive years, and the weather had been so dry, that all of the corn had been lost to the moles, and they did not dare to go back to planting unless it rained much first. They implored us to speak to Heaven that it would rain, and so we prayed, and we promised them that we would do so. We also wanted to know from where they had brought their corn. They told us that it was from where the sun sets, that it existed in that whole country, moreover that the shortest way to it was on that trail.

16 We asked them, "Where would it be good for us to go?"[2] and that they inform us of the trail, because they did not want to go there. They told us that the way to go was up that river, which went to the north, and that in seventeen days of travel we would not find anything to eat except for a fruit that they called *chacán*, which they crush between some stones, and even after taking this measure it cannot be eaten, being rough and dry.[3] That was the truth, because they showed it to us there, and we could not eat it. They also told us that while we went up the river, we would always be among people who were their enemies and spoke their

---

[1] Lit. *les havian faltado las Aguas*, or "the waters had been lacking to them." Bandelier and many others incorrectly interpret this to say it had not rained for two years, but the author only said that the "waters," or rain, had been insufficient, not that there had not been any.

[2] Lit. *por donde iriamos bien?*, or "where should we go well?"

[3] Historians and translators have not identified this terrible, inedible fruit. It has nothing in common with the phonetically similar *achacha* that is native to Bolivia. Rolena Adorno and Patrick Charles Pautz cleverly note in their translation that Cabeza de Vaca may have written *que la machacan*, "which they pound," but this got changed to *que llama Chacán*, "which they call chacán," due to a printer's error. Oviedo calls this fruit *massarones*, another name which does not help identify it at all. He writes that it was "very bad," "totally stringy," and "not even fit for animals."

same language. They would not have anything to eat to give us, but they would receive us very willingly, and they would give us many cotton robes and hides and other things of that which they had. Still, it seemed to them that we should in no way take that road.[1]

17 In doubt about what we ought to do, and which road would most be to our purpose and advantage, we remained with them for two days. They gave us beans and gourds to eat. Their manner of cooking them is so new, that as such, I wanted to put it here, so that one can see and understand how different and strange are the ingenuity and workings of humans. They do not understand pots,[2] and to cook what they want to eat, they fill a

---

[1] I do not believe Cabeza de Vaca's explanation of their options is clear, or even correct, but if one locates present-day Presidio (La Junta, the village of the cow people) on a Texas map and reads Oviedo's account, the picture becomes rather clear. The road that followed the Rio Grande upriver was the road "of the cows." Approximately 200 miles (320 km) along the road is a mountain pass that gives present-day El Paso ("the pass") its name. When the castaways reached the pass, they would have to choose between crossing the river and going west, or staying on the road of the cows (i.e. following the Rio Grande) to the north. There was corn in both directions. Oviedo states that the castaways followed the river upstream for 15 days, then crossed over to the west, for if they had gone north, there would have been nothing to eat for 30 to 40 days. A few years later, the Coronado Expedition discovered a complex of native villages called Tiguex on the Rio Grande in the vicinity of Albuquerque, New Mexico. This was apparently where the natives of La Junta said they had obtained their corn and where the castaways would finally be able to find food.

[2] Lit. *ellos no alcançan Ollas*, "they do not reach pots." *Alcanzar* can mean to reach something by extending the arm and hand to grab it, to pursue and catch up to it, or to mentally comprehend it. In this way, it is similar to "grasp" in English, which can indicate having either a literal or figurative hold on something. Also see our note on *no alcanzan* in 32:1.

medium-sized gourd full of water. They throw many stones that heat up easily into the fire, and they become heated,[1] and when they see that they are burning, they take them with some wooden tongs, and they throw them in the water that is in the gourd, until it boils with the heat that the stones carry. When they see that the water boils, they pour it in that which they are making to eat.[2] During all of this time, they take out some stones and throw in other burning ones, so that the water boils to cook that which they want, and this is how they cook.

The author may not have *seen* pots at La Junta and assumed the natives did not know how to make them, but archeology shows that the natives of La Junta did have pottery. It would be expected that people who lived in "real houses," used wooden tongs, understood agriculture, and earned praise from the author for their "ingenuity" would understand pottery.

[1] Lit. *toman el fuego*, "take the fire."

[2] Oviedo describes the dish being made here as a "thick soup" or porridge.

Chapter 31
Gifts of Turquoise

Of how we followed the road of the corn

After two days of staying with them, we determined to go in search of corn,* and we did not want to follow the road of the cows, because it went to the north, and this to us was a very great detour, because we always held it for certain that going toward the sunset would be how to find what we wanted. And so, we went on our way, and crossed all the land as far as the South Sea.* The fear of the great hunger that would come to pass - which did, in fact, befall us - was not enough to hinder us for the whole seventeen-day journey that [the Indians] had told us of. For all of these [days] up the river, they gave us many cowhides. We did not eat of that fruit, but our sustenance every day was as much as a handful of deer fat, which, out of necessity, we always tried to keep. And so we passed the whole seventeen-day journey. At the end of it, we crossed the river and traveled another seventeen [days].

2 At sunset, on some plains, and among some very large mountains that form them, we found a people that eat nothing but powdered straw for a third of the year. Since that was the season when we traveled there, we also had to eat it until, at the end of this journey, we found some fixed houses, where there was much corn gathered, and they gave us a great quantity of it, and of their flour, and of gourds, beans, and cotton robes. We loaded those who had brought us there with all of it, and with this, they returned the most contented [people] in the world. We gave many thanks to our Lord God for having brought us there, where we had found so much sustenance.

3 Among these houses, there were some of them that were of earth, and the others were of cane matting. From here, we traveled more than a hundred leagues* of land, and we always found

fixed houses, much sustenance from corn and beans, and they gave us many deer[1] and many cotton blankets - better than those of New Spain. They also gave us many beads of some coral that is in the South Sea, many very good turquoises that they get from the north, and finally, they gave here all that they had.

4 They gave to me[2] five emeralds[3] made into arrowheads; with these they made their ceremonies* and dances. They appeared to me to be very good. I asked them where they had come from. They said that they brought them from some very tall mountains that were to the north, and traded for them with parrot plumes and feathers. They said that there were villages with many people and very large houses.

5 Among these people, we saw the most decently-treated women in any part of the Indies that we have seen. They wear cotton shirts that reach down to the knees, and over them, half-sleeves of a few strips of deerskin, without hair, that touch the ground. They wash them with using some roots as soap, which clean them well, and so they keep them very well cared for. [The shirts] are open in front and closed with straps.[4] They walk shod with shoes.

---

[1] I suspect this is an error and that the text should have read "deer hides" instead of "deer."

[2] Bandelier, possibly conflating this gift with the one mentioned in 32:1, writes, "to Dorantes."

[3] As the author notes, they were ceremonial items, not meant to be used as projectiles. We should consider it possible that the author misidentified some copper or turquoise-bearing stones as emeralds.

[4] Oviedo adds that the women's shirts "cover their breasts completely" and that the castaways reasoned that the women in this place must have "learned" modesty from whoever was in the direction they were going. This, plus the fact that they were seeing more fixed houses, corn, and cotton blankets, made them think they were near a more advanced form of civilization.

6 All of these people came to us so that we would touch them and bless* them. They were so importune in this that we endured it with great difficulty,* because all, suffering and healthy, wanted to be blessed. It occurred many times that the women who went with us would give birth, and then, being born, bring the baby to us for us to touch and bless it. They always accompanied us until leaving us in the care of others, and among all of these people, it was held for very certain that we came from Heaven.*[1]

7 While we walked with these, we would travel the whole day without eating until night, and we would eat so little that they were amazed. They never sensed that we were tired and, in truth, we were so inured to hardship that we did not sense it either.

8 We had much authority and respect with them, and to protect this, we spoke to them few times. The Negro* always spoke to them; he inquired about the road that we wished to go on, the villages that were there, and the things that we wanted to know. We came across a great number and variety of languages; our Lord God favored us with all of them, because they always understood us and we understood them, with us asking them and them responding by signs, as if they understood our tongue and we theirs. Although we knew six languages, we could not take advantage of them everywhere, because we found more than a thousand differences.[2]

---

[1] Here Bandelier inserts an additional sentence: "What they do not understand or is new to them they are wont to say it comes from above." I do not know where this sentence comes from, for it does not exist in either *La Relación* or Oviedo's account, but it matches Oviedo's tone perfectly. Also see 32:3: "They told us that it had come from the sky," and 27:5.

[2] The ability to speak and be understood in unknown languages is, like the healing of the sick, a gift given to the disciples of Christ in the New Testament. The author's implication that he and his companions were

9 In all of these lands, those who were at war with others would become friends upon seeing us, so as to receive us and bring us everything that they had. In this way, we left the whole country at peace.

10 We told them, by signs so that they understood us, that there was a man in Heaven who we called God, the one who had created Heaven and Earth, that we worshipped Him and held Him to be our Lord, that we did as He commanded us, that all good things came from His hand, and that it would be very good for them if they did likewise. We saw such a great readiness in them, that if there had been a language with which they could have understood us perfectly, we would have left all of them Christians.

11 This we gave them to understand as best as we could. From then on, when the sun came out, they would lift their hands together to the sky with a great uproar, then pass them all over their bodies. They did the same when it set. They are a well-conditioned people, ready to follow anything that is well-prepared.

serving as the Lord's disciples to evangelize the natives of America is unmistakable. On the other hand, he admits to a certain amount of manipulation, which Christ never sanctioned, in having Estevanico be the main one to ask questions about the land, so as to hide the Spaniards' ignorance of such matters.

Chapter 32
News of Other Christians

Of how they gave us deer hearts

In the village where they gave us the emeralds, they gave to Dorantes more than six hundred deer hearts, opened, of which they always had a great abundance for their sustenance, and because of this, we named it the Village of the Hearts.[1] Through it is the entrance to many provinces on the South Sea,*[2] and if anyone going to look for it does not enter through there, they will be lost, because the coast does not have corn.* They eat ground weeds, straw, and fish[3] that they catch on rafts, because they do not un-

---

[1] The Coronado Expedition established a camp called St. Jerome of the Hearts at a place Coronado's men believed to be the Village of the Hearts mentioned by Cabeza de Vaca. Coronado route interpreters place this camp in the Sonora River valley, near present-day Ures, which is about 40 miles (64 km) northeast of Hermosillo. Here, however, I concur with Krieger that Ures is a poor fit with the information given, and a location approximately 40 miles south of it works better. After crossing the Rio Grande at El Paso, the castaways apparently traveled west to west-southwest through northern Chihuahua, southern New Mexico, and southern Arizona, then turned south, entering the Sonora Valley and staying in it until they came out of the Sierra Madre Occidental. Friar Bartolomé de las Casas, a contemporary of Cabeza de Vaca's, wrote, "The hearts, I incline to think, are used by the people of these provinces as offerings rather than for food." That might better explain why the natives had such a large number of them on hand.

[2] In reality, the travelers were approaching the Gulf of California, not the ocean proper.

[3] Lit. *Polvo de Bledo, i de Paja, i de Pefcado*, "dust of *bledo*, of straw, and of fish." *Bledo* is the Spanish name of the Latin *Blitum*, a genus of flowering plants in the amaranth family. The author's wording states that the straw and fish were also ground, or "dust."

derstand canoes.¹ The women cover their privates with grass and straw. They are a very lowly and timid² people.

2 We believe that near the coast, in the direction of those villages that we came to, there are more than a thousand leagues*³ of inhabited land, and that they have plenty of food, because they plant beans and corn three times a year. There are three kinds of deer, one of which is the size of the steers of Castile. There are fixed houses, which are called *buhíos*.⁴ They have a plant - it is from some trees the size of apple [trees] - and it is only necessary to take the fruit and wipe the arrow with it, and if it does not have fruit, they break a branch and do the same with its milk. There are many of these trees that are so poisonous that if they pound its leaves and wash them in some nearby water, all of the deer and any other animals that drink of it burst afterward.⁵

----

¹ Lit. *no alcançan Canoas*, "they do not reach canoes." See the note in 30:17 regarding *no alcanzan*.

² Lit. *apocada, i triſte*. Both adjectives can be translated various ways, including "mean-spirited" for *apocada* and "sad (gloomy, melancholy)" for *triſte* (*triste*). I chose translations that seem to fit best in context.

3 While a league in *La Relación* is usually a unit of distance, it was also used to measure area. A league of area was equal to about 6.9 square miles (17.9 km²).

4 Although this is written to sound as if Cabeza de Vaca is introducing a new term to his readers, this is the fourth appearance in *La Relación* of the word *buhíos*. It is translated in the other instances as "huts."

5 This was the so-called *yerba de flecha*, or arrow poison plant, known as *Sebastiana bilocularis* in Latin. It is native to Arizona, Sonora, and Baja California. Pedro de Castañeda, chronicler of the Coronado Expedition, writes that some natives in the vicinity of the encampment they named Hearts attacked the Spaniards and "killed a soldier with a poisoned arrow, which had made only a very little wound in one hand." In another conflict, 17 soldiers died from poisoned arrows. "They would

3 We stayed in this village three days. One day's journey from there was another, in which such rains overtook us that we could not cross one river, because it rose so much. We stayed there five days.[1] In this time, Castillo saw, around the neck of an Indian, a little buckle from a sword belt, with a shoeing nail sewn in it. He took it, and we asked him what it was. They told us that it had come from the sky.* We asked him further about who had brought it from there. They answered that some men who had beards like us had come from the sky and arrived at that river, and that they brought horses, lances, and swords and had lanced two of them. We asked them, as slyly as we could, what had happened to those men. They responded that they had gone to the sea and put their lances below the water, and that they also had been put below, and that later they saw them on the waves going toward the sunset.[2]

4 We gave many thanks to our Lord God for that which we heard, because we had been doubtful of hearing news of Christians. On the other hand, we found ourselves greatly confused and sad, believing that people were some who had come from the sea

---

die in agony from only a small wound," Castañeda writes, "the bodies breaking out with an insupportable pestilential stink."

[1] Oviedo writes that the castaways were at this location for 15 days, and it "was around Christmas." As I will explain in a footnote to Paragraph 9, I take this river to be the Matape.

[2] In 1530, Nuño Beltrán de Guzmán began his conquest of the New Galicia – a province in present-day Mexico that was independent of New Spain and consisted approximately of the modern states of Jalisco, Nayarit, Guadalajara, and Sinaloa. Guzmán was notorious for his wholesale enslavement of the natives for export to other provinces. The castaways are probably some 350 miles (560 km) from Culiacan, the northernmost town in New Galicia, at this point in the narrative, but the men these natives saw were undoubtedly from one of Guzmán's slaving parties.

only for discovery. In the end, as we had such a certain report of them, we hastened on our way. We always heard more news of Christians, and we told [the Indians] that we came to look for them, in order to tell them not to kill them or take them as slaves, or to take their lands or do any other bad thing to them. They were put greatly at ease by this.

5 We walked over a lot of land, and found all of it deserted, because its inhabitants had run away to the mountains, without daring to take their houses or to labor, for fear of the Christians. It was something that made us very sad - seeing such fertile land, very pretty and full of waters and rivers, and to see the places deserted and burned, and the people so thin and sick, displaced and in hiding. Since they did not plant, they were so hungry that they sustained themselves on tree bark and roots. We nearly reached this level of hunger all along this road, because they were ill-able to provide for us, being so unfortunate that it seemed as if they wanted to die. They brought us blankets that they had hidden from the Christians and gave them to us, and even related to us how the Christians had entered the land other times, and had destroyed and burned the villages, and taken half of the men and all of the women and children, and that those who could escape their hands ran fleeing.

6 Since we saw them so frightened, not daring to stay anywhere and neither wanting nor able to plant or work the land, almost having determined to let themselves die, believing that to be better than to stay there and be treated with such cruelty, and they showed the greatest pleasure with us, although we feared that those who were on the frontier with the Christians and fought with them would mistreat us as payback for what the

Christians had done against them.[1] But, as our Lord God was served in taking us to them, they began to respect and defer to us, as the former ones - even a little more so - at which we were left not a little amazed. By this it is clearly seen that in order for these people to be attracted to become Christians and obedient to the Imperial Majesty, they should all be brought with good treatment, and that this is a very certain way, not otherwise.[2]

7 These took us to a village that is in the cleft of a mountain, which one must climb by a very rough [trail]. There we found many people who had gathered together out of fear of the Christians. They received us very well and gave us whatever they had, and they gave us more than two thousand loads of corn, which we gave to those miserable and hungry ones who had brought us there.[3]

---

[1] This ungrammatical sentence would make more sense to me if the word "although" were moved, to make it read "... and although they showed the greatest pleasure with us, we feared ..."

[2] As mentioned in the prologue, every conquistador and governor's royal commission included a command to treat the natives well and to attempt to teach them Christianity. Slavery was allowed, but only if the natives were hostile and could not be controlled any other way. Every Spanish administrator in the New World violated the crown's edicts concerning slavery to some degree, but no one was as flagrant about it as Nuño de Guzmán, who was eventually removed from office and imprisoned for his atrocities. Thus, the author is touching on an extremely sensitive political issue here, and even though the position he is taking is the only one he *could* take in a report written to the king, the historical record shows that it was one that Cabeza de Vaca held sincerely, to the detriment of his career and reputation.

[3] Oviedo writes that this village was 40 leagues, or 138 miles (221 km) from Culiacan. This is approximately where the boundary between Sonora and Sinaloa is now.

8 The next day[1] we dispatched four messengers from there to the land, as we were accustomed to do, to call and convene as many people as they could to a village that was a three-day journey from there. With that done, we parted the next day from all of the people who were there, and we always found traces and signs where the Christians had slept. At noon, we happened upon our messengers, who told us that they had not found anyone - that all had run to the woods, hidden, fleeing so that the Christians would not kill them and make them slaves - and that the previous night, staying behind some trees, they had seen the Christians and were watching what they were doing, and that they saw how they carried many Indians in chains. Those who came with us became upset with this, and some of them returned to give notice through the land how Christians were coming; many more would have done this if we had not told them not to, nor to be afraid. This assured them and greatly relaxed them. At that time, some Indians had come with us from a hundred leagues away, and we could not conclude with them so that they could return to their homes.[2] To assure them, we slept there that night, and the next day, we traveled and slept on the trail.

9 The following day, those who we had sent out as messengers guided us to where they had seen the Christians. Arriving at the hour of vespers,* we clearly saw that they had told the truth,

---

[1] The author gives a date check in 36:5. Working back from it, the date is now April 9, 1536 at the latest.

[2] As Cabeza de Vaca mentions elsewhere, the natives' custom was that their duties as escorts were not completed until the travelers were safely in the company of other natives. He does not explain why the natives who came so far could not "conclude" their duties at the Village of Hearts (32:1), the village on the flooded river (32:3), or the village in the cleft of a mountain (32:7), or why he chose to explain how this custom prevented the natives from leaving them right after noting that some natives did, in fact, do just that.

and we knew the people were horsemen from the stakes on which the horses had been tied. From here, which is called the Petutan River, to the river where Diego de Guzmán reached, there can be up to it - since where we knew of Christians - eighty leagues, and from there to the village where the waters took us, twelve leagues, and from there to the South Sea was twelve leagues.[1]

10 Through all this land, where the mountains reach, we saw large samples of gold, antimony, iron, copper, and other metals. Where there are fixed houses, it is hot - so much so that it is

---

[1] The author is describing the route he and his companions took from the flooded river mentioned in Paragraph 3, which was a day's journey from the Village of the Hearts, which the author called "the entrance to many provinces on the South Sea." At that river, the castaways were out of the Sierra Madre Occidental and were following the plain between that range and the Gulf of California, going southeast. As mentioned earlier, I take the flooded river to be the Matape. The next river, "where Diego de Guzmán reached," was the Yaqui. Diego de Guzmán was the nephew of Governor Nuño de Guzmán; he went as far as the Yaqui River in 1533. There are many ways to measure the distance between the Matape and the Yaqui, but 12 leagues is in the right ballpark. Identifying the next river, which Cabeza de Vaca called *Petután*, is troublesome. Cabeza de Vaca's estimate of there being 80 leagues between the Yaqui River and his current location cannot be right, since Culiacan is less than 80 leagues from the Yaqui River, and based on information Cabeza de Vaca gives in the next chapter, the castaways are now about 20 leagues from Culiacan. Many commentators take the Petutan River to be the Fuerte River, which is fewer than 40 leagues from the Yaqui, and is also about 40 leagues from Culiacan, but this is too far from Culiacan to fit the distances given in Chapter 33. Author Robin Varnum observes that the Sinaloa River, which is about 65 leagues from the Yaqui and about 24 leagues from Culiacan, fits the distance estimates better. I concur. On the other hand, the Sinaloa River may be the one where Captain Alcaraz was camped in 33:3. In the documents of the Coronado Expedition, the first district north of Culiacan is called *Petatlán*.

very hot in January. From there to the south of the country, which is unpopulated as far as the North Sea, is wretched and poor, where we endured great and incredible hunger, and those who inhabit and roam that land are the cruelest and of the worst inclination and customs. The Indians who have fixed houses, and those behind them, make nothing of gold and silver, nor do they find any use for them.

Chapter 33
Contact with Other Spaniards

How we saw signs of Christians

A fter we clearly saw a sign of Christians and knew how close we were to them, we gave many thanks to our Lord God for desiring to remove us from such a sad and miserable captivity. Anyone can imagine the pleasure we felt at this, considering the time we stayed in that land and the dangers and hardships* we endured.

2 That night,[1] I entreated one of my companions to go after the Christians, who were going through where we had left the land secured - it had been three days on the trail.[2] They made themselves out to be sick over this, excusing themselves because of tiredness and exhaustion.[3] Although each one of them could do it better than I, being stronger and younger,[4] seeing their deter-

---

[1] April 12, 1536, at the latest.

[2] Lit. *havia tres dias de camino,* "it had been three days of road (or of travel)." In saying that the other Christians "were going through where we had left the land secured," the author is saying that the other Christians are now in their rear, or to their northwest, and I believe the second part of this sentence means they are in a place where the Four Ragged Castaways had been three days previously. Bandelier renders this as "who were moving through the part of the country pacified and quieted by us, and who were three days ahead of where we were," but I do not think that is right. Smith writes, "... should go back three days' journey ... where we had given assurance of protection," which is how I also see it.

[3] Lit. *trabajo,* "work." See the glossary for a note on Cabeza de Vaca's propensity to give *trabajo* many meanings beyond its literal one.

[4] Cabeza de Vaca was about 45 at this time. His complaint about not being able to get people – in this case, Dorantes or Castillo – to do as he

mination, the next morning I took the Negro* and eleven Indians with me, and following the signs of the Christians we had found, I went to three places where they had slept. I walked ten leagues* that day.[1]

 3 The next morning, I reached four Christians on horseback, who were highly agitated on seeing me so strangely dressed and in the company of Indians. They kept looking at me for a long time, so astonished that they neither spoke to me nor were able to ask me anything. I told them to take me to where their captain was, and so we went a half league from there, where Diego de Alcaraz, the captain, was. After having spoken to him, he told me that [he] was very distraught there,[2] because it had been many days that he had been unable to take Indians, and he did not [know] where to go, because they were getting hungry and deprived.[3] I told him how Dorantes and Castillo, who were ten

---

asks continues a recurring theme not only of *La Relación*, but also the author's life in general.

[1] As explained in the glossary, a league represented the distance a man could walk in an hour, so this means he walked practically from dawn to dusk, with only a few quick stops for food and water. Ten leagues is about 35 miles (56 km).

[2] Lit. *eſtaba mui perdido alli*, "[I/he/it] was very lost there." As is common in Spanish, the subject of the sentence is not written here, and is determined by the context and the conjugation of the verb. The primary meaning of *perdido* is "lost," but it has many secondary meanings, including "confused" and "done for," similar to how one might say, "I am at a loss."

[3] Whenever Spaniards went out into the wilderness, they could only bring so much food with them, so they depended on natives for a large part of their food supply. Amazingly, these slavers did not anticipate that the people they had been terrorizing would go into hiding and therefore

leagues from there, remained behind with many people that had brought us. He then sent three horsemen and fifty Indians that they had brought, and the Negro returned with them to guide them. I stayed there and requested that they give me a testament of the year and the month and day that I had arrived, and the manner in which I came, and they did so.[1] From this river to San Miguel,[2] which is in the jurisdiction of the province called New Galicia, there are thirty leagues.[3]

---

not be able to give them sustenance. Oviedo writes that there were "as many as twenty horsemen" in this camp.

[1] Even after eight years of being lost in the wilderness, Cabeza de Vaca had not forgotten his responsibility, as senior officer of the Narváez Expedition, to make an official report at this important time. Oviedo writes that the report was sent to "Their Majesties," but it has not been found. We do not know what date it bore, but working backward from 36:5, it was no later than April 14, 1536.

[2] I.e. San Miguel de Culiacan, which the castaways will visit soon.

[3] Approximately 100 miles (160 km). The river where Alcaraz was camped may be the Sinaloa, or it may be one of the smaller rivers in the vicinity. Oviedo gives the distance as "a good thirty-five leagues or more from there," which would probably make it the Fuerte River.

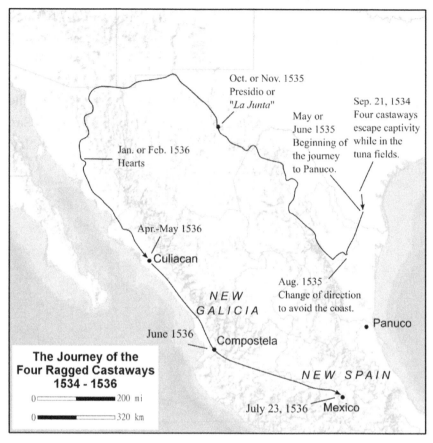

Figure 7 - Map of the Journey of the Four Ragged Castaways

Chapter 34
Saying Goodbye to the Indians

Of how I sent for the Christians

Five days later,[1] Andrés Dorantes and Alonso del Castillo arrived with those who had gone for them, and they brought more than six hundred people with them, who were from the village that the Christians had made to go up to the woods and had gone about hidden in the land. Those who had come there with us had taken them out of the woods and turned them over to the Christians. They had dismissed all of the other people who they had brought to that point.

2 When they came to where I was, Alcaraz entreated me to send out a call to the people of the villages that were on the bank of the river, who went about hidden in the woods of the country, and for us to order them to bring food (although this was not necessary, because they always took care to bring us all that they could). We then sent out our messengers to call them, and six hundred people came, and they brought us all the corn* they could get their hands on, and brought it in some mud-covered pots, which they had buried and hidden. They brought us everything else that they had, but we did not want to take of any of it except the food, and we gave all the other to the Christians to distribute among themselves.

3 After this, we had many great quarrels with them, because they wanted us to make the Indians who brought us into slaves. Upon leaving in anger, we left many Turkish bows[2] that we brought, and many pouches and arrows (and among them the five

---

[1] April 19, 1536, at the latest.

[2] A Turkish bow is a style of bow known for its extreme curvature. Obviously, the author is referring to the bows' shape, not their origin.

emeralds) that we did not remember from them, and so we lost them. We gave many cowhide robes to the Christians, and other things that we brought. We saw the Indians were very troubled because they would have returned to their homes and secured them and sowed their corn. They did not want to without going with us until they could leave us, as they were accustomed, with other Indians, because if they returned without doing this, they feared that they would die [and] that in going with us, they did not fear the Christians or their lances.

4 This weighed on the Christians, and they had their interpreter* say to them that we were the same as them, and we had been lost for a long time, and were people of poor luck and valor, and that they were the lords of that land, who must be obeyed and served. But the Indians gave little or no regard to all that they said to them; rather, they talked amongst themselves, saying that the Christians were lying, because we came from where the sun rose, and they where it sat; that we healed the sick and they killed those who were well; that we came naked and barefoot, and they were dressed and on horses and with lances; and that we had no greed for anything, and all that they gave us we turned and gave later, and were left with nothing, and the others never ceased to rob everything they could find, and never gave anything to anyone. In this manner, they related all these things and praised us, in contrast to the others.

5 They so responded to the interpreter of the Christians, and made the same known to the others in a language that they have among them, by which we understood them. Those who use it, we properly call Primahaitu (which is like saying Basque),[1]

---

[1] Basque is the name of a people and language indigenous to a certain region of Spain. The author is merely drawing a parallel between the indigenous peoples and languages on two different continents, not saying that the languages or people themselves are the same.

which, more than four hundred leagues* of those we traveled, we found used among them, without there being another in all those lands.

6 Finally, it was never settled[1] with the Indians to believe that we were of the other Christians. With great effort* and annoyance, we made them return to their homes and charged them to be assured and stay in their villages, and sow and work the earth, which, for being so deserted, was now very full of woods, which without doubt is the best of all there is in these Indies, and most fertile and productive[2] - they sow three times per year. They have many fruits and very beautiful rivers, and many other very good waters. There are great signs and signals of gold and silver mines. The people of them are very well-conditioned; they serve the Christians (those who are friends) out of very good will. They are well disposed, much more than those of Mexico, and finally, it is a land that lacks nothing to become very good.

7 Upon seeing the Indians off, they told us that they would do as we charged them, and would settle in their villages if the Christians left them alone. So I say and affirm with great certainty that if they do not do so, it will be the fault of the Christians.

8 After we had sent the Indians away in peace, thanking them for the trouble they had gone through with us, the Christians sent us away,[3] out of caution, to an alcalde, Cebreros,[4] and two others with him, who took us through the woods and uninhabited lands to sever our communication with the Indians, and

---

[1] Lit. *nunca pudo acabar*, "never was it able to finish."

[2] Lit. *abundoſa de Mantenimientos*, "abundant of sustenances."

[3] Oviedo writes that Cabeza de Vaca's party stayed at Alcaraz's camp for one day. This would mean they left on April 20, at the latest.

[4] Lázaro de Cebreros, one of the conquistadors of Sinaloa and founders of Culiacan.

so we would not see or understand that which they were doing. And so it seems how much the plans of men are fooled, in that we went about looking for their liberty, and when we thought that they had it, something very different happened. They had planned to attack the Indians we had sent away assured of peace. And as they thought, they did; they took us through those woods for two days, without water, lost and without a trail. All of us thought we would be lost to thirst, and seven men succumbed to it. Many friends that the Christians brought with them could not arrive until almost the next day at noon, to [a place] where we found water that night. We traveled with them twenty-five leagues,[1] more or less, and at the end of them we came to a village of peaceful Indians. The alcalde who brought us left us there, and he went another three leagues[2] to a village called Culiacan,[3] where Melchior[4] Díaz, chief alcalde and captain of that province, was.

---

[1] About 87 miles (138 km). This is too far to travel in two days, especially if the first day started at noon. This segment of the journey began on April 21, at the latest.

[2] 10 miles (16 km). Oviedo gives the distance from this valley to Culiacan as 8 leagues, or 28 miles (44 km), but that may be too far, considering that the next passage has Melchior Díaz arriving there the same night.

[3] Culiacan, the capital of the Mexican state of Sinaloa, had a population of about 839,000 in 2020. It was founded in 1531 as *San Miguel de Culiacán* by Nuño de Guzmán. As the northernmost Spanish settlement on the continent, it was not only the terminus of Cabeza de Vaca's journey, but also the origin of explorations under Coronado a few years later. Culiacan is about 700 miles (1,120 km) in a straight line from the Guadalupe River, where the castaways lived as captives of the Iguaces and Mariames. It is 650 miles (1,040 km) from Culiacan to Mexico City.

[4] The Cervantes Virtual Library edition of *La Relación*, which I usually rely upon for spelling and accentuation of personal names, spells his first name "Melchor," but it is spelled "Melchior" in Barcia's text. Modern writing uses both spellings about equally.

Chapter 35
Melchior Díaz, the Alcalde of Culiacan

Of how the chief alcalde received us well the night that we arrived

Whereas the chief alcalde* was informed of our departure and arrival, he left later that night[1] and came to where we were staying. He wept much with us, giving praise to our Lord God for having used such mercy with us. He spoke to us and treated us very well, and on behalf of Governor Nuño de Guzmán and himself offered to us all that he had and could do, and showed much sorrow for the poor welcome and treatment that we had found from Alcaraz and the others. We felt for certain that if he had been there, that which was done to us and the Indians would have been avoided.

2 That night passed, and we left the next day.[2] The chief alcalde entreated us greatly to stay there - that this would be a very great service to God and Your Majesty, because the country is unpopulated, unworked, and all very ruined, and the Indians went about hidden and running in the woods, not wanting to come settle in their villages - and for us to send out a call for them and command them on behalf of God and Your Majesty to come and populate the plain and work the land. This seemed very difficult to us to put into effect, because we did not bring one Indian of ours, nor did those who accompanied us when we left understand these things. In the end, we ventured for this two Indians of those who had been brought there as captives, who were from the same part of the country. These had been found with the Christians when we first came to them, and saw the people who had accom-

---

[1] April 23, 1536, at the latest.

[2] The first edition contains the additional words, "for Anhacan," an unknown place.

panied us, and knew from them of the great authority and power that we had held and carried throughout that land, and the marvels that we had done, and the sick that we had cured, and many other things. With these Indians, we sent others of the village to jointly go and call out to the Indians who went up to the mountains, and those of the Petaan River, where we had found the Christians,[1] and say to them to come to us, because we wanted to speak with them. To ensure their going, and that the others would come, we gave them one of the large gourds[2] that we had carried in our hands, which was our principal insignia and symbol of great status, and with this, they left and went about there for seven days.

3 At the end,[3] they came and brought with them three lords of those who had gone up to the mountains, who brought fifteen men, and they brought us beads, turquoises, and feathers. The messengers told us that they had not called out to the natives of the river where we had left, because the Christians had made them flee again to the woods.

4 Melchior Díaz said to the interpreter to speak to those Indians on our behalf, and he told them he came on the behalf of God, who is in Heaven,* and that we had gone about the world for

---

[1] Note that according to 32:9 and 33:2-3, Alcaraz's camp, i.e. the place where the castaways "found the Christians," was not at the "Petutan" river, but one that was ten leagues further north. As explained in the footnotes to 32:9, I take the "Petaan" (*Petachan* in the first edition, *Petután* in 32:9, and *Petatlán* in the Coronodo Expedition documents) to be the Sinaloa River, the first large stream northwest of Culiacan.

[2] Lit. *Calabaçon* in the Barcia source text or *calabazo* in the Cervantes digital copy. This is slightly different from *calabaza*, the usual word for "gourd." Some dictionaries render *calabazón* as "a large winter pumpkin."

[3] May 1, at the latest.

many[1] years, telling all the people that we had found to believe in God and serve Him, because He is Lord of all things in the world, and that He gave rewards and paid the good, and eternal pain of fire to the wicked, and when the good died, He carried them to Heaven, where no one ever dies, nor has hunger, nor cold, nor thirst, nor any other need, only the greatest glory that can be imagined, and that those who do not want to believe or obey His commandments, He casts below the earth in the company of the demons in a great fire, which never ceases, but torments them forever. Moreover, if they wanted to be Christians and serve God in the manner that we directed, the Christians would take them as brothers and would treat them very well, and we would command that no one would injure them[2] or take their lands from them, but that the Christians would become their great friends, but if they did not want to do this, the Christians would treat them very badly, and would take them as slaves to other lands. To this they responded to the interpreter that they would be very good Christians and serve God.[3]

---

[1] The first edition reads, "nine."

[2] *No les hiciefsen ningun enojo*, "they would do them no injury (offense)." *Enojo* is from the verb *enojar*, "to offend, annoy, irritate, to make angry."

[3] This paragraph relates the reading of the *requerimiento*, which was a major component of Spain's colonization efforts in the 16th century. This document asserted Spain's divine right to settle and colonize the western hemisphere and demanded that the natives acquiesce and obey their new overlords. All Spanish conquistadors were required by the crown to carry a copy of the *requerimiento* and have it read to the natives before engaging them in hostilities. At its worst, the *requerimiento* was nothing but a farcical justification for barbarism and conquest, cloaked in theological terms. Nevertheless, by acknowledging that the indigenous peoples of Spain's overseas territories were not subhuman brutes, but people with eternal souls, just like the Spaniards, it laid a crude and prim-

5 When asked who they worshipped and offered sacrifices, and to who they asked for water for their corn* fields and for their health, they responded, to a man who was in the sky. We asked them what he is called, and they said Aguar, and that they believed that he had created all the world and the things in it. We asked them in return how they knew this, and they responded that their fathers and grandfathers had told them, that they had known this for a long time, and that the water and all the good things were sent to them by him. We told them that one of whom they spoke, we called God, and that they were to call Him such, and serve and worship Him as we directed, and they would find themselves very well for it. They responded that they understood everything very well, and would do so.

6 We directed them to come down from the mountains, go safely and in peace, populate all the land, build their houses, among them build one for God, and put in the entrance a cross like the one we had there, and when the Christians came there, they were to go out to receive them with crosses in their hands, not bows or weapons, and to take them to their houses, and give them of what they have to eat, and in this manner they would do no harm to them, but would be their friends. They said that they would do as we had directed. The captain gave them blankets and treated them very well, and so they returned, taking those two

---

itive, yet important, foundation for the idea of universal human equality. Furthermore, it sometimes did, as in this instance, result in natives keeping their homes and a form of their previous way of life in a state of coexistence with the Spaniards, instead of being summarily slaughtered, enslaved, or displaced. While the crown's command to extend the *requerimiento* to the natives was often treated lightly or ignored entirely, especially by the likes of Nuño de Guzmán, this paragraph indicates that Melchior Díaz treated it seriously. Díaz's story is continued in the epilogue at the end of this translation.

who had been captives and had gone as messengers. This happened in the presence of the scribe that they had there and many other witnesses.[1]

_____

[1] Oviedo's paraphrased edition of the Joint Report essentially ends here. He adds a few closing paragraphs of commentary, however, which hint that his source text contained some material also included in the next chapter.

Chapter 36
On to Mexico City

Of how we had them make churches in that land

As the Indians returned, all those of that province, who were friends of the Christians, who had heard of us, came to us to see, and brought us beads and feathers, and we directed them to build churches and put crosses in them, because until then, they had not built them. We had them bring the children of their principal lords and baptize them, and then the captain made a solemn pledge to God to not make or consent to any foray, nor to take a slave of the land and people who we had made secure, and that he would keep and comply with this unless His Majesty and Governor Nuño de Guzmán,[1] or the viceroy[2] in his name, should decree something that better served God and His Majesty.

---

[1] By the time the castaways reached Culiacan, King Charles had already issued orders for Governor Guzmán's arrest, some of his confederates had already been imprisoned or arrested, and the man charged with taking custody of Guzmán, Diego Pérez de la Torre, was on his way to New Spain. Whether Melchior Díaz knew about Guzmán's "lame duck" status as governor when he offered the natives the *requerimiento* and the promises associated with compliance, in contrast with Guzmán's policy of wholesale enslavement, I do not know, but it was no secret at this time that Guzmán was out of the court's favor.

[2] Between 1526 and 1528, the crown, suspicious of what Hernán Cortés's ultimate ambitions were, took measures to reduce his power. These measures made affairs in New Spain much worse, because the men, such as Guzmán, who were entrusted with authority proved to be ruthless, corrupt, and unjust. The king and queen then decided to name a viceroy ("vice-king") to rule over all of North America. The man they chose was Antonio de Mendoza. He arrived in Mexico City on November 14, 1535 and was, therefore, still relatively new on the job when the castaways emerged from the wilderness. Cortés was given the title "Marquis of the

2 After the children were baptized, we left for the town of San Miguel, where, upon our arrival,[1] Indians came, who told us how many people came down from the mountains and occupied the plain, and built churches and crosses and all that we had directed. Every day we had news of how this was being done and more fully carried out.

3 After we had been there fifteen days, Alcaraz came[2] with the Christians who had gone on that foray and related to the captain how the Indians were down from the mountains and had occupied the plain, and how they found villages with many people, which had earlier been unpopulated and deserted, and that the Indians had gone out to receive them with crosses in their hands, taken them to their houses, and gave to them of what they had, and that they slept with them there that night. Astonished at such a change, and at how the Indians told them how they were now

---

Valley of Oaxaca" and was allowed to command an army and conduct explorations. Cabeza de Vaca and his comrades no doubt listened with great interest as these developments were explained to them.

[1] The first edition of *La Relación* adds, "April 1, 1536." See my footnote to the next paragraph.

[2] The castaways had been in San Miguel de Culiacan for 15 days when Alcaraz arrived, but how much longer they stayed there afterward is unknown. They left on May 15 (36:5), so they arrived on May 1 at the latest, but it was likely earlier. If the first edition is correct, they arrived on April 1, but I consider it very likely that that this date was removed from the second edition because Cabeza de Vaca realized it was wrong. As a rule, I assume that any changes made between the first and second editions were corrections, meaning where there are any discrepancies between the two editions, the second should be given more weight.

secure, he ordered that nothing bad be done to them, and so they departed.[1]

4 May our Lord God in His infinite mercy desire that in the days of Your Majesty and under your power and rule, these people come to be truly and entirely willing subjects of the true Lord who created and redeemed them. We hold for certain that it will be so, and that Your Majesty will be the one who will put it into effect (that it will not be difficult to do), because we traveled two thousand leagues*[2] through the land and on the sea on the boats, and another ten months after leaving captivity,[3] without stopping, going about through the land, we did not encounter sacrifices or idolatry.[4] In this time we traversed from one sea to the other, and

---

[1] Cabeza de Vaca portrays Captain Diego de Alcaraz as untrustworthy and blames him for his poor treatment of both the natives and his own party earlier. Alcaraz's subsequent participation in the Coronado Expedition was documented by Castañeda and is summarized in the epilogue. Castañeda also had a poor opinion of him.

[2] 2,000 leagues is roughly 7,000 miles (11,200 km). This estimate can only be close to right if the author included his trans-Atlantic travel from Spain to Cuba. The actual distance from Tampa Bay to Culiacan, along the author's estimated route, is about 3,000 miles (4,800 km).

[3] The author is being imprecise. He and his fellow castaways fled from captivity under the Mariames and Iguaces in September 1534 (see 19:3) and remained in south Texas as willing guests of other tribes, principally the Avavares, until about June 1535 (see 22:6). Their ten-month journey from south Texas to the outskirts of Culiacan ended in April 1536.

[4] Here the author is, once again, touching upon a hot political issue, the importance of which may be lost to modern readers. Conquistadors and governors in the Spanish Empire were only allowed to go to war against and enslave natives who refused to accept the *requerimiento* (see 35:4) and who defied Spain's claim to their territory. The natives who chose vassalage, however, also had to renounce certain heathen practices, including cannibalism, human sacrifice, and idolatry. Continuing in them,

from the information that we were able to understand, with great diligence, from one coast to the other at the most wide, there could be two hundred leagues.[1] We were able to understand that

---

even if they otherwise accepted Spanish rule, still left the natives open to severe chastisement. Nuño de Guzmán, who was a lawyer before becoming a governor, no doubt claimed that the natives in his province were guilty of these heinous acts, because that was the only way he could legally justify his slaving enterprise. Oviedo states, "They wrote this report, certifying that throughout all that land, where they had travelled, they did not see idolatry nor sacrifice of men. Moreover, they did not hear of such things *until they arrived at the city of Compostela*" (emphasis mine). Compostela was where they met Guzmán (see Paragraph 6). Remember, however, the Mariames and Iguaces had a custom of killing all of their daughters and sometimes killing their sons (18:4), which would have sounded uncomfortably similar to the Aztecs' practice of human sacrifice. Of it, Oviedo writes, "These natives do not have any other form of idolatry," and Cabeza de Vaca writes, "Only [the Mariames] and the others, their neighbors who are called the Iguaces, follow this custom; no one else in their land keeps it." It seems that both writers wanted to make sure that the Mariames' practice of infanticide did not taint the king's and the viceroy's opinion of the submissive natives of Sonora and Sinaloa, and was not used as a pretext for enslaving them.

[1] 200 leagues is about 700 miles (1,120 km). This is a reasonable estimate of the distance from the Gulf of Mexico at the River of Palms to the Gulf of California at Culiacan, but it is far from being the "most wide" measurement of the distance from the Atlantic to the Pacific Oceans across North America. When Coronado and his captains and scouts began exploring northward, they always believed they were closer to the Pacific Ocean than they actually were, because they did not understand that the continent got wider and wider the further north one went. The first edition reads "two thousand leagues," which is certainly not what the author meant, and is why it was corrected in the second edition.

on the South* coast[1] there are pearls and many riches, and that the best and richest is near it.

5 We stayed in the town of San Miguel until the fifteenth day of the month of May. The reason we stopped there so long was because from there to the city of Compostela, where Governor Nuño de Guzmán resided, are a hundred leagues,[2] all of which were deserted and [inhabited by] enemies, and people, including twenty horsemen, had to go with us. They accompanied us up to forty leagues, and from there forward, six Christians, who brought five hundred Indian slaves, came with us.

6 We arrived in Compostela. The governor received us very well, and gave us clothing from what he had.[3] For many days, I could not put it on, nor could we sleep except on the floor.

7 Ten or twelve days later,[4] we left for Mexico.[5] We were treated well by the Christians the whole way, and many came out

---

[1] Lit. *la Costa del Sur*, "the coast of the South [Sea]."

[2] About 350 miles (560 km). Compostela was Guzmán's capital. The colonial city of Compostela is now Tepic, the capital of the state of Nayarit. It is about 300 miles (480 km), or 87 leagues, from Culiacan.

[3] It would be interesting to know what Cabeza de Vaca and Guzmán talked about and how much of their discussion, if any, was about slavery. By the time Cabeza de Vaca wrote *La Relación*, Guzmán had used his connections in Spain to escape further punishment for his crimes, and was a free man. Cabeza de Vaca made his position on slavery clear in *La Relación* without dragging Guzmán's name through the mud.

[4] The author gives no information about the dates or travel times between Culiacan and Mexico City, but if they traveled at a constant speed, they arrived in Compostela around June 6 and left around June 17.

[5] Hernán Cortés discovered the Aztec city of Tenochtitlan in 1519. The valley in which Tenochtitlan was situated was called Mexico. He conquered the city and renamed it Mexico in 1521. Originally, "Mexico" referred only to the city now known as Mexico City, while the province of which it was the capital was called New Spain.

to see us on the roads and gave thanks to God for having freed us from such dangers. We arrived in Mexico on Sunday, one day before the eve of Saint James,[1] where we were treated very well and received with great pleasure by the viceroy and the marquis of the Valley.[2] They gave us clothing and offered us all that they had, and on the day of Saint James, there was a party, a game of canes,[3] and bulls.[4]

---

[1] Lit. *Visepra de Santiago*, "Vesper of St. James." The feast day of Saint James the Apostle is July 25. A public festival is held beginning the evening (vespers) before, or July 24. The author's group arrived on Sunday, July 23. The festival of Santiago is still a major holiday in northern Spain, but its observance has diminished elsewhere.

[2] Viceroy Antonio de Mendoza and Marquis Hernán Cortés, as explained in the footnotes to Paragraph 1.

[3] The game of canes, or *juega de cañas*, was a Spanish tournament game similar to jousting, in that the participants rode horses at each other armed with lances and shields, except they threw the lances at each other, rather than clashing directly.

[4] I.e., bullfights.

Chapter 37
The Voyage to Europe

Of what happened when I desired to come

After we rested in Mexico two months, I wanted to come to this realm. Upon going to embark in the month of October, a storm came which hit the ship crossways, and it was lost. Seeing this, I decided to remain and pass the winter, because in those parts the weather is very rough for navigating in it.

2 After winter passed, during Lent,[1] we left Mexico - Andrés Dorantes and I[2] - for Veracruz,[3] in order to embark. There we had to wait until Palm Sunday,[4] when we boarded. We were on board more than fifteen days for lack of wind, and the ship we were on took on a lot of water. I left it and went over to others which were arriving, and Dorantes remained in that one.

3 On the tenth day of the month of April, three ships left the port. They sailed together for a hundred and fifty leagues.*[5] On the way, two ships had taken a lot of water, and one night we lost them from the convoy, because the pilots and captains, ac-

---

[1] Lent is the 46-day period preceding Easter. In 1537, Easter was on April 1, so Lent began on February 14.

[2] Before Dorantes left Mexico, Viceroy Mendoza arranged to have him leave Estevanico with him. This is discussed further in the epilogue.

[3] Founded by Hernán Cortés on May 18, 1519, Veracruz was the first Spanish town in New Spain and was also the principal port. It is almost certainly where Cabeza de Vaca went to embark the previous October as well.

[4] March 25, 1537, the Sunday before Easter.

[5] About 500 miles (800 km). This is roughly half the distance between Veracruz and Havana. If the ships were following the coast, they had passed Campeche and were beginning to round the Yucatan Peninsula.

cording to how it later appeared, did not dare to go further with their ships, and returned again to the port where they had departed, without giving notice of that, neither did we know more of them.

4 We continued our voyage, and on the fourth day of May, we arrived at the port of Havana, which is on the island of Cuba, where we stayed waiting on the other two ships, believing that they would come, until the second day of June.[1] We left there in great fear of running into the French, who had taken three of our ships there a few days before.[2] When we arrived off[3] the island of Bermuda, a storm which tends to take everyone who passes

---

[1] Oviedo writes that while at Havana, "these gentlemen" (though it was only Cabeza de Vaca) sent a letter to the *audiencia real* at Santo Domingo, which was an important government body in North America. It was this letter, which historians call the Joint Report, that Oviedo used as his source. Thus, there must have been at least two specimens of the Joint Report, for I believe Cabeza de Vaca retained one in his possession to present to the king. The copy might have been made in Havana, but I believe it is more likely it was made in Mexico. Neither specimen survives.

[2] Portugal was the first European nation to take to the high seas; Spain was next. In 1494, these two nations signed the Treaty of Tordesillas, wherein they divided the world's oceans and undiscovered territories between themselves. Portugal disclaimed interest in most of the western hemisphere, except for Brazil, while Spain agreed not to colonize Brazil or Africa. Although these two nations were competitors, the treaty worked, and they enjoyed friendly relations with each other. As other European nations gained the ability to sail the oceans, however, they challenged the Portuguese-Spanish duopoly. The first nation to do so was France. In 1520, King Francis I of France sanctioned "privateering," the raiding and capturing of Spanish and Portuguese ships by private French vessels.

[3] Lit. *sobre*. While it normally means "over" or "above," in nautical contexts, it means "off of."

through there, according to the people who travel there, took us. For a whole night, we took ourselves to be lost. It pleased God that, when morning came, the storm ceased, and we continued on our way.

   5 At the end of twenty-nine days since we departed Havana,[1] we had traveled a thousand and one hundred leagues, which is said that there are from there to the village of Azores.[2] The next day, we passed the island called "of the Raven."[3] We came upon a French ship; at the noon hour, it commenced to follow us with a caravel[4] that it had taken from the Portuguese, and gave us chase. That afternoon, we saw other new sails, and they were so far away, we could not know if they were Portuguese or of the same as those who were following us. When night came, the French one was a cannon[5]-shot away from our ship. When it was

---

[1] July 1.

[2] 1,100 leagues is about 3,800 miles (6,080 km), which is roughly the distance from Havana to the Azores, a group of islands in the Atlantic Ocean west of Portugal. Spanish ships sailing from Europe to North America sailed down the coast to the Canary Islands, then turned west. Ships returning home, however followed a more northerly route that took them past the Azores. These routes were taken to make the best use of the prevailing currents and winds in the Atlantic Ocean.

[3] Lit. *del Cuervo*. It is better-known by its Portuguese name, Corvo. This tiny (7 square miles, or 17 square kilometers) island is about 1,200 miles (1,920 km) west of Lisbon.

[4] The caravel is the ship that launched the Age of Discovery. A Portuguese design, it was fast and highly maneuverable and could sail in contrary winds and currents. Due to its shallow keel, it could also navigate close to coasts and sail up rivers. Its only drawback was its limited carrying capacity. Two of Christopher Columbus's three ships from his fabled 1492 voyage were caravels.

[5] Lit. *Lombarda*. The lombard was a smooth-bore cannon used by Spain and Italy.

dark, we stole the defeat by diverting ourselves from it.¹ Since it was so close to us, it saw us and traced our path, and we did this three or four times. It could have taken us if he had wanted, but he left it for morning. It pleased God that when morning came, we found the French [ship] and ours together, surrounded by the new sails that I said that we had seen the afternoon before, which we knew were of the Portuguese fleet. I gave thanks to our Lord for having me saved from the hardships* of the land and dangers of the sea. Since the French [captain] knew it was the Portuguese fleet, he let go of the caravel that he had taken, which was loaded with Negros, who he had brought with them so that we would believe that it was Portuguese and we would wait for it. When he let it go, he told its captain and pilot that we were French and of his convoy. As he said this, they put sixty oars of their ship into the water, and so, by oar and sail, it began to go, and it went so [quickly] that it could not be believed.

6 The caravel that [was] let go went to the galleon and said to the captain that our ship and the other were French, so when our ship approached the galleon, and since the whole fleet saw that we went to them believing for certain that we were French, they put themselves at the point of war and came up to us. When they came close we hailed them.² [It] knew that we were friends; they had found themselves deceived for that corsair having escaped by having been told that we were French and of his com-

---

¹ Notwithstanding the well-known tradition of referring to ships as "she," the word *Navio* ("ship") is masculine, and the author consistently uses masculine pronouns when referring to them. With *Caravela* ("caravel"), however, a feminine noun, he switches to feminine pronouns. I use "it" when the author is referring to a ship and "he" in references to the captain.

² Lit. *les falvamos*. The verb *salvar* usually means "to save," but it can also mean to make a *salva*, or salute, either with or without artillery or small arms. The greeting, "*Salve!*" is translated as "Hail!"

pany. And so four caravels went after it, and the galleon came to us. After being greeted, the captain, Diego de Silveira, asked us where we came from and what merchandise we brought. We responded that we came from New Spain and that we brought silver and gold. He asked us how much there was; the captain told him that we brought three hundred thousand *castellanos*.[1] The captain responded, "Faith, you come back very rich, although you have a bad craft and miserable artillery. That dog of a French renegade has lost a fat morsel, the bastard! Now, go ahead, since you escaped; follow me closely, and, God helping, I shall lead you back to Spain."[2]

7 A little later, the caravels that had pursued the French [ship] returned, because it seemed that they had traveled much, and so as not to leave the fleet, which was guarding three ships that came loaded with spices.

8 And so we arrived at Terceira Island,[3] where we stayed to rest for fifteen days, taking refreshment and waiting for another ship that came loaded from India, which was in the convoy of the three ships that the fleet carried. When fifteen days passed, we departed from there with the fleet and came to the port of Lisbon on the ninth of August, eve of Master Saint Lawrence, the year of one thousand five hundred and thirty seven years.

---

[1] The denomination of Spanish gold coins is a complex topic. Suffice it to say that 300,000 of any gold coin represents an extremely large amount of wealth.

[2] The quoted words are written in Portuguese in the source text. Since I do not read Portuguese, I have copied Bandelier's translation of them verbatim.

[3] Lit. *Isla Tercera. Tercera* and *Terceira* are the Spanish and Portuguese words, respectively, for "third." Since the Azores are a Portuguese possession, English-speaking countries use the Portuguese spelling of the name. Terceira is said to be the third island of the Azores to have been discovered.

The Account of Cabeza de Vaca

9 Because the truth is so - what I told in this above Account[1] - I have signed my name. *Cabeza de Vaca.* The Account was signed in your name, and with your coat of arms, where it was published.[2]

---

[1] Lit. *Relación*, Cabeza de Vaca's title for this work.

[2] I have formatted this paragraph the way it appears in Barcia's published text of *Naufragios*. I imagine that in Cabeza de Vaca's manuscript, his signature was on a line by itself, and the publisher or editor's note following his signature was written below it.

Chapter 38
Of Narváez's Ships

Of that which happened to the rest that entered the Indies

Since I have made an account of everything mentioned above on the voyage, and the entrance and exit from the country, until returning to this realm, I want to likewise try to remember and relate what happened to the ships and the people that remained in them, which I did not remember to do in what I told previously, [1] because we never had news of them until after exiting. We found many of the people in New Spain, and others here in Castile, from whom we learned the outcome and the conclusion of it and in what manner it happened.

2 After we left the three ships (because the other was already lost on the rough coast, where they were in great danger) there were almost a hundred people left with a few supplies. Among them were ten married women, and one of them had said to the governor many things that happened on the voyage, before they took place. She said to him, when he entered the country, not to enter it, because she believed that neither he nor any of those who went with him would settle the land, and that if anyone left it, that it would be by great miracles of God, but she believed that few or none would escape. The governor then responded to her that he and all those who entered with him were going to fight and conquer many very strange people and lands, and that he held it for certain that many would die conquering them, but those who remained would have good luck and would become

---

[1] The conclusion of the previous chapter and the beginning of this one make it look like this chapter was a supplement to the original finished work. In Barcia's printing, however, Chapter 38 is presented immediately following Chapter 37, without being set off by any marks or notes indicating it was supplemental.

very rich, because of the news that he had obtained of the riches that were in that land. He spoke further and implored for her to tell him: the things that she had said past and present - who had told them to her? She answered and said that in Castile a Moor woman of Hornachos had told it to her, which she had been telling us before we left from Castile, and the whole voyage had happened to us in the same manner that she had told us.

3 After the governor had left as his lieutenant, and captain of all the ships and people who had left there, to Carvallo,[1] native of Cuenca of Huete, we parted from them. Upon leaving, the governor ordered that, by all means, all would then gather onto the ships and would continue the voyage straight to Panuco, always going by way of the coast and looking for the best port that they could find, so that in finding it, they would stop in it and wait for us. In that time that they gathered on the ships, they said that those people who were there, seeing and hearing very clearly how that woman said to the others that since their husbands entered the interior country and put themselves in such great danger, not to take them into account anymore,[2] that they should look for whom they would marry, because thus she had to do, and so she did it, that she and the rest married and became concubines to those who remained on the ships.

4 After they left from there, the ships made sail and continued their voyage. They did not find the port further on, and came back. Five leagues* below from where they had disem-

---

[1] Spelled "Caravallo" in 4:11.

[2] Lit. *no hicieſen en ninguna manera cuenta de ellos*, or "not to make in any manner account of them." The Spanish phrase *hacer quenta* means to keep an account or record of something. A modern colloquial equivalent of *no hacer cuenta de ellos* would be "to write them off."

barked, they found the port,[1] which extended six or eight leagues inland,[2] and was the same that we had discovered, where we found the Castilian boxes about which I have written above, where the bodies of the dead men were, those who were Christians. In this port and on this coast, the three ships, and the other which came from Havana, and the brigantine went about looking for us close to a year.[3] Since they did not find us, they went to New Spain.[4]

---

[1] Smith includes a footnote here, which reads, "This 'below' should be 'above,'" but Smith is wrong. The ships sailed north from where the men disembarked and did not find the port. They found the port after they came back to the original spot and then went south for another five leagues, so the port was "below" where they disembarked.

[2] Also see Paragraph 5. The description of the port fits Tampa Bay and nowhere else. Johns Pass, where I believe Narváez disembarked his men, is 16 miles (26 km), or about 4.6 leagues, north of the middle of Tampa Bay's main channel. Recall from 4:1 that the men walked north (or northeast, per Oviedo) and found a bay, i.e., Old Tampa Bay.

[3] On one occasion, the Spaniards aboard one ship spotted a post on the beach with what looked like a letter stuck in a split on the top of it. Five men went ashore to investigate it. The "letter" turned out to be a trap set by natives. Four of the Spaniards were killed. The fifth, Juan Ortiz, was captured. He was recovered 12 years later, as told in the epilogue.

[4] On May 29, 1529, almost thirteen months after Narváez sent the ships away, Lope Hurtado, the royal treasurer at Santiago, Cuba, wrote King Charles a long letter covering a multitude of topics. One sentence of that letter states, "A caravel arrived here, which came in search of Narváez, and brought eight Indians that it took from that coast where Narváez embarked, and these Indians say, by signs, that Narváez is in the interior country, and that they do nothing but eat, drink, and sleep, and I do not know what we believe of it."

5 This port that we speak of is the best in the world, and enters the land seven or eight leagues,[1] is six fathoms* at the entrance, and near the land it is five, and the bottom of it is mud. There is no sea inside nor fierce storm. It holds many ships; it has a very great quantity of fish. It is a hundred leagues from Havana, which is a village of Christians in Cuba, and is at north-south with this village,[2] and here the breezes always prevail. They come and go from one part to another in four days, because the ships come and go on the quarter.[3]

6 Now that I have given the account of the ships, it will be good for me to tell who are, and of what place in this realm, those who Our Lord was served in escaping from these hardships.* The first is Alonso del Castillo Maldonado, native of Salamanca, son of Doctor Castillo and of Mrs. Aldonza Maldonado. The second is Andrés Dorantes, son of Pablo Dorantes, native of Bejar and citizen of Gibraleon. The third is Álvar Núñez Cabeza de Vaca, son of Francisco de Vera and grandson of Pedro de Vera - the one who won Canaria.[4] His mother was called *Doña[1]* Teresa Cabeza de Va-

---

[1] 24 to 28 miles (39 to 44 km). There are various ways to interpret what "enters the land" means, but this is about the distance from the easternmost point of Tampa Bay, at the mouth of the Alafia River, straight across to the Gulf coast at the Pinellas Peninsula. It is also about the distance from the mouth of Tampa Bay to its northern end at Safety Harbor. No other bay on Florida's Gulf coast is anywhere near this large.

[2] Havana is at 82.35° W longitude. Tampa Bay is approximately at the same longitude; they are "north-south" with each other. The distance between them is a little over 300 miles (480 km), or about 90 leagues.

[3] That is, the winds are so strong that ships lower or furl their sales to one-quarter size in order to maintain a safe speed.

[4] Spain began its conquest of the Canary Islands on Gran Canaria – one of the larger islands in the group – in 1478. Pedro de Vera was appointed governor in 1481. During his time in office, the indigenous resistance was suppressed and Spain's conquest of the island was completed. Ca-

ca, native of Jerez de la Frontera. The fourth is called Estevanico; he is an Arabian Negro,* native of Azamor.²

---

beza de Vaca did not exaggerate in saying his grandfather "won" the island.

¹ *Doña* and its masculine counterpart, *Don*, are terms of respect that are always connected to the person's first name, so the author's mother could be addressed as either Doña Teresa or Señora Cabeza de Vaca. In the 16th century, these terms were functionally equivalent to the British "Dame" and "Sir." They are still widely used today, but their usage is different, especially in countries that have abolished titles of nobility, such as Mexico. His mother's status as a noblewoman may be the reason that Cabeza de Vaca chose her surname rather than his famous grandfather's.

² See the footnotes to 5:3, 7:11, and 16:1 for more information about Castillo, Dorantes, and Estevanico, respectively. To learn what became of them following the expedition, read the epilogue.

Epilogue to the Narváez Expedition

The emergence of the Four Ragged Castaways from the wilderness solved the eight-year-old mystery of what became of Pánfilo de Narváez and his expedition after he sent the ships away in Florida. The men drew a map, which has not survived, for Viceroy Mendoza and gave their account of their journey, first verbally, then as a written testament. This epilogue relates what became next of each of the four castaways, plus certain other people mentioned in the story, and what the immediate effects were of their discoveries.

Estevanico and the Coronado Expedition

Mendoza and the others who heard the castaways' story were more interested in some parts of it than others. They heard how in Florida and Texas, the Spaniards died of illness and exposure and that there were no precious metals or gems. The natives there were unfriendly or hostile and fought with and enslaved the Christians. They lived in small, poorly-organized, nomadic bands, always seemed to be on the brink of starvation, and had no interest in hearing about the Christians' beliefs in God and the afterlife. On the other hand, Cabeza de Vaca and his colleagues described northern Mexico as fertile and populated by friendly natives. Some of these natives farmed, some lived in "real houses," and many seemed receptive to the Gospel. More importantly, the lands had some mineral resources, and the residents traded with natives to the north who reportedly had copper in large quantities and knew how to smelt and mold it into useful and decorative items.

Viceroy Mendoza was eager to explore and conquer this new land to the north, but he also thought that before committing to a large-scale expedition of any kind, some more scouting work should be done. No one was more qualified to do it than the four castaways themselves, but Cabeza de Vaca planned to return to Castile to petition the king for the governorship of Narváez's territory. Dorantes planned to go also; some historians believe he had ambitions of being Cabeza de Vaca's second-in-command. Castillo had already left New Spain. Not wanting to lose access to the knowledge these travelers had, Mendoza bought Estevanico from Dorantes so that he could serve as a guide to whoever ended up leading the next undertaking. In a letter to King Charles, Mendoza vouched for Estevanico as being a "person of reason," apparently in contrast to the natives he would have been forced to rely upon had he not been able to secure one of the castaways.

As Cabeza de Vaca writes in Chapter 37 of *La Relación*, he and Dorantes left Mexico during Lent of 1537 to board a ship at Veracruz. They ended up on separate ships headed to Castile, but Dorantes's ship turned around. When Mendoza heard about this, he wrote to Dorantes at Veracruz and asked him to lead the expedition he had been planning. Initially, Dorantes agreed, but some months later, Mendoza wrote a letter to King Charles advising him that his plans with Dorantes fell through, for reasons he did not know.

The castaways' arrival in Mexico coincided with another major event occurring in Mendoza's first year in office – the downfall of Nuño Beltrán de Guzmán, the governor of New Galicia. King Charles ordered Guzmán's removal because of his abuses against the natives of his province. His replacement, Diego Pérez de la Torre, was already on his way to Mexico to arrest Guzmán when the castaways met with the viceroy. Guzmán allowed Pérez to arrest him in Mexico. He remained in prison there until June 30, 1538, when he was released to answer a summons to appear in Seville. By that time, however, Pérez was already dead, having been killed in a battle with natives. This unfortunate occurrence gave Mendoza the opportunity to appoint a new governor. He chose Francisco Vázquez de Coronado, a friend of his who came over with him from Castile.

Coronado[1] would also be leading the expedition to the north, but he needed some time to organize it, not to mention to organize his province by making appointments, visiting town councils, etc. before leaving on a long trip. Furthermore, the scouting mission Mendoza wanted had not yet been made. Mendoza ultimately chose Friar Marcos de Niza to lead the scouting mission. With the matter of who would lead the expedition and the scouting trip finally settled, Coronado, Marcos, and Estevanico left for New Galicia in September 1538, more than two years after Cabeza de Vaca and his colleagues arrived in Mexico City to give their report.

In March 1539, Marcos took his small exploratory party, including Estevanico, out of Culiacan and began retracing the castaways' steps. While they were still in Sonora, Marcos stopped to inquire about the lands in the vicinity and toward the coast, while Estevanico continued northward. One day, a messenger came to Marcos carrying a cross the size of a man. This was a signal he and Estevanico had worked out to indicate that the Moor had found something extremely important, and the friar ought to hurry. Marcos left his camp and went north. Estevanico kept sending crosses back, but also kept advancing, not waiting for Marcos to catch up. After Marcos crossed two deserts, he was met by a native bearing sad news: Estevanico had been killed by natives at a nearby town called Cibola.

The way it was explained to Marcos, Estevanico always sent a gourd decorated with feathers and bells ahead of himself to herald his arrival. When the chief at Cibola saw the gourd, he became angry and forbade Estevanico from entering the city. Estevanico ignored the warning, and so he was killed. George Parker

---

[1] In his day, he was referred to as "Vázquez."

Winship theorizes that Estevanico was killed because his gourd identified him as allies of natives who were Cibola's enemies. When Coronado arrived at Cibola later, he was told a different story: that Estevanico was violent with the native women. Pedro de Castañeda, a soldier in Coronado's army, wrote that Estevanico came carrying turquoises and in the company of native women, and the chief was offended when he asked for turquoises and women from the people of Cibola. None of these reasons for his death are mutually exclusive, so they all could have played a part in it. All of the contemporary sources agree, however, that Estevanico was killed by the natives of Cibola. Coronado was in Cibola 14 months after the fact, learned what he could, and called the Moor's death "perfectly certain." The natives even told the Spaniards that they kept Estevanico's bones as proof that Christians could be killed. A modern theory that he faked his death in order to escape from Spanish slavery ignores all of this testimony, or rejects it for no sound reason.

Friar Marcos claimed that he came within sight of Cibola, but, fearing for his life, did not approach the town. When he returned to Compostela to report on his findings, however, he described it as very large and grand – larger than the city of Mexico – and said that it was the smallest of seven cities in a kingdom that was one of many such kingdoms in the vicinity. Marcos's report - which Marcos quite possibly enhanced in retelling it to his friends and associates – soon took on a life of its own and generated excited rumors about seven cities of gold. Mendoza and Coronado poured much of their own personal wealth into getting the main expedition ready, and they had no trouble finding men to go on it. Based on the level of excitement in New Spain, many people expected that Cibola would be the third great kingdom of wealth discovered in the New World, after Mexico and Peru.

Before Coronado went to Mexico to visit with Mendoza about his expedition, he sent Melchior Díaz, who was still alcalde of Culiacan, with a company of soldiers to further explore the territory between Culiacan and Cibola. Díaz and his men started out on November 17, 1539. They found the country too difficult to cross in the winter, and turned around before reaching Cibola. Díaz subsequently rejoined Coronado, who marched out of Culiacan in April 1540.

In May, Coronado and his army reached a location in the Sonora River valley which they believed to be near the place the Four Ragged Castaways called *Corazones*, or Hearts. Coronado set up a camp and left most of the army there while he advanced with a company to Cibola. He found Cibola in July. It was a huge disappointment. Castañeda writes, "when they saw the first village, which was Cibola, such were the curses that some hurled at Friar Marcos that I pray God may protect him from them." Coronado conquered the city, wrote a letter to the viceroy, and gave the letter to Melchior Díaz to deliver. When Díaz reached Hearts, he relayed Coronado's orders for most of the army to advance to Cibola. Díaz gave the letter to someone else to take to Mexico and took command of the approximately 80 men who remained at Hearts.

Around the end of September, Díaz took 25 men to explore the territory to the west of Hearts. They marched around the north end of the Gulf of California, crossed the Colorado River, and followed the river to its mouth on the Gulf. Díaz and his company were the first non-indigenous people to explore this part of the continent.

One day, Díaz threw his lance from horseback at a dog that was chasing some sheep the soldiers were trying to herd. The tip of the lance stuck in the ground, and Díaz could not stop his horse in time. The lance pierced Díaz's thigh, ruptured his bladder, and came out at his groin. His men began taking him back to Hearts, but he died after twenty days of agony on January 8, 1541.

History remembers him as a capable leader. Castañeda wrote that Díaz "merited the position he held."

Díaz had left Diego de Alcaraz, the captain Cabeza de Vaca met in Chapter 33 of *La Relación*, in charge of the village of Hearts. Castañeda describes Alcaraz as "a man unfitted to have people under his command." Some of the men at Hearts mutinied, and Alcaraz sentenced two of them to be hanged, but they escaped. Natives also killed a soldier with a poison arrow. Alcaraz seized some of the natives responsible for the attacks, but after they gave him some blankets, he let them go. They subsequently attacked and killed 17 more soldiers. Some of the remaining men then deserted and went back to Culiacan. The emboldened natives then launched a nighttime attack in which Alcaraz was mortally wounded.[1]

The Coronado Expedition explored much of present-day Arizona and New Mexico, including Albuquerque, Santa Fe, and the Grand Canyon. Coronado never found any cities of gold. He also took part of his army into Texas, in the vicinity of Lubbock, and even went up into Kansas. While in the High Plains region of Texas, he encountered some natives who said they knew and remembered Cabeza de Vaca and his three colleagues.[2] For centuries, historians took this as evidence that the Four Ragged Castaways passed through that part of Texas. This led to some very odd route interpretations that usually placed the boat landings between Alabama and Louisiana and the prickly pear fields in places like the Piney Woods of east Texas. This encounter is now used as

---

[1] "Whoever fights against them must be very wise that [the Indians] do not sense weakness or greed for what they have. During war, one must treat them very badly, because if they are aware of any fear or greed, these are people who know the time to avenge themselves, and to take strength from the fear of their foes" – Cabeza de Vaca, *La Relación* 25:3.

[2] See 30:14 and the footnotes.

evidence of how far some native tribes traveled for the purposes of hunting and trade.

The De Soto Expedition

Cabeza de Vaca arrived in Castile in August 1537. He intended to petition for Narváez's title to the province of Florida to be transferred to him. Instead, he found that Hernando de Soto was awarded that grant in April. Cabeza de Vaca consulted with De Soto and was reportedly offered a position on the expedition, but he declined. One of De Soto's chroniclers, known as "A Gentleman of Elvas," writes that De Soto did not meet Cabeza de Vaca's financial demands and also that Cabeza de Vaca wanted to head his own expedition, not serve in someone else's. After this disappointment, Cabeza de Vaca wrote his memoir of the Narváez Expedition, - *La Relación*, the account translated herein.

The De Soto Expedition sailed from Cuba on May 18, 1539. It landed south of Tampa Bay and went north, passing through approximately the same territory Narváez did. As luck would have it, a cavalry patrol found a Spaniard living with the natives. He was Juan Ortiz, a member of the Narváez Expedition who went with the ships when Narváez took the army inland in 1528. While the ships were scouring the Florida coast, looking for any sign of Narváez and his army, Ortiz went ashore with four other Spaniards. They were attacked. The other four were killed; Ortiz surrendered and was captured. He lived with the natives for twelve years – almost twice as long as Cabeza de Vaca and his colleagues did. By the time he was rescued, Ortiz was fluent in several native languages, so he was a great asset to De Soto until he died of natural causes.

De Soto continued north to Apalachee. One of his captains, Juan de Añasco, discovered physical evidence of Narváez's camp at the Bay of Horses somewhere in the Apalachee Bay area.[1] The similarity between De Soto's travels and Narváez's ends there. De Soto traveled through Georgia, South Carolina North Carolina, back to Georgia, Alabama, Mississippi, and Arkansas. He died near the Mississippi River on May 21, 1542 and was buried in the river. His successor, Luis de Moscoso, took the expedition into east Texas, then turned around and went back to the Mississippi River. The Spaniards, disappointed once again at finding no gold, built boats, floated down the river, and sailed to Panuco.

Dorantes and Castillo

Cabeza de Vaca is not exactly a household name in the United States today, but he is familiar to students of early American, Texas, and Florida history. Estevanico is somewhat well-known because of his connection to the Coronado Expedition and for being one of the first explorers of Arizona and New Mexico. The other two ragged castaways, on the other hand, Andrés Dorantes and Alonso del Castillo, are now obscure. This was not always so in Dorantes's case. He comes across in *La Relación* as energetic, determined, and a natural leader. This depiction of him is even more evident in Oviedo's paraphrase of the Joint Report. Viceroy Mendoza probably saw these same qualities when he asked Dorantes to lead the expedition that ultimately became Coronado's. For a time, Dorantes was at least as well-known in New Spain as Cabeza de Vaca was. Contemporary sources including Mendoza, Castañeda, and Juan Jaramillo typically wrote of the acts, not of the Narváez Expedition or the Four Ragged Castaways, but of "Cabeza de Vaca and Dorantes" or even "Dorantes and Cabeza de Vaca." References to him appear in numerous

---

[1] See the footnotes to 9:1.

documents, lists, and personal histories written in New Spain for the rest of the 16th century.

Alonso del Castillo, on the other hand, who comes across in the Narváez Expedition narratives as a meeker, humbler, and perhaps more introspective counterpart to Cabeza de Vaca and Dorantes, faded into obscurity soon after the expedition ended. What is known of him is that soon after he arrived in Mexico, he went to Guatemala. Seven months later, he was back in New Spain. Viceroy Mendoza arranged for him to marry a widow who owned a sizable *encomienda* - the right to collect tribute or taxes from the conquered natives of a particular area. A royal decree dated February 11, 1540 confirms Castillo's marriage and owner-ship of the *encomienda*. In 1541, he briefly visited Spain to attend to some family estate matters. He then lived the rest of his life quietly in New Spain, where he and his wife had three daughters. The last record of his life is a testimony of merits and services he submitted to the Council of the Indies on November 17, 1547, when he was around 47.

Dorantes's fame resulted in more being written about him. Much of his record is contradictory, but it is known that he main-tained a relationship with Mendoza, who also found a widow for him to marry named María de la Torre. He owned two *encomien-das*, but he apparently received them as a royal grant during a 1539 visit to Spain, rather than owning them via his wife. He is reported to have gone to New Galicia with Mendoza in 1541 to participate in the Mixton War. His known children include one son and three or four daughters. Assertions that he had more than fourteen children may include step-children from María's earlier marriage, or may simply be wrong. A witness's testimony in 1573 that he had known Dorantes's wife and son for 18 years, but never knew Andrés because he was already dead, leads to the conclusion that he died in or before 1555, probably in his 50s. An assertion made in some online biographies that he survived María by twenty years and remarried cannot be right.

Cabeza de Vaca

There is no hard evidence that Cabeza de Vaca gave a copy of the Joint Report of the Narváez Expedition to King Charles after his return to Castile in August 1537, but we should assume that he did. Some time later, he wrote *La Relación*. He may have had another copy of the Joint Report made, or he may have borrowed the royal copy, for there are a few similarities between *La Relación* and the summary written by Gonzalo de Oviedo that hint that Cabeza de Vaca's eyes were on one document while his pen was on the other, such as both documents incorrectly stating that April 12, 1528 was a Tuesday (see 2:3).

While Cabeza de Vaca was in Mexico, he met with Juan de Zumárraga, the bishop of Mexico. Zumárraga, a Franciscan friar, had originally been sent to New Spain with the title of "Protector of the Indians." At the time, Hernán Cortés was out of power and the officials governing in his place, including Nuño de Guzmán, were subjecting the natives to all sorts of abuse. There are no records of what transpired between Cabeza de Vaca and Zumárraga, but there can be little doubt that they considered each other to be allies. Cabeza de Vaca developed intense sympathies for the natives he encountered, even those who had been cruel to him. His views and input would have strengthened Zumárraga's case that the natives ought to be evangelized rather than enslaved.

Two other key figures in the advocacy of the natives at that time were Sebastián de Fuenleal and Bartolomé de las Casas. Fuenleal was president of the *audiencia real* in Santo Domingo from 1528 to 1531 and president of its sister body in Mexico from 1531 to 1535. His administration brought the atrocities of Guzmán and his confederates in New Spain to an end, although New Galicia was beyond his jurisdiction. After Antonio de Mendoza came to rule as viceroy, Fuenleal went to Spain. He became friends with Cabeza de Vaca and was placed on the Council of the Indies, the powerful body that determined Spanish policies in all of its overseas provinces.

Las Casas, a Dominican friar, was the original "Protector of the Indians." In the 1520s and 1530s, he went from post to post, including Santo Domingo, Nicaragua, New Spain, and Guatemala, tirelessly advocating for treating the natives as rational human beings and attempting to convert them to Christianity of their own free will, not as an alternative to enslavement. In 1540, he traveled to Spain to advocate for the abolition of slavery in the Spanish Empire. Even though the views of men like Las Casas, Zumárraga, and Fuenleal were fiercely opposed by many within Spain's ruling class, Cabeza de Vaca no doubt could see during his time in Spain that his humane approach to dealing with natives was gaining momentum.

New Andalusia was the name given to a Spanish colony in South America that consisted essentially of Buenos Aires and nearby portions of present-day Argentina, Uruguay, and Paraguay that were on the Rio de la Plata and the Parana River. In 1539, the governor, Juan de Ayolas, went on an expedition on which he and his entire party were killed by natives. The colonists, who only knew that the governor went missing, wrote to King Charles to ask for help. In March 1540, Charles offered Cabeza de Vaca the position of captain-general to take an expedition to aid the colony and search for Ayolas. If Ayolas was dead, Cabeza de Vaca was to be the governor; otherwise, he would be the lieutenant governor.

Cabeza de Vaca invested 14,000 ducats into the expedition, which was his entire net worth plus all he was able to borrow. He sailed on November 2, 1540 with three ships, adding a fourth ship at a routine stop at the Canary Islands. In March 1541, he landed at Santa Catarina Island, Brazil, which was under Spanish control at the time and had been granted to him for twelve years as partial compensation for his services. While at this location, he learned that Governor Ayolas had been killed and the colony at Buenos Aires had evacuated to Asuncion, in present-day Paraguay.

Never one to leap without looking, Cabeza de Vaca gathered intelligence and sent out search parties to discover how to reach Asuncion, which was either 600 miles (960 km) over land, or 1,600 miles (2,560 km) by water – about half on the ocean and half upriver. He decided upon the shorter route and left in October 1541 with 250 soldiers and 25 horses, accompanied by wives, friars, and natives. He led his forces across the country, treating the natives with respect and trading with them for their food and supplies, rather than taking them by force, like so many of his contemporaries did.

Cabeza de Vaca arrived at Asuncion on March 11, 1542, two years after he was sent to aid the colony. He immediately clashed with Domingo Martínez de Irala, who was now the acting governor, and the other officials who had been running the colony. One witness, a German named Ulrich Schmidel, writes that Cabeza de Vaca refused Irala and the other officials' requests for him to show them his royal credentials - a claim that seems consistent with Cabeza de Vaca's ability to be brittle, but inconsistent with his scrupulousness in following correct procedure. Within a few days, he was demanding that these officials stop imposing novel taxes upon the colonists, such as a butter tax and a honey tax. When the officials argued with him over ending these taxes, he had some of them arrested and imprisoned. His standing dove even further when he refused a native tribe's offer of a hundred of their girls to be distributed to his soldiers as a goodwill offering. On April 25, 1543, after a year of constant strife between Cabeza de Vaca and Irala, the colonists seized their governor and put him in chains.

While Cabeza de Vaca was contending with his own citizens over Indian slavery policies, his views were being endorsed back in Spain. In November 1542, in response to the growing calls for reform coming from Las Casas and others, the Council of the Indies passed, and King Charles signed, the "New Laws for the Good Treatment and Preservation of the Indians." In brief, the New Laws freed the native slaves in the New World. Landowners could not force natives to work and had to pay them wages for their labor. The *encomienda* system (see pg. 235) would be phased out by making all *encomienda* grants expire upon the death of the grant holder, where they had previously been hereditary. Also in 1542, the first edition of Cabeza de Vaca's *La Relación* was published in Zamora, Spain.

From April 1543 to March 1544, Irala's confederates kept Cabeza de Vaca imprisoned under conditions that were harsher than any treatment he suffered at the hands of the Mariames. He was confined in a dark cell and allowed no visitors except for a single native attendant. When he was finally released, he was unable to walk, and had to be dragged to the caravel that would take him to Spain. As he was being led aboard, he announced, with his characteristic unflappability, that a Captain Saluzar would serve as lieutenant governor in his absence. One of the leaders in the conspiracy, Garcia de Venegas, became enraged at this, drew his dagger, and threatened to kill him if he uttered another word. He was then chained to the deck of the ship.

The record of Cabeza de Vaca's voyage home includes an incident that occurred as the ship was sailing to the Azores that is reminiscent of the Biblical story of Jonah. A storm came, lasting four days. Cabeza de Vaca's jailers began to believe that the tempest was a sign of God's wrath against them for their sins against their governor. Venegas set him free, confessed that he had uttered thousands of lies about him, and begged for his forgiveness. "As soon as they had taken the chains off the governor," the account states, "the sea and winds subsided, and the tempest, which had lasted four days, calmed down."

Although he was no longer in chains, Cabeza de Vaca still had to answer the charges leveled against him. Officially, he was accused of treason. One of the arguments to support this charge was that he supposedly flew a coat of arms that was larger than the king's. This was, of course, only a pretext: he was hated for his anti-slavery views and policies. If Schmidel is to believed, he was also hated because he was vain, boastful, and arrogant.

On his way to Castile, Cabeza de Vaca might have felt that his chances of acquitting himself were good, given the political climate at the time of his departure, the sinister behavior of his enemies at Asuncion, his friends and allies on the Council of the Indies, and the exonerating testimony he could count on from the penitent Venegas. Alas, fate turned against him. Viceroy Mendoza, exercising the prudence and caution he was known for, implemented the New Laws of 1542 slowly in North America. He realized that imposing them all at once would put too much stress on the landowners and elite and, by extension, his province's economy and stability. His South American counterpart, on the other hand, Blasco Núñez Vela, the Viceroy of Peru, enforced the laws abolishing slavery strictly and all at once. The result was a full-scale revolt and Núñez's head being marched through the streets on a pike. Spain prevented Peru from breaking away, but it also repealed the New Laws and took a much more accommodating stance on slavery. To make matters worse for Cabeza de Vaca, his friend on the Council of the Indies, Bishop Fuenleal, died, as did another ally, Cardinal Loaysa, the president of the Council. The latter was replaced by a pro-slavery enemy of Friar Las Casas, who was so hated in Spain he had to flee to Mexico.

Cabeza de Vaca spent six years in Spain awaiting action from the Council. On March 18, 1551, the Council issued its decision: Álvar Núñez Cabeza de Vaca, being guilty, was stripped of his office of governor of the Province of Rio de la Plata (as New Andalusia had been renamed), banned from holding public office in the future, banished for life from going anywhere in the Indies, and sentenced to five years in the Spanish penal colony in Oran, Algiers. Furthermore, he was liable for any civil actions that might be brought against him by those who he wronged.

Cabeza de Vaca filed appeals in April and May 1551, which the Council denied, but he did not surrender his liberty easily. He petitioned successfully for the councilors to hear new testimony in his favor, and on August 23, 1552, the Council commuted his punishment. He was granted full release from custody, his sentence to Oran was revoked, and the scope of his banishment was amended so that he was only forbidden from returning to his former South American province. An account stating, "*le dieron por libre y quito*," which means "they set him free and he got out," was mistranslated to English as "he was set at liberty and acquitted," giving rise to a common misconception that he was found not guilty at his original trial.

In 1555, the second edition of *La Relación* was published in Valladolid, Spain. Cabeza de Vaca was about 65 years old at that time. The historian Pierre de Charlevoix writes, "the emperor granted him a pension of two thousand crowns, and gave him a place in the Royal Audience of Sevilla, where he died at an advanced age." He died around 1560.

Chronology

All dates given in *La Relación* and in this chronology are from the Julian calendar, which was the standard in Spain and the rest of Europe at the time. The Julian calendar is identical to our modern Gregorian calendar in every respect, with the same months and number of days per month, except that the Julian calendar had 100 February 29 leap days every 400 years, while the Gregorian calendar has 97. To convert 16th-century dates from the Julian calendar to the Gregorian, add 10 days; i.e. November 6, 1528 "Old Style" becomes November 16, 1528 "New Style."

Dates given explicitly by Cabeza de Vaca are in **bold**.
Dates derived from Cabeza de Vaca are in *italics*.
The chapter and paragraph are given for all explicit dates and some derived dates.
Dates from other sources are in normal type.

1511
Pánfilo de Narváez aids Diego Velázquez de Cuellar in the conquest of Cuba.

1513
April 2   Juan Ponce de León officially discovers Florida.

1519
April   Hernán Cortés, sent from Cuba by Velázquez to explore New Spain, betrays Velázquez and establishes a new Spanish province with himself as governor.

June-July   Alonso Álvarez de Pineda, sailing for Francisco de Garay, maps the coast of the Gulf of Mexico and founds a short-lived colony at Panuco.

1520

April   Narváez, sent by Velázquez to take New Spain from Cortés, arrives at Veracruz, but loses an eye in battle, is captured, and is imprisoned.

1521

Mar-July   Ponce de León makes a failed attempt to colonize Florida.

Aug. 13   Cortés conquers the Aztecs and establishes the capital of New Spain at Mexico City.

1522

Dec. 26   Cortés's men establish a town at Panuco.

1523

Sep-Dec   Garay is stopped from settling at Panuco, but obtains Narváez's release. Narváez goes to Spain to complain about Cortés.

1525

King Charles separates Panuco from New Spain and gives it to Nuño Beltrán de Guzmán.

1526

July 5   A royal licentiate arrives to take over the government of New Spain.

Sep-Dec   Lucas Vázquez de Ayllón makes a failed attempt to colonize the Atlantic coast of Florida.

Dec. 11   Narváez is authorized to explore, conquer, and settle from the cape of Florida to the River of Palms.

1527

Feb. 15	Álvar Núñez Cabeza de Vaca is commissioned as treasurer of Narváez's expedition.
May	Guzmán arrives at Panuco as governor of the province.
June 17	Narváez and his fleet depart from San Lucar de Barrameda, Spain (1:1).
August?	The fleet arrives at Santo Domingo.
October?	The fleet departs from Santo Domingo.
Nov. 2?	Two of Narváez's ships, 60 men, and 20 horses are lost in a tropical storm or hurricane at Trinidad, Cuba.
Nov. 5	Narváez regroups at Trinidad. The decision is made to spend the winter at Xagua (1:10).
Dec. 13	A new government is created in New Spain, with Guzmán at its head.

1528

Feb. 15	Cabeza de Vaca writes a letter to King Charles about the losses at Trinidad.
Feb. 20	Narváez meets the fleet at Xagua (1:10-2:1).
Feb. 22	The expedition departs from Xagua (2:2).
Apr. 7	The expedition sights land off the coast of Florida (2:3 – the text incorrectly gives the date as April 12).
Apr. 9	The fleet drops anchor near Tampa Bay (2:3). Accountant Alonso Enríquez makes contact with some natives (3:1).
Apr. 10	Narváez goes on land; a gold rattle is found (3:1).
Apr. 11	Narváez formally takes possession of Florida for Spain (3:2).
May 1	Narváez decides to send the ships to look for a port while the army marches toward Apalache (4:6).
June 25	Narváez and his army arrive at Apalache (5:9).

July 20	Narváez and his army begin marching to Aute (7:4).
July 29	Narváez and his army arrive at Aute (7:10).
Aug. 4	The men begin building boats to leave Florida (8:4).
Sep. 20	The boats are finished (8:4).
Sep. 22	The men leave the Bay of Horses in five boats (8:7).
Oct. 29	The boats are driven away from the coast (10:2).
Nov. 1	The boats become separated. Cabeza de Vaca sees Narváez for the last time (10:3).
Nov. 5	Castillo and Dorantes's boat reaches land (13:1).
Nov. 6	Cabeza de Vaca's boat reaches land (10:8).
Nov. 6?	Enríquez's boat reaches land.
Nov. 9?	Peñalosa and Téllez's boat reaches land. Everyone on it is massacred (19:6).
Nov. 10?	Inspector Alonso de Solís and two others drown in a failed attempt to leave the Island of Misfortune (12:3).
Nov. 11?	Cabeza de Vaca's group meets with Castillo and Dorantes's. They lose their boat and send four good swimmers to walk to Panuco while the others wait out the winter on the Island of Misfortune (13:3-4).
Nov. 12?	Narváez's boat joins Enríquez's party on the coast. They cross Cavallo Pass. Narváez and his boat are lost at sea (17:7).
Nov. 13?	Figueroa and the other swimmers cross Cavallo Pass.
Nov. 16?	Figueroa and Méndez reach Cedar Bayou (17:6).

1529

Mar. 1	The Quevenes capture Hernando de Esquivel (17:9).
Apr. 1	Dorantes and Castillo regroup on the Island of Misfortune (15:5). They lead a party off the island (16:1).
Apr. 9?	Dorantes's party crosses Cavallo Pass (17:5).

Apr. 12?	Dorantes's party reaches Cedar Bayou (17:5).
Apr.-May	Dorantes, Castillo, and Estevanico become slaves of a cruel tribe in the vicinity of Aransas Pass.
May	A ship sent to search for Narváez returns to Santiago, Cuba with no sign of him; only rumors.
Dec.	Guzmán abandons his office in Mexico and begins his conquest of New Galicia.

1530

May	Dorantes flees to the Iguaces.
July 15	After a successful visit to Spain, Cortés returns to New Spain with the titles of Marquis of the Valley of Oaxaca and captain-general.
August	Estevanico flees to the Iguaces (18:6). Dorantes flees to the Mariames (18:3).

1531

Jan. 10	The government of New Spain is reorganized again, with Sebastián de Fuenleal at its head.
Jan. 25	Guzmán is formally recognized as governor of New Galicia.
Feb.?	Castillo flees to the Iguaces (18:6).

1533

March?	Cabeza de Vaca meets Dorantes near the River of Nuts (17:3).
Sep.?	The four castaways are prevented from escaping together (19:1).

1534

Sep. 20	Cabeza de Vaca escapes from the Mariames (19:3).
Sep. 23	The four castaways leave the Anagados and join the Avavares (20:1).

1535

May?	The four castaways leave the Avavares (22:6, 22:11).
July?	The four castaways cross the Rio Grande for the first time (27:4).
Jul-Aug.?	The four castaways change direction to go inland (28:7).
Sep.?	The four castaways cross the Sierra Madre Oriental (29:4).
Oct-Nov.?	The four castaways arrive at La Junta on the Rio Grande (30:2).
mid-Nov.?	The four castaways cross the Rio Grande at El Paso (31:1).
Nov. 14	Antonio de Mendoza arrives in Mexico to take his throne as viceroy of New Spain.
Dec.	The four castaways, at a river in Sonora, see and hear evidence of Spaniards having visited that area (32:3).

1536

April?	Cabeza de Vaca and Estevanico arrive at a Spanish camp outside of San Miguel de Culiacan, New Galicia.
May 15	The four castaways depart from Culiacan for Compostela (36:5).
June	The castaways depart from Compostela for Mexico (36:7).
July 23	The castaways arrive in Mexico (36:7).
Oct.	Cabeza de Vaca goes to Veracruz to sail for Spain, but ends up staying in New Spain for the winter (37:1).

1537

Feb.- Mar.	Cabeza de Vaca and Dorantes leave Mexico for Veracruz (37:2).
***Apr.* 10**	Cabeza de Vaca and Dorantes sail from Veracruz on separate ships. Dorantes's ship turns around halfway to Havana and returns to Veracruz (37:3).
Apr. 20	Hernando de Soto is authorized to explore, conquer, and settle the territory from Florida to the River of Palms.
May 4	Cabeza de Vaca's ship arrives at Havana, Cuba (37:4). A copy of the Joint Report is sent from there to the *audiencia real* in Santo Domingo.
June 2	Cabeza de Vaca's ship departs from Havana (37:4).
July 2	Cabeza de Vaca's ship is threatened by French privateers at the Azores (37:5).
Aug. 9	Cabeza de Vaca's ship arrives at Lisbon, Portugal (37:8).

1538

June 30	Guzmán is released from prison in New Spain to answer a summons to appear in Seville.

1539

Feb. 7	Friar Marcos de Niza begins his march from Culiacan to explore the northern wilderness, with Estevanico as his guide.
May 21	Marcos learns of Estevanico's death at Cibola.
May 30	De Soto lands near Tampa Bay, Florida.
Sep. 2	Marcos certifies his report on Cibola in Mexico.
Nov. 17	Melchior Díaz leads a party north from Culiacan to prepare the way for Coronado's army.

1540

Cabeza de Vaca writes *La Relación*.

March	Cabeza de Vaca is appointed captain-general and provisional governor of New Andalusia.
Apr. 22	Coronado marches with his army out of Culiacan.
July 7	Coronado reaches and conquers Cibola.
Nov. 2	Cabeza de Vaca departs from Spain for Buenos Aires.

1541

Jan. 8	Díaz dies of injuries from an accident.
March	Cabeza de Vaca arrives at Santa Catarina Island. There, he learns that Governor Ayola is dead and the colony of New Andalusia is now at Asuncion.
June	De Soto crosses the Mississippi River.
August	Coronado is in Quivira (Kansas).
October	Cabeza de Vaca begins his journey to Asuncion.

1542

La Relación is published in Zamora.

March	Cabeza de Vaca arrives at Asuncion and assumes the office of governor.
April	Cabeza de Vaca prohibits native slavery and concubinage in New Andalusia.
Nov. 20	The "New Laws" are passed, ending the enslavement of natives in the Spanish Empire.

1543

April	Cabeza de Vaca is seized and imprisoned by confederates of Domingo de Irala.

1544

March   Cabeza de Vaca's captors begin transporting him to Spain for trial, accused of treason.

Sep. 18   Blasco Núñez Vela, Viceroy of Peru, is seized and deposed in an uprising against the New Laws.

1545

The New Laws are repealed.

1546

January   Cabeza de Vaca is brought to the Council of the Indies under arrest.

1547

Alonso del Castillo dies in New Spain?

1551

Mar. 18   The Council of the Indies judges Cabeza de Vaca guilty, forbids him from holding office, banishes him from the Indies for life, and sentences him to five years' service in a penal colony.

Mar.-Apr.   The Council denies at least two appeals from Cabeza de Vaca.

1552

Aug. 23   Cabeza de Vaca's punishment is commuted.

1555

The second edition of *La Relación* is published in Valladolid.

Andrés Dorantes dies in New Spain?

1560?

Cabeza de Vaca dies in Seville.

Glossary

The following words appear regularly in *La Relación* and require some explanation, but to explain them in footnotes would be too repetitive. The first appearance in each chapter of a word appearing in this glossary is indicated with an asterisk (*).

Alcalde

An *alcalde* is a municipal official in the Spanish form of government. Compared to present-day American officials, his office combined the executive powers of a city mayor and the judicial powers of a local judge, over the territorial jurisdiction of a county. The office of county judge in Texas was originally patterned after the alcalde.

Ceremonial dances/ceremonies – *areitos*

The *areito* or *areyto* was a ceremony involving music and dance among the Taino natives of the Caribbean islands. Cabeza de Vaca uses it as a general word for an indigenous ceremonial dance. In this translation, *areitos* is translated as "ceremonial dances," except where the author pairs it with *bailes*, the usual Spanish word for "dances," in which case the translation is "ceremonies and dances."

Corn – *maíz*

This is the cereal grain known as "corn" in the United States, Canada, Australia, and New Zealand, and as "maize" in other English-speaking countries, including the United Kingdom. Some translations render *maíz* as "corn" in some places and "maize" in others, but this implies a distinction that does not exist in the Spanish text.

Fathom – *braza*

Both the English fathom and the Spanish *braza* represent the distance from tip to tip of a man's outstretched arms. ("Arms" is *brazos* in Spanish.) A fathom is usually reckoned as six feet, but the Spanish *braza* may have been closer to 5½ feet.

Gourd – *calabaza*

Calabaza is the Spanish name for the genus *Cucurbita*, which includes gourds, pumpkins, squash, and zucchini. Other translations render *calabaza* variously by one or another of these terms from passage to passage. All of these words mean different things to English readers, however. To best represent the text, *calabaza* is translated herein uniformly as "gourd."

Hardship/difficulty/trouble/effort/labor – *trabajo*

Appearing in singular or plural form 62 times in *La Relación*, the noun *trabajo* is one of Cabeza de Vaca's favorite words. It is derived from the verb *trabajar*, which means "to work." Literally, *trabajo* means "job," "labor," or "effort." Most of the time, however, Cabeza de Vaca uses it to connote suffering: not just working hard, but enduring a difficult ordeal. This translation uses a variety of words in place of *trabajo*, with the most frequent choices being "hardship," "difficulty," and "trouble." More literal translations such as "effort" are used wherever the context allows. *Trabajo* also occurs occasionally in other forms, such as the adjective *trabajoso*, which is translated as "difficult."

Heaven/the sky – *el cielo*

There is no distinction in Spanish between the English concepts of "the sky" and "Heaven." The only guide to translation is context. This translation tends to use "the sky," as it is more generic, unless the context indicates that "Heaven" is more appropriate.

Interpreter – *Lengua*

The Spanish noun *lengua* means "tongue," which, just as in English, can also mean "language." Cabeza de Vaca uses it, capitalized as *Lengua*, as a synonym for "interpreter." The usual Spanish words for "interpreter" are *intérprete* or *traductor* ("translator").

League – *legua*

The league represents the distance a man can walk in an hour. The Spanish common league (*leagua común*), which is apparently what Cabeza de Vaca used, was 3.46 miles (5.54 km). The statute league (*legua legal*) of 2.6 miles (4.16 km) that some readers may be familiar with was used for measuring the dimensions of parcels of land. The common league was used to measure distances traveled.

Make the sign of the Cross/bless – *santiguar*

The Spanish word *santiguar* refers both to the familiar Cross-shaped hand motion Catholics make when blessing someone and to the blessing itself. This translation generally renders it as "make the sign of the Cross," especially when the context makes it clear that the hand motion is being described. *Santiguar* is sometimes translated herein as "bless," mostly for brevity's sake when the word appears multiple times in the same paragraph, but also in a few places where the gesture does not seem to be what the author is emphasizing.

Negro – *negro*

Negro is the Spanish word for "black." *El negro* and *un negro* literally mean "the black one" and "a black one," respectively. In the instances where Cabeza de Vaca uses *el negro* to refer to a specific black person (usually the Moor, Estevanico), translating it as "the black one" or "the black" in these instances would not result in normal-sounding English, and translating it as "the black man" or "the black person" loses accuracy with the addition of another noun. Even though the dated term "Negro" has not been widely used in the U.S. as a reference to black people since the late 1960s, it is still validly used in historical contexts. "Negro" is capitalized in this translation when it is used as a personal noun, to conform to standard English usage.

South Sea and North Sea – *Mar del Sur* and *Mar del Norte*

These are the historical names for the Pacific and Atlantic Oceans, respectively. The Pacific Ocean was discovered at Panama, which lies east-to-west, so it was given the name "South Sea," while the Atlantic was called the "North Sea." These names continued to be used even after Spanish explorers discovered more of the North American continent and found that the Pacific was actually the ocean to the west of it. When Cabeza de Vaca uses the terms "North Sea" and "South Sea," he is simply calling them by their well-known names, not describing their position relative to his location at the time.

Tuna

Tuna is the Spanish word for the dark red, egg-shaped fruit of the prickly pear cactus, known as *opuntia* in Latin. "Tuna leaves" are the pads of the prickly pear, known as *nopales* in Spanish.

Vespers - *Vifperas*

Vespers is the name of the evening prayer service in several Christian denominations, including Roman Catholicism. "At the hour of vespers," a phrase Cabeza de Vaca uses sometimes, is synonymous with "at sunset," another term he sometimes uses.

Bibliography

Relation of Alvar Nuñez Cabeca de Vaca, translated by Buckingham Smith, New York, 1871. This volume not only includes Smith's translation of *La Relacion*, but also his translations of some related documents, including Narváez's petitions to the king for the conquest of Florida, a copy of the *requerimiento* claiming Spain's right to subjugate the Indians, and Cabeza de Vaca's royal commission as treasurer of Narváez's expedition. It also includes a biography of Cabeza de Vaca covering the events of his life before and after the Narváez Expedition.

The Narrative of Alvar Núñez Cabeza de Vaca, translated by Fanny Bandelier, with *Oviedo's Version of the Lost Joint Report Presented to the Audiencia of Santo Domingo,* translated by Gerald Theisen. Published by the Imprint Society, Barre, Massachusetts, 1972.

Collección de documentos inéditos para la historia de España (1842) and *Colección de documentos inéditos de Indias* (1883). These two huge, multi-volume works are "Collections of unedited documents" in Spanish of the history of Spain and the Indies, respectively. They contain typescripts (i.e., typeset versions of manuscripts) of hundreds of royal decrees, petitions to the crown, letters, depositions, and other sorts of official papers.

"The First Europeans in Texas, 1528-1536," by Harbert Davenport and Joseph K. Wells, published in *The Southwestern Historical Quarterly*, Volume XXII, July 1918 to April 1919.

Álvar Núñez Cabeza de Vaca: American Trailblazer, by Robin Varnum, published by University of Oklahoma Press, 2014.

We Came Naked and Barefoot: The Journey of Cabeza de Vaca across North America, by Alex D. Krieger, published by University of Texas Press, 2003.

The Journey of Coronado, by Pedro de Castañeda, translated by George Parker Winship, published by A. S. Barnes & Company, New York, 1904.

A Narrative of the Expedition of Hernando de Soto Into Florida, by A Gentleman of Elvas, translated by Richard Hackluyt, 1609 (e-book).

Index

A

accountant. *See* Enríquez, Alonso

acorns, 133

Acubadaos, 149

Aguar, 206

Aguenes. *See* Deaguanes

Alaniz, Gerónimo de, 22, 24, 91, 93

Alcaraz, Diego de, 196, 199, 203, 210

Anagados, 119, 121

antimony, 167, 193

ants, 113

Apalache, 21, 30, 32, 35, 37–39

Arbadaos, 133

arrow poison plant, 188

Astudillo, 77

Asturian. *See* cleric from Asturias

Atayos, 127, 148

Aute, 39, 40, 42, 45, 46

Avavares, 122, 123, 130, 149

Avellaneda, 42

Azores, 217

B

Bad Thing, 131, 132

Bay of Horses, 51

Bay of the Cross, 49

beans, 39, 177, 181, 183, 184, 188

bear, 37

Benítez, 90

bison, 116

blackberries, 84, 103

bull, 214

C

Cabeza de Vaca, Álvar Núñez, 4, 7–9, 11, 19, 22, 24, 25, 28, 35, 45, 50, 55, 56, 61, 63, 64, 67, 68, 72, 75, 85, 86, 89, 91–94, 96, 99, 101, 109, 118, 120, 122, 124, 125, 128, 129, 133, 134, 168, 169, 174, 176, 184, 195, 196, 199, 215, 220, 221, 224

Camoles. *See* Camones

Camones, 120, 149

Canarreo, Cuba, 14

cannibalism, 79, 82, 107

Caoques. *See* Capoques

Cape Corrientes, Cuba, 14

Cape San Antonio, Cuba, 14

Capoques and Han, 68, 69, 71-73, 75, 79-83, 87, 91, 147

Caravallo, 25, 222

Carvallo. *See* Caravallo

Castillo, Alonso del, 29, 43, 49, 75, 86, 89, 93, 99, 100, 102, 112, 119, 122, 123, 127, 128, 133, 177, 189, 196, 199, 224

cattle, 38, 119, 167, 178, 183

Cebreros, 201

cedar, 37

Cerda, Álvaro de la, 13, 19

Charruco. *See* Chorruco, Indians of

Chaves, 89

children of the sun, 130, 164, 165, 170, 172-174, 185, 200, 204

Chorruco, Indians of, 91, 147

Cienfuegos, Cuba. *See* Xagua, Cuba

cleric from Asturias, 89, 109, 132

Coayos. *See* Comos

commissary. *See* Suárez, Friar Juan

Comos, 127, 149

Compostela, 213

copper, 166, 169, 193

coral, 184

corn, 20, 21, 28, 35, 37-39, 47, 55, 60, 65, 133, 163, 177, 179, 183, 184, 187, 188, 191, 199

Corral, 79

cotton, 181, 183, 184

crabs, 103, 107

Cuba, 6, 216

Culiacan, 197, 202, 210, 213

Cutalches. *See* Cutalchiches

Cutalchiches, 127, 129, 149

D

Deaguanes, 96, 143, 147

deer, 17, 20, 30, 37, 46, 92, 113-116, 123, 145, 156, 170, 171, 179, 183, 184, 187, 188

Díaz, Melchior, 202, 203, 204

dog, 67, 111, 134, 137, 150

Doguenes. *See* Deaguanes

Dorantes, Andrés, 43, 49, 55, 75, 86, 89, 93, 95, 99, 101, 110, 112, 119, 120, 122, 128-130, 133, 166, 187, 196, 199, 215, 224

Dorantes, Diego, 89, 95, 110

duck, 38

Dulchanchelín, Chief, 30, 31

E

egret, 38

emerald, 184, 187, 200

Enríquez, Alonso, 4, 17, 21, 22, 28, 49, 102, 104, 105, 120

Espíritu Santo, 94

Esquivel, Hernando de, 95, 104, 107, 109, 110, 120

Estevanico, 89, 100, 112, 119, 121, 122, 128, 130, 133, 177, 196, 197, 225

Estrada, 89

F

falcon, 38

Fernández, Álvaro, 77

Fernández, Bartolomé, 22

figs, natives of the, 132, 150

Figueroa, 77, 104, 107, 109, 132

fish, 17, 39, 53, 54, 69, 71, 73, 79, 81, 113, 133, 187

flint, 129

Florida, 3, 15, 19, 41

flycatcher, 38

fool's gold, 167

friars, 5, 27, 102, 105, 108, 120

fruit, 92, 124, 133, 134, 153, 180, 183, 188, 201

G

God: faith in, 45, 46, 54, 121, 123, 127, 132, 137; giving thanks to, 32, 43; goodness of,
45, 54, 63, 86, 93, 100, 118, 127, 203; native instruction in, 186; other references to,
23, 185, 204, 206, 209, 211, 221; prayer to, 86, 130, 175; suffering of Christ, 134;
thanks to, 28, 99, 123, 127, 177, 183, 189, 195; will of, 9, 31, 46, 61, 71, 76, 77, 86,
100, 118, 124, 162, 191, 218, 224; works of, 128

gold, 17, 21, 193, 194, 201, 219

goose, 38

gourds, 39, 177, 181, 183, 204

governor. *See* Narváez, Pánfilo de

grubs, 113

Guaniguanico, Cuba, 14

Guaycones, 148

Gutiérrez, 89

Guzmán, Diego de, 193

Guzmán, Nuño de, 203, 209, 213

H

Han. *See* Capoques and Han

hare, 37, 170, 171

Havana, Cuba, 13, 15, 19, 217, 223, 224

hawk, 38

healing, 85, 86, 122, 123, 127-131, 157, 164, 168, 169, 175, 200

Hearts. *See* Village of the Hearts

heron, 38

horse, 6, 8, 10, 13, 14, 17, 19, 22, 27, 29, 31, 32, 35, 39, 40, 43, 45, 46, 48, 49, 51, 53,
64, 71, 145, 189, 193, 196, 200, 213

Huelva, Diego de, 89, 95, 110

I

Iguaces, 102, 111, 117, 148, 212

inspector. *See* Solís, Alonso de

iron, 167, 189, 193

Island of Misfortune, 67, 77, 81, 85, 102, 120, 141, 147

J

juniper, 37, 48

L

laurel, 37

León, Francisco de, 90

lion, 37

Lisbon, Peru, 219

live oak, 37, 40

lizards, 115

López, Diego, 79

M

Maliacones, 127, 133, 149

Malicones. *See* Maliacones

Mareames. *See* Mariames

Mariames, 95, 102, 104, 109-111, 117, 118, 122, 148

marten, 55, 59, 89

Méndez, 77, 95, 104

Mendica, 147

mesquite, 153

Mexico City, 201, 213, 215

Miruelo, 13, 14, 19

mole, 180

mosquitos, 84, 114, 115

mouse, 176

mullet, 52, 67

N

Narváez, Pánfilo de, 3, 11, 13, 14, 17, 19, 22, 24, 25, 27-30, 32, 35, 38, 40, 41, 43, 46, 49, 54, 55, 56, 59, 60, 61, 104, 120, 221, 222

native customs: conflict resolution, 142; death and funeral, 72, 82, 83; food and beverage preparation, 150, 153, 168, 171, 181; hospitality, 87, 142; marriage and

children, 83, 111, 141; other, 113, 150, 152; robbery, 159, 161, 163, 165, 170, 173; self defense and war, 142, 143, 145, 146, 232
native dress and adornment, 81, 87, 93, 112, 179, 184, 188
New Galicia, 197
New Spain, 20, 72, 184, 219, 221
newts, 113
nuts, 96, 99, 128, 133

O

oak, 37
of the figs. *See* figs, natives of the
opossum, 37
Oviedo, Lope de, 67, 68, 91, 93, 96, 99
oysters, 29, 43, 84, 86

P

Palacios, 79
palmetto, 28, 37, 47
Palos, Friar Juan de, 27
Pantoja, 7, 62, 106, 107
Panuco, 77, 104, 108, 222
parrot, 170, 184
pearl, 213
peas: Texas ebony, 124
Pedro, Don, 39
Peñalosa, 50, 55, 63, 120
Petaan. *See* Petutan River
Petutan River, 193, 204
pine, 37, 48, 167
poplar, 41
Porcalle, Vasco. *See* Porcallo, Vasco
Porcallo, Vasco, 6, 7, 107
Primahaitu, 200

Q

quail, 170
Quevenes, 96, 104, 107, 144, 147
Quitoles, 149

R

rabbit, 37
red ochre, 92, 161
River of Palms, 3, 13, 22, 53
River of the Magdalene, 42
roots, 69, 73, 79, 81, 91, 112
Ruiz, Gonzalo, 79

S

sable. *See* marten
salamanders, 113
San Miguel de Culiacan. *See* Culiacan
Santiago, Cuba, 6
Santo Domingo, Hispaniola, 5, 7
scribe. *See* Alaniz, Gerónimo de
seafood, 48
seaweed, 103
Sierra, 79
signs, communicating by, 18, 21, 30, 68, 72, 75, 185, 186
Silveira, Diego de, 219
silver, 161, 194, 201, 219
snake, 113, 125, 134
Solís, Alonso de, 5, 19, 22, 28, 35, 50, 68, 70
Sotomayor, 107
spiders, 113, 172
Suárez, Friar Juan, 5, 19, 20, 22, 23, 27, 28, 40, 49, 104
Susolas, 127, 128, 149
sweetgum, 37

T

Tavera, 76

Téllez, 50, 56, 63, 120

Teodoro, Doroteo, 48, 56

Terceira Island, 219

Tostado, 89

treasurer. *See* Cabeza de Vaca, Álvar Núñez

Trinidad, Cuba, 7, 8, 9, 11

tunas, 100, 114, 117-119, 121-125, 127, 129, 133, 137, 138, 163, 164, 167, 172

turquoise, 184, 204

V

Valdivieso, 89, 95, 110

Valenzuela, 29

Velázquez, Juan, 31

Veracruz, 215

Village of the Hearts, 187, 189

W

walnut, 37

worms, 172

X

Xagua, Cuba, 11

Y

Yguaces. *See* Iguaces

About the Author

David Carson is a lifelong Texas resident who has been enamored with the history of his state ever since his first Texas History class in seventh grade. His view of history is that while its course is sometimes determined by leaders acting on a grand scale, more often than not, our present lives have been shaped by decisions that originally affected just a small area and a few hundred people or less. When studying a historical event, he tries as best as possible to interpret the exact spot where it happened, visit that spot, and literally put himself in the place of the figures he is studying.

In 2013, Mr. Carson launched the web site, TexasCounties .net, with the purpose of presenting information about Texas and Texas history on the county level. For his first major project, he performed the most detailed reconstruction of the "Old San Antonio Road" - a branch of the historic 300-year old *Camino Real* or "King's Highway" – that has been performed to date, tracing its route through twenty Texas counties from the Sabine River to the Rio Grande.

His next project was to trace the route of the Narváez Expedition through the nineteen or more counties that Narváez, Cabeza de Vaca, and the other Europeans visited during their eight years in Texas. This book, his first, is a direct product of that effort.

Made in the USA
Las Vegas, NV
09 August 2024

93602364R00164